*THE YEAR AFTER THE ARMADA*
*AND*
*OTHER HISTORICAL STUDIES*

ROBERT DEVEREUX, SECOND EARL OF ESSEX.
*(After a contemporary portrait in the collection of the Earl of Verulam.)*

# THE YEAR AFTER THE ARMADA

**✻✻ AND OTHER HISTORICAL STUDIES**
BY MARTIN A. S. HUME, F.R.HIST.S.

SECOND EDITION

"'There is no book so bad,' said the bachelor, 'but that something good may be found in it.' 'There is no doubt of that,' replied Don Quixote."—*Don Quixote*, pt. ii.

KENNIKAT PRESS
Port Washington, N. Y./London

THE YEAR AFTER THE ARMADA

First published in 1896
Reissued in 1970 by Kennikat Press
Library of Congress Catalog Card No: 71-110909
SBN 8046-0891-1

Manufactured by Taylor Publishing Company    Dallas, Texas

# PREFACE.

Circumstances have led me to follow the course of modern history into somewhat unfrequented channels, and in the pursuit of my main object it is occasionally my good fortune to come across a piece of unused or unfamiliar contemporary information—some faded manuscript or forgotten news-letter—which seems to throw fresh light upon an important period or an interesting personality of the past. It is true that in some cases the matters recounted are not of any great historical significance, but even then there is generally some quaint glimpse to be caught of bygone manners or events which redeems the document from worthlessness. From such treasure-trove as this, and from other sources which have generally been overlooked or neglected by English historians, the studies contained in the present book have been drawn; and it is hoped that some fresh knowledge as well as amusement may be gained from them.

## PREFACE.

If the reader is only half as much interested in perusing as I have been in writing them, I shall consider myself very fortunate.

Some of the studies have already appeared in Magazines, but the principal portion of the book is now printed for the first time.

MARTIN A. S. HUME.

LONDON, *September*, 1896.

## CONTENTS.

|  | PAGE |
|---|---|
| THE YEAR AFTER THE ARMADA | 1 |
| JULIAN ROMERO—SWASHBUCKLER | 73 |
| THE COMING OF PHILIP THE PRUDENT | 123 |
| THE EVOLUTION OF THE SPANISH ARMADA | 175 |
| A FIGHT AGAINST FINERY | 205 |
| A PALACE IN THE STRAND | 261 |
| THE EXORCISM OF CHARLES THE BEWITCHED | 289 |
| A SPRIG OF THE HOUSE OF AUSTRIA | 321 |
| THE JOURNAL OF RICHARD BERE | 343 |

## LIST OF ILLUSTRATIONS.

THE EARL OF ESSEX ... ... ... ... *Frontispiece*
(*After a contemporary portrait in the collection of the Earl of Verulam.*)

PHILIP AND MARY ... ... ... *To face p.* 125
(*After the painting by Antonio Mor.*)

QUEVEDO ... ... ... ... *To face p,* 256
(*After the portrait by Velasquez, at Apsley House.*)

CHARLES II. OF SPAIN ... ... *To face p.* 291
(*After the portrait by Claudio Coello, at the Madrid Museo.*)

PHILIP IV. OF SPAIN ... ... ... *To face p.* 323
(*After the portrait by Velasquez, in the National Gallery.*)

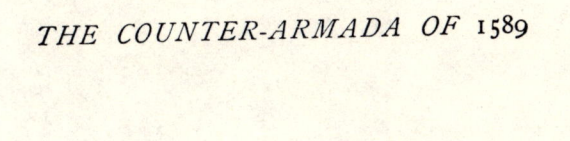

*THE COUNTER-ARMADA OF* 1589

# THE YEAR AFTER THE ARMADA.

### THE COUNTER-ARMADA OF 1589.[1]

ON the night of Sunday, the 28th of July, 1588, the great Armada was huddled, all demoralised and perplexed, in Calais roads. Only a week before the proudest fleet that ever rode the seas laughed in derision at the puny vessels that alone stood between it and victory over the heretic Queen and her pirate countrymen, who for years had plundered and insulted with impunity the most powerful sovereign in Europe. Gilded prows and fluttering pennons, great towering hulls which seemed to defy destruction, the fervid approbation of all Latin Christendom, and the assurance of Divine protection, combined to produce in the men of the Armada absolute confidence in an easy conquest. But six

[1] For the sake of uniformity, throughout this narrative the dates are given in the "old style," then used in England, ten days earlier than the dates cited by the Spanish and Portuguese authorities.

days of desultory fighting in the Channel had opened their eyes to facts thitherto undreamed of. Handy ships, that could sail several points closer to the wind than their unwieldy galleons, could harass and distress them without coming to close quarters. At first they shouted that the English were afraid of them, but as the sense of their own impotence gradually grew upon them their spirits sank. Brave they were, but, said they, of what use is bravery against foes who will not fight with us hand to hand in the only way we wot of? And so from day to day, whilst they straggled up the Channel, their boasting gave place to dismay and disorganisation. They saw their ships were being sunk and disabled one after the other, whilst the English vessels were suffering little damage and had safe ports of refuge behind them. Thus at the end of the week they found themselves with a dangerous shoally coast to leeward, in an exposed roadstead surrounded by the reinforced English fleet. They were ripe for panic, for their commander was a fool and a craven in whom they had no confidence; and when the English fireships drifted down upon them with the wind, flaring in the darkness of the summer night, abject paralysing terror turned the huge fleet into a hustling mob of ships, in which the sole thought was that of flight. From that moment the Armada was beaten. The storms on the northern and Irish coasts, the cold, the rotten food and putrid water, pestilence and panic, added dramatic completeness to their discomfiture; but superior ships, commanders, and seamanship had practically defeated them when they slipped their cables and anchors and crowded through the narrow sea with the English fleet to windward and sandbanks on their lee.

But the Armada had represented the labour, the thought, and the sacrifice of years. Every nerve had been strained to render it irresistible. Spain and the Indies had been squeezed to the last doubloon, careful Sixtus V. had been cajoled into partnership in the enterprise, and the Church throughout Christendom had emptied its coffers to crush heresy for once and for ever. All along the coast of Ireland from the Giant's Causeway to Dingle Bay the wreckage of the splendid galleons was awash, and many of the best and bravest of Spain's hidalgos, dead and mutilated, scattered the frowning shore; or, alive, starved, naked, and plundered, were slowly done to death with every circumstance of inhumanity by the Irish kerns or their English conquerors. It could hardly be expected, therefore, that on the receipt of the dreadful news Spain should calmly resign itself to defeat. Such lessons as this are only slowly and gradually brought home to the heart of a nation ; and after Mendoza's lying stories of victory had been contradicted, and the fell truth ran through Spain as the battered, plague-stricken wrecks of what was left of the Armada crept into Santander, the first heart-cry was for vengeance and a re-vindication of the national honour.

Medina Sidonia was the scapegoat (perhaps not undeservedly, though Parma should bear his share of blame), and as he went in state and comfort through Spain to his home in the south, the very children and old women in the streets jeered and spat upon him for the chicken-hearted coward who had disgraced their country in the eyes of the world. Only the over-burdened recluse in the Escorial was patient and resigned under the blow. He had, as he thought, done his best for the cause of God; and if for some inscrutable reason all his labour, his sacrifice, and his prayers were to be in vain, he could only suffer dumbly and bend his head to the Divine decree. One after the other the provinces and municipalities came to him with offers of money to repair the disaster. In November the national Cortes secretly sent him word, "that they would vote four or five millions of gold, their sons and all they possess, so that he may chastise that woman, and wipe out the stain which this year has fallen on the Spanish nation."[1] But the Cortes and the Town Councils always tacked upon their offers two conditions, born of their knowledge that peculation and mismanagement were largely responsible for the disaster of the Armada. "First that his Majesty will act in earnest; and secondly that their own agents may have the spending of the money which they shall vote, for in this way his Majesty will not be so robbed and all affairs will go far better."[2] But the last condition was one that Philip could never brook: the secret of his failure through life was that he wished to do everybody's work himself and he was smothered in details. Besides this there were difficulties, diplomatic and others, in the way, of which the people at large were unaware. The star of Henry of Navarre was rising, and all France was now alive to Philip's real object in the invasion of England. Philip knew that in any repetition of the attempt he would prob-

[1] Venetian Calendar of State Papers. [2] Ibid.

ably not have to confront England alone. So the cries for vengeance grew fainter, and national feeling was gradually turned purposely in other directions.

But these cries had been loud enough to reach England. Exaggerated rumours of the intention to renew the Armada were industriously sent from all quarters by zealous spies and agents, and an uneasy feeling grew that perhaps, after all, England had not finished her foe; for Elizabeth's advisers had no means of exactly gauging the depth of Philip's purse, and they knew the papal coffers were overflowing. It is true that immediate danger was over. The hasty English levies had been sent home again, bragging of the prowess they would have shown if the hated Spaniard had dared to land, and the panic and fright had given place to perfectly natural congratulations on the special protection vouchsafed by the Almighty to the Virgin Queen and her people. The heroics were over, and England was free, for the present at all events, to don its work-a-day garb again.

But the easy victory had inflamed men's minds. There had been very little fighting even on the fleet, and none at all on shore; and it is not pleasant to be balked of a set-to when all is ready, and to turn swords to bill-hooks without once fleshing them in an enemy's carcase. So the idlers in England who were loath to go to work again, the turbulent youngsters who were burning for an excuse to have a go at somebody, and the lavish gentlemen who were thirsting for loot, began on their side to talk about vengeance and retaliation. It mattered little to them that for a long course of years England had been the aggressor, and that Philip had exhausted all diplomatic and conciliatory means, including even secret murder, and the subornation of treason, in England, to arrive at a peaceful *modus vivendi*. For thirty years he had suffered, more or less patiently, robbery, insult, and aggression in his own dominions at the hands of Elizabeth. The commerce of his country was well-nigh swept from the sea by marauders sallying from English ports or flying the English flag. His own towns, both in the Spanish colonies and in old Spain, had been sacked and burnt by English seamen without any declaration of war; and rebellion in the ancient patrimony of his house had been, and was still, kept alive by English money and English troops.

Englishmen, then as now, had the comfortable and highly commendable faculty of believing their own side always to be in the right, and they knew in this particular case that it was much more profitable to plunder than to be plundered, to attack rather than defend. Elizabeth's caution and dread of being forced into a costly national war had over and over again caused her to discountenance this tendency on the part of some of her advisers, though she was ready enough to share the profits when her official orders were disregarded and her own responsibility evaded. Only the year before the Armada she had peremptorily ordered Drake, when he was ready to sail for Cadiz, not to imperil peace by molesting any of the territories or subjects of his Catholic Majesty. But when he came into Dartmouth, after "singeing the King of Spain's beard," towing behind him the great galleon *San Felipe*, with its 600,000

## THE COUNTER-ARMADA OF 1589.

ducats in money, the Queen smiled upon him as if he had never disobeyed her. But for her positive orders of recall indeed, Drake on this very voyage would have made the Armada impossible by destroying, as he was able and ready to do, all the ships preparing for it in Lisbon harbour.

Only just before the Armada, in June, 1588, the idea of diverting and dividing Philip's forces by attacking him in his own country, ostensibly in the interest of Dom Antonio, the Portuguese pretender, was broached by Lord Admiral Howard in a letter to Walsingham, now in the Record Office. The scheme assumed definite form soon after the flight of the Armada, when, in September, Sir John Norris presented to the Queen a complete plan for fitting out an expedition with this object by means of a joint-stock company, which might be made both patriotic and profitable at the same time. Such a proposal was one eminently likely to suit the Queen, frugal and evasive of responsibility as she was. Norris and his associates suggested that the capital of the company should be £40,000 at least, out of which the Queen was to subscribe £5,000, and to appoint a treasurer, who was to supervise the expenditure of the whole. The Queen's contribution was only to be spent by permission of this treasurer, and if the enterprise fell through for want of subscribers she was to have her money returned to her or the munitions of war which had been purchased with it. The Queen, as was her wont, discreetly hesitated about it; and it was not until addresses had been presented from Parliament begging her to adopt some such action that she consented to take shares in the enterprise. But her treasury was well-nigh empty; and willing as she was that anything should be done to weaken her enemy, her poverty and Tudor frugality forbade her from undertaking to defray any very large portion of the cost herself. So she answered her petitioners that although she would sanction the enterprise and subscribe something to it, the main cost must be borne by others.

The story of this ill-starred expedition is usually disposed of in a few lines by English historians, although its success would have completely changed the status of England on the Continent. What is known of it hitherto is practically confined to the official documents and letters in the Record Office, which have only become accessible of late years, a few letters in the Bacon and Naunton Papers, and a curious tract printed in Hackluyt and ascribed to Captain Anthony Wingfield, minutely describing and apologising for the proceedings. The account was written in the same year, 1589, as the expedition took place; and the writer, whoever he was,[1] evidently witnessed the events he relates. His

[1] In a subscription reprint of sixty copies of this tract published in 1881 under the editorship of the Rev. Alexander Grosart, the authorship appears to be ascribed, I know not on what grounds, to a certain Robert Pricket, who served probably as a gentleman volunteer and follower of the Earl of Essex. He had seen previous service in the Netherlands, and was the author of several poetical works, one being a panegyric on the Earl of Essex. The tract is entitled "*A True Coppie of a Discourse*, written by a gentleman employed in the late voiage of Spaine and Portingale. Sent to his particular friend and by him published for the better satisfaction of all such as having been seduced by particular report have entered into conceipts tending to the discredit of the enterprise and Actors of the same. At London. Printed for Thomas Woodcock, dwelling in Paules Churchyard, at the sign of the blacke Beare 1589."

description is most graphic and interesting, and presents the English view of the enterprise in its best possible light, although all his explanations and palliations cannot succeed in conjuring away the utter failure of the expedition, or the bad conduct of the men who took part in it. The English account, however, all indulgently unflattering as it is, is not the only one extant. The publication of the latest volume of the Calendar of Venetian State Papers puts us into possession of the version of the affair current in the Spanish Court and conveyed to the King from his officers in Portugal; and in addition to this I possess the transcript of an unpublished contemporary manuscript which exists in the library of Don Pascual de Gayangos at Madrid, written by a Castilian resident in Lisbon at the time of the invasion, containing a detailed diary of the event.[1] This manuscript, I believe, has never yet received the attention it deserves from historians, but it is nevertheless valuable as confirming in the main the English accounts, but relating the incidents from an entirely different point of view. I have also recently discovered in the Pombalina Library in Lisbon still another contemporary manuscript diary of the English invasion, written by a Portuguese gentleman in Lisbon who was present at the scenes he describes, and whose standpoint is widely different from those of the Castilian and the Englishman.[2] The Spaniard

---

[1] It is called "Relacion de lo subcedido del armada enemiga del reyno de Inglaterra a este de Portugal çon la retirada a su tierra, este año de 1589." MS. Gayangos Library. Transcript in possession of the author.
[2] "Memoria do successo da vinda dos Ingreses ao reino de

is full of scorn and contempt for the chicken-hearted Portuguese in Lisbon who, though sympathising with the native pretender, slunk into hiding at his approach; whilst the Portuguese diarist insists vehemently upon the loyalty of the Portuguese nobles to Philip, and ascribes the instability of the common people to their weakness and incredulity, to their fear of the anger of Saint Antonio if they opposed his namesake the pretender, to their desire to protect their wives and families, to any other reason but the obvious one that high and low, rich and poor, in the city were in a state of trembling panic from first to last, utterly cowed and appalled by the few Spaniards whom they hated as much as they feared.

In 1578, ten years before the Armada, the rash young King Sebastian of Portugal had disappeared for ever from the ken of men on the Moorish battlefield which had seen the opening and closing of his mad crusade. For centuries afterwards the Portuguese peasants dreamt of his triumphant return to lead to victory the hosts of Christendom. But he came not, unless indeed one of the many claimants who long afterwards assumed his name was indeed he; and in the meanwhile, when his uncle, the childless Cardinal King Henry, died, Portugal wanted a monarch.

It had a large choice of descendants of Dom Manoel, grandfather of the lost Sebastian, but the Magna Charta of the Portuguese, the laws of Lamego (apocryphal as we now believe them to have been), were then universally accepted, and strictly excluded

Portugal." Biblioteca Nacional, Lisbon. Pombalina, 196, fol. 271. Transcribed by the author.

## THE COUNTER-ARMADA OF 1589.   13

foreigners from the throne; and all the claimants were aliens but two, the Duchess of Braganza, daughter of the elder son of Dom Manoel, and doubtless the rightful heiress; and Dom Antonio, a churchman, prior of Ocrato, the questionably legitimate offspring of Manoel's second son.

When the Cardinal King died in 1580, Philip II., who for two years had been intriguing, suborning, and threatening the leading Portuguese to acknowledge his right to the succession, stretched out his hand to grasp the coveted crown. Of the two native claimants one, the Duchess of Braganza, was timid and unready; the other, Dom Antonio, was ambitious, bold, and eager. Around him all that was patriotic grouped itself. The poorer classes bitterly hated the foreigner, and particularly the Spaniard, whose King was really the only other serious claimant to the throne. The churchmen were devotedly attached to the ecclesiastical claimant, the nobles were Portuguese before all, and Antonio was acclaimed the national sovereign. But not for long; the terrible Alba swept down upon Lisbon, as years before he had come down upon the Netherlands, and crushed the life out of Portuguese patriotism. There was no religious question to stiffen men's backs, and no William of Orange to command them here. The Portuguese were made of different stuff from the stubborn Dutchmen, and Alba rode roughshod over them with but little resistance. Antonio was soon a fugitive, hunted from town to town, holding out for weeks in one fortress, only to be starved into another; proclaimed a bastard and a rebel, with a great price set upon his head; and yet for eight long months he wandered amongst the mountain peasantry, as safe from betrayal as was Charles Edward amongst the Scots Highlanders. At last Antonio gave up the game and fled to France, and thence to England. He came in July, 1581, and was immediately made much of by the Queen and Leicester. In vain did Mendoza, Philip's ambassador, demand his surrender as a rebel. The Queen said she had not quite made up her mind to help him, but she had quite decided that she would not surrender him to be killed. He was too valuable a card in her hand for her to let him go, and she made the most of him. He was treated with royal honours, and covert aid was given to him to strengthen the Azores, which were faithful to him. He had taken the precaution to bring away the crown jewels of Portugal with him, the spoils of the two Indies, but he had no money. The greedy crew that surrounded the Queen soon scented plunder, and money for warlike preparations, the purchase of ships, and the like, was speedily forthcoming on security of diamonds and pearls such as had rarely been seen in England. Elizabeth and Leicester, in presents and by a quibble, managed to grab some of the best; and most of those pledged to the London merchants ultimately fell into the Queen's hands.[1]

[1] Mendoza, writing to Philip from London, August 8, 1582, gives one instance of this amongst several. He says: "The Queen lent Dom Antonio £3,000 when he was here, and I understand she peremptorily demands payment of the sum, taking possession of the diamond which was pledged here for a sum of £5,000 lent by merchants, who offer to relinquish their claim to the Queen, if she will lend them £30,000 free of interest for six years out of the bars brought by Drake, which they will repay in five yearly instalments of £6,000 each. So far as I can learn, this talk of the loan is a mere fiction and a cloak under which the Queen may keep the diamond for the £8,000 on the ground that the merchants advanced the £5,000

## THE COUNTER-ARMADA OF 1589.

Some were left with Walsingham for safety, but when they were demanded Walsingham alleged that he was personally responsible for some provisions Antonio had ordered, and made difficulties about giving them up. So long as the money lasted Antonio might spend it in England and leave his diamonds, but some specious excuse was always invented to prevent any openly hostile expedition to attack Philip leaving an English port under Antonio's banner. The rascally Dr. Lopez, who was afterwards hanged at Tyburn for attempting to poison the Queen, was Dom Antonio's go-between and interpreter at Court, and he, greedy scamp as he was, made a good thing out of it until the money began to run short, when, in his usual way, he sold his knowledge to Philip, and attempted more than once to poison the unhappy Pretender. Antonio, indeed, was surrounded by spies though he knew it not,[1] but he found he was being frustrated, betrayed, and defrauded in every way in England, and his precious jewels the meanwhile were slipping away. So, in dudgeon with the greedy English, he fled to France and took

by her express order, without which they would not have done so. This plan was invented by Cecil in order to prevent Dom Antonio from getting his diamond back again."
This diamond is probably identical with the celebrated stone given by Charles I. when Prince of Wales to the Count-Duke of Olivares, favourite of Philip IV., when Charles and Buckingham went on their foolish visit to Madrid. A contemporary account (Soto's MS. in the Academy of History, Madrid) describes the diamond as being of the purest water, weighing eight carats and called "the Portuguese," from its having been one of the crown jewels of Portugal. It had a great pearl pendent from it.
[1] See Calendar of Spanish State Papers of Elizabeth, vol. 3, for particulars of them.

such of his vessels as he could gain possession of with him. Catharine de Medici, the Queen-mother, was, for form's sake, a claimant to the Portuguese throne herself, but her shadowy claim was soon abandoned when she had an opportunity of cherishing such a thorn as Antonio promised to be in the side of her powerful late son-in-law Philip. Antonio still had jewels, and whilst they lasted he was treated with consideration and regal splendour in that gay and dissolute Court. He certainly got more return for them there than he got in England. Many were scattered in bribes amongst the easy-going ladies and painted mignons of the Court, and most of the rest went to pay for two costly naval expeditions fitted out in France in the Queen-mother's name, to enable Antonio to hold the islands faithful to him.[1] But Santa Cruz swooped down upon Terceira as Alba had pounced upon Lisbon, and the merry-making crew of revellers was soon disposed of. Then poor Antonio fell upon evil days. The emissaries of Philip, false friends of Antonio, tried time after time to put him out of the way by poison and the dagger, but he was ever on the watch; and for help and safety, still sanguine and hopeful, drifted from France to England and from England to France,

[1] The first of these, in 1582, commanded by Strozzi, consisted of 55 ships and 5,000 men. Terceira, which was held for Dom Antonio, welcomed it at once, and in the midst of the rejoicings to celebrate the event the Spanish fleet under Santa Cruz appeared and scattered the French like chaff, Strozzi being killed, Antonio barely escaping, and the fleet almost entirely destroyed. The second expedition in the following year under Aymar de Chastes with 6,000 men was, curiously enough, beaten by Santa Cruz in the same place and under exactly similar circumstances ("Un prétendant portugais du xvi. siècle").

## THE COUNTER-ARMADA OF 1589.    17

the plaything in the game alternately of Elizabeth and Catharine, to be taken up or cast aside as the interests of the players dictated.

Philip's open attempt to invade England in 1588 seemed once more to offer him a chance of success, and his hopes rose again. One gem, and one only, of all the rich store he brought from Portugal was left to him; but that was the most precious of them all, the eighth greatest diamond in the world, the chief ornament in the Russian imperial crown to-day.[1] It was his last stake, and he decided to risk it on his chance. It was pledged to Monsieur de Sancy, whose name it ever afterwards bore, and with the money so raised Antonio started for England to tempt Elizabeth to link his desperate cause with her hopes of revenge upon Spain.

This was in the autumn of the Armada year, 1588, and, all unconscious of his vile treachery to him, Antonio once more evoked Lopez's influence at Court to gain the ear of the Queen and the support of his close friend Walsingham. The venal Jew, who was for ever craving rewards and favours, persuaded the Queen, no doubt for a weighty consideration, to listen anew to the pretender's proposals.[2]

[1] It is a curious co-incidence that this gem was long afterwards carried away from England by another fugitive King, James II., who sold it, as Antonio had done, to provide for his needs. It had formerly belonged to Charles the Bold of Burgundy, the great-grandfather of Philip II.

[2] After the return of the expedition Lopez writes (July 12, 1589) to Walsingham, deeply regretting that the Queen had been induced by his advice to spend so much money to no purpose, and hinting that he had intimated to Dom Antonio that he and his Portuguese were not wanted in England. On the same day he himself craves for help in his need and again asks for a thirty years' monopoly of the import of aniseed and

The adventurer-king was confident that if he could once set foot again in his own country with an armed force the whole population would flock to his standard, and he was ready to promise anything, and everything, for the help he wanted. Already in 1582, when Catharine de Medici had aided him to fit out the fleet under Strozzi at Bordeaux which was to hold Terceira and restore Antonio to the throne, the desperate gamester had promised her the great empire of Brazil as a reward for her help; and now, if my Spanish diarist is to be believed, he offered to make himself a mere vassal of Elizabeth if he were successful.

In the Record Office there is a bond by which Antonio undertakes, in February, 1589, to reimburse to the adventurers all the cost of the enterprise and the pay of the soldiers, but the Spanish manuscript gives the substance of an agreement between Dom Antonio and the Queen which promises much more than mere repayment. The diarist I quote says:—

"The Queen, cautious and astute as she was, caught at the fine promises that Dom Antonio held out and insisted that an agreement should be entered into; which was done, in substance as set forth in the following clauses. This agreement was brought, written in the English language, by a certain Portuguese named Diego Rodriguez who

sumach into England. He was executed in 1592, and was in high favour almost up to the day of his arrest. In the Mendoza Papers in the National Archives in Paris, to which I have had access, are documents proving that he made a regular trade of poisoning—or attempting to poison, as he does not seem to have been very successful in the cases recorded.

# THE COUNTER-ARMADA OF 1589.

came hither as treasurer to this expedition and passed over to the service of our lord the King on the eleventh of June. The clauses, translated into Castilian, say as follows :—

"First her Majesty the Queen of England undertakes to provide a fleet of one hundred and twenty vessels and twenty thousand men—15,000 soldiers and 5,000 sailors—with captains for both services, to go and restore Dom Antonio to the throne of Portugal.

"Dom Antonio undertakes that within eight days from the arrival of the said fleet in Portugal the whole country will submit to him in accordance with the letters he has received from the principal people in the said kingdom.

"Item, That on arriving in Lisbon the city will be reduced at once without any defence and all Castilians in it killed and destroyed, and, for the friendship and aid thus shown him in recovering his kingdom, he undertakes to fulfil the following things —namely :—

"First that within two months of his arrival in Lisbon he will hand to her Majesty the Queen as an aid to the costs of the fleet five millions in gold.

"Item, In testimony of the help she has given him he will pay every year to the Queen for ever three hundred thousand ducats in gold, placed and paid in London at his cost.

"Item, that the English should have full liberty to trade and travel in Portugal and the Portuguese Indies and the Portuguese equal freedom in England.

"Item, That if the Queen should not desire to fit out a fleet against the King of Spain in England she shall be at liberty to do so in Lisbon and shall be helped in all that may be necessary.

"Item, That the castles of São Gian, Torre de Belem, Capariza, Oton, São Felipe, Oporto, Coimbra and the other Portuguese fortresses shall be perpetually occupied by English soldiers paid at the cost of Dom Antonio.

"Item, That there shall be perpetual peace between her Majesty the Queen and Dom Antonio and they shall mutually help each other on all occasions without excuse of any sort.

"Item, That all the Bishoprics and Archbishoprics in Portugal shall be filled by English Catholics and the Archbishopric of Lisbon shall be at once filled by the appointment of Monsieur de la Torques (*sic*).

"Item, On arriving at Lisbon every infantry man shall receive twelve months pay, and three extra, as a present from Dom Antonio and they shall be allowed to sack the city for twelve days, on condition that no man of any rank shall presume to harm any Portuguese or molest the churches or houses wherein maidens are dwelling; and also that they pay in money for whatever they may need in the country. Which agreement her Majesty ordered to be duly executed under date of last day of December 1588."[1]

The Spanish scribe waxes very indignant at this document, showing, as he says it does, the sagacity of the Queen and the blind infatuation of Dom Antonio,

---

[1] It is certain from letters of Dom Antonio's friends in London, now in the Archives Nationales (K 1567), that it was not until the end of December that Antonio was confident that the fleet was really intended to aid him.

"who gives up the substance for the shadow of kingship, and is content to make the Portuguese subjects slaves so that he shall be called King." But he is most shocked at the sacrifice to this "pestilent sect" of the two instincts dearest to the Portuguese heart, namely, devotion to their Church and their greed of gain; the first of which, he says, will be destroyed by relationship with the accursed heretics, and the second attacked by the substitution for "our lord the king who does not spend a maravedi of Portuguese money, but brings Castilian money into Portugal," of a King who has promised to pay away more than the Portuguese can ever give him. "And besides," he says, plaintively, "we Castilians and Portuguese are not so estranged in blood of boundaries after all, for only a line divides us, and if it be hard for the Portuguese to endure connection with their Castilian kinsmen who bring riches into the country and take nothing from it how much worse will it be to put up with a nation so greedy and insolent as the English, separated from them by land and sea, and foreign to them in customs, language, faith and laws?"

He ridicules the idea of five millions (of ducats) in gold being paid, and says he supposes that a mistake of a nought has been made, which probably was the case; but even then, he asks, where is such a sum as 500,000 ducats to come from, "let alone the 15 months' pay"? However correct or otherwise in detail this agreement may be, it is certain that some such terms were made, and it may be safely assumed that Elizabeth, with her keen eye to the main chance, would take care to make the best bargain she could out of the sanguine eagerness of Dom Antonio, who would be ready to promise "mounts and marvels" for ready aid.[1] My Portuguese diarist also ridicules the impossible terms promised by the Pretender, but adds the false finishing-touch, evidently spread by the Castilians for the purpose of arousing the indignation and resistance of the Portuguese, that the churches were to be plundered and the Portuguese inhabitants of Lisbon despoiled.

It would appear strange at first sight that Elizabeth should have made any proviso for the benefit of English Catholics whom she had sometimes treated so unmercifully, but on other occasions she had favoured the idea of English Catholic settlements being established across the seas under her sway; and the great body of Catholic sympathisers resident in England had not acted altogether unpatriotically in the hour of panic and terror on the threat of invasion. It would, therefore, not have been an impolitic move to earn their gratitude and further loyalty by opening a new field for them outside of her own country but, in a manner, under her control.

On the 23rd of February, 1589,[2] the Queen issued a warrant of her instructions for the expedition, ap-

---

[1] There is a rough memorandum in Burleigh's writing, September 20, 1588, in the Record Office, setting down the details of the proposed expedition, in which he mentions that four thousand men are to be sent for from Holland, as well as two thousand horsemen volunteers. At the foot of the memorandum Burleigh sets down the "Articles of offers from King Antonio.
"1. To attempt to burn ye shippes in Lysbon and Civill."
"2. To tak Lysbon."
"3. To tak the Ilands."
[2] Calendar of State Papers (Domestic). Record Office.

## THE COUNTER-ARMADA OF 1589.

pointing Sir John Norris [1] and Sir Francis Drake to the chief command thereof, and in it lays down precise rules for their guidance. She says that the objects of the expedition are two : namely, first to distress the King of Spain's ships, and second to get possession of some of the Azores, in order to intercept treasure passing to and from the East and West Indies. Also to assist the King Dom Antonio to recover the kingdom of Portugal, "*if it shall be found the public voice in the kingdom be favourable to him.*"

On the same date authority was given to Norris and Drake to issue warrants to the adventurers for their shares in the enterprise ; and the Queen herself undertook to repay them if the expedition were stopped at her instance. Courtiers and swashbucklers touted their hardest for subscriptions to this joint-stock warfare, and pressure was put upon country gentlemen to subscribe liberally as a proof of their patriotism—a pressure not to be disregarded in those doubtful times.[2] The Queen's subscription ultimately reached £20,000, besides seven ships of the Royal Navy. Promises of money and arms were forthcoming in abundance, and flocks of idlers, high and low, offered their valuable services. The scum of the towns, the sweepings of the jails, were pressed for the voyage, and Pricket (or Wingfield),

---

[1] Norris had greatly distinguished himself in Ireland and the Netherlands, notwithstanding Leicester's persistent attempts to ruin him ; and, from his conduct there and during this expedition, he would appear to have been brave, but turbulent and of doubtful discretion.

[2] Philip was informed late in December by his spies in England that Drake was to contribute 12,000 crowns, the Earl of Essex 10,000, Norris 8,000, and London Merchants 24,000, and that the Queen had advanced £20,000.

in his apology for the expedition, lays most of the blame of failure on the kind of men they had, and complains bitterly of the justices and mayors sending them " base disordered persons sent unto us as living at home without rule." He says many idle young men, having seen their fellows come back after a few months in the Netherlands full of their brave deeds and tales of the wars, "thought to follow so good an example and to spend like time amongst us," and finding soldiering a harder trade than they had bargained for, were not likely to make good troops.

The misfortunes of the enterprise began before it was fairly launched. As may be supposed, promises of support, given under such circumstances as those which I have described, were hardly likely to be strictly kept, and the performance in this case fell far short. Pricket (or Wingfield) bemoans this as follows: "For hath not the want of 8 out of the 12 pieces of Artillerie which was promised unto the adventure lost her Majestie the possession of the Groyne and many other places as hereafter shall appear whose defensible rampiers were greater than our batterie (such as it was) could force and therefore were lost unattempted. It was also resolved to send 600 English horse out of the Low Countries whereof we had not one, notwithstanding the great charge expended in their transportation hither. . . . Did wee not want seaven of the thirteene old Companies we should have had from thence? foure of the ten Dutch Companies and sixe of their men-of-warre for the sea from the Hollanders? which I may justly say we wanted in that we might have had so many good souldiers, so many good shippes, and so many able bodies more than we had

"Did there not, upon the first thinking of the journey, divers gallant courtiers put in their names for adventurers to the summe of £10,000, who seeing it went not forward in good earnest, advised themselves better and laid the want of so much money on the journey?"

But the expedition was got together somehow. Men were cajoled into the belief that they were going on a great plundering excursion, and would soon return home again loaded, as Wingfield says, with "Portogues" and "Milrayes" which should make them independent for life. There were no surgeons, no carriages for the hurt and sick, and from the first the discipline was of the loosest. Provisions were said to be shipped for two months, but in some of the ships the men declared they were starved from the first day.

Even amongst contemporaries much difference of statement exists as to the number of ships and men that composed the expedition, although this difference is partly accounted for by a fact which will presently be mentioned, and which has hitherto escaped notice. We should probably not be far out when we put the number of soldiers who left Plymouth at about 16,000 and the sailors at 2,500.[1]

[1] On the eve of departure Norris and Drake officially told the Council that the total number of all sorts was 23,375. Captain Fenner, Drake's vice-admiral, gives the number as 21,000 (Bacon Papers). Captain Baillie, of the *Mary German*, in a letter to Lord Shrewsbury says the landsmen alone were 20,000; whilst Drake himself, in one of his many letters begging for supplies, says, "20,000 men cannot be kept for a trifle." Camden, the historian, speaks of 12,500 soldiers, and Speed, following Pricket's tract, puts the number of landsmen at

Of the men-at-arms all but the three or four thousand old soldiers, mostly from the Netherland wars, were idle vagabonds whose first idea was loot and whose last was fighting. In addition to these there were 1,200 gentlemen or more, the flotsam and jetsam of the Court, younger sons of slender fortunes, and gallants whose hearts were aflame to do good service to their country. Seven [1] of the bravest of the Queen's ships, of three hundred tons burden each, twenty other armed ships, and a large number of transports and galleys of light draft, would have completed the fleet, but sixty German smacks and sloops, which had been wintering in Holland on their way to Spain, were pressed into the service and added to the number, which finally reached nearly two hundred sail. The 1st of February was the date originally fixed for starting, but when that date arrived nothing was ready but the army of idlers, who wanted feeding, so that when the fleet could have sailed it was found that most of the stores had been consumed, and in some ships not a week's provision remained. Money ran short, and Drake and Norris wrote, day after day,

---

11,000 and mariners at 2,500. There is a letter in the British Museum from one of the Portuguese nobles (Count de Portalegre) to Philip II., in which the army before Lisbon is spoken of as 12,000 men; and the Spanish diarist whose MS. I have mentioned says 16,000 men-at-arms left England and very few sailors. The terrible mortality from sickness, &c., and the comparatively small number that came back made English writers of the time anxious to minimise the disaster by underrating the numbers of the expedition.

[1] English accounts usually say six, but I am inclined to believe the Spanish account is correct, as Drake writes to the Council (Record Office, Domestic Calendar), after the six ships had been appointed, asking for a larger vessel, the *Victory*, "in respect of the King Dom Antonio."

during all the month of March and first two weeks in April, heartrending letters to the Council and to Walsingham. The provisions were run out, they said; the enterprise must fall through if help be not sent at once. They point out the dishonour and disgrace of such a lame ending, and again and again beg for more provisions.

The innkeepers and victuallers of Canterbury, Southampton, Winchester, Plymouth, and elsewhere wrote dunning letters to the Queen for money due for stores supplied. The Dutch shipmasters commanding the flyboat transports contributed by the States formally protested and refused to put to sea with such insufficient provender as they had; and, just as it looked as if the expedition would break down for good, there came providentially into the harbour a Flemish ship with a cargo of dried herrings, another with five hundred pipes of wine, and above all a sloop loaded with barley. These provisions were promptly transferred to the fleet to the dismay of the masters, who protested for many a day afterwards, fruitlessly, against the confiscation of their cargoes. The expedition was declared ready for sea, but then came tales of contrary winds that kept them in and out of harbour for several days more; and one day, whilst they were thus detained, the Queen's kinsman, Knollys, comes post haste from London. Had anybody seen or heard anything of the young Earl of Essex, the Queen's last new pet? Curiously enough nobody had, although only the day before a party of young gallants had dashed into Plymouth from London all dusty and travel-stained, and had been received with open arms by the courtiers and officers on the fleet. Hot-blooded Essex, with all the thoughtlessness of his twenty-two years, tired of sickly dallying with an old lady and of squabbling with Raleigh, tired of his debts, his duns and duties as prime favourite, had made up his mind to see some fun, and had fled against the Queen's orders. No one had seen him of course, but the *Swiftsure*, with Sir Roger Williams, the general second in command of the army, mysteriously left the harbour as soon as Knollys had told his tale. But a few hours later the Earl of Huntingdon came with warrants of arrest and all manner of peremptory papers, and Drake saw the matter was serious. Boats were sent scouring after the *Swiftsure*, but could get no news of the missing earl. The other ships stayed in Plymouth ten days longer for a fair wind, but the *Swiftsure* came back no more until the expedition was at an end. Drake and Norris wrote nearly every day until they sailed disclaiming any knowledge of Essex or his intention to join the force, and expressing their deep sorrow; but the Queen did not believe them, and from that time had nothing but hard words and sour looks for an adventure that had robbed her of her favourite. At length, on the 13th of April 1589, (O.S.), the expedition finally left Plymouth, but even then it was only a feint in order that the men might be kept together and not stray on shore and get out of hand. "The crosse windes held us two daies after our going out, the Generalls being wearie thrust to sea in the same wisely chosing rather to attend a change out there than to lose it when it came by having their men on shoare."

Knocking about in the Channel in bad weather

was, however, not to the taste of some of the ruffians who thought they were bound over summer seas to a paradise of plunder; and three thousand men in twenty-five ships, probably most of them owned by the recalcitrant Dutchmen, deserted and were heard of no more—at least so far as the expedition was concerned. This desertion to some extent explains the divergence between the accounts given of the numbers of the expedition.

The rest of the fleet on the third day caught a fair wind and stretched across the Bay of Biscay in fine spring weather. They were four days before their eyes were gladdened by the sight of Cape Finisterra, but in the week they had been at sea their provisions were running out. Murmurs at the short commons were heard on all the ships, and it was seen that the only way to keep the scratch crews from open mutiny was to give them a chance of plunder.

So, instead of obeying the Queen's strict injunctions—for Drake was a far better hand at commanding than obeying—and landing poor Dom Antonio on the country he assured them was yearning for him, they bore down upon Corunna, on the northwest coast of Spain. For months before this, as the difficulties attending the fitting out of a new Armada became more evident, terror-stricken rumours had pervaded Spain that the dreaded Drake, who had now become a sort of supernatural bogey to the Spanish people, was about to descend upon this or the other place on the coast and wreak a terrible vengeance for the Armada. Early in January even false news came to Madrid that an English fleet had appeared outside Santander, and at the end of the month the Venetian ambassador in Madrid writes to his Doge that news had just arrived from Lisbon that forty sail of English ships were out, divided into squadrons of eight or ten ships each, and were doing much damage. It was feared, he said, that they would all unite under Drake and make an attempt first upon Portugal and then will go to the Azores, and finally to the Indies. The fitting out in Spain of fifty ships to protect the seas was hurried on; but, says the Venetian, "it is thought that two months must elapse before they can be ready, and then one does not see what they can do against such light ships as the enemy's."

Philip was dangerously ill and sick at heart. Fear reigned supreme in his councils—fear that Drake the terrible would ravage the coasts whilst Henry of Navarre crossed the Pyrenees. The Portuguese nobles were known to be disaffected, and a rising in favour of Dom Antonio was feared. Philip, with the energy of despair, did what he could, ill as he was, immersed in mountains of papers dealing with trivial detail. But he could do little. The Portuguese nobles who were at all doubtful were ordered to come to Madrid, the Spanish grandees were enjoined to raise and arm their followers and hold themselves in readiness to march either towards the Pyrenees or to Lisbon. Then rumours came that the Moorish King of Fez was to act in concert with the English, and seize the Spanish possessions on the African coast opposite Gibraltar.

It will thus be seen in the distracted condition of affairs that Spain was practically defenceless against a sudden descent on the coast, but most defenceless of all at the extremely remote northwest corner of Spain, where Drake decided to land. The fear was mostly for Portugal, where, we are told, "the population is so impatient of the present rule that neither the severity of penalties, garrisons of soldiers, nor the ability of governors have succeeded in quieting the contumacious spirits. This causes a dread lest Drake who is acquainted with those waters may furnish pretexts for fresh risings and they (the Spaniards) wish to be ready to crush them."[1] The troops they raised, says the Venetian ambassador, were inferior in quality of horses and men: raw levies pressed unwillingly into the service, whilst Portugal was in violent and open commotion awaiting the arrival of Drake the deliverer.

But whilst all panic-stricken regards were directed upon Portugal, Drake and his joint-stock Armada suddenly appeared where they were least expected, before Corunna, and cast anchor; and the men, nothing loath, were put on shore in a little bay within a mile of the town. There was no one to stay their landing, and they had come nearly to the gates before a hasty muster of townsfolk met them. These, all unprepared and surprised as they were, soon retreated when they saw the force that was coming against them, and shut themselves up behind the gates and walls of the town. The place was weak and ill-garrisoned, commanded by the Marquis de Cerralba, and could not hope to hold out against a regular siege, but there were three galleons loaded with arms in the harbour, which the new commander-in-chief in Madrid, Alba's son Fernando, said would be a much greater loss than the town

[1] Venetian Calendar.

itself. The English slept the first night in the cottages and mills belonging to a hamlet on the bank of one of the small streams discharging into the bay, and out of gunshot of the walls. They were, however, quite unmolested by the terrified townsfolk, although the galleon *San Juan* and her consorts in the harbour kept up a fire upon them as they passed to and fro.

The place indeed was utterly taken by surprise. The Cortes of Galicia were in session at the time, the people peacefully pursuing their ordinary avocations; the soldiers of the garrison were nearly all on furlough, scattered over the province; "and, in short, every one was so far from expecting an attack that they had no time to turn the useless out of the town nor put their dearest possessions in safety." The wife and daughter, indeed, of the Governor Cerralba at the first alarm fled in their terror two leagues on foot, through the night, to a place of safety, but after that none dared to move. The lower part of the town fronting the harbour was protected on the land side only by weak walls, and was unfit for protracted defence. The townspeople therefore agreed that if the place were attacked on the water side it would be untenable, and arranged that as soon as those in the higher town on the hill should espy the English boats approaching they were to signal the low town by a fire, so that the people below might make their escape to the better defensible upper portion of the town. Some artillery was landed by the English to stop the fire of the Spanish ships, and on the morning of the second day the town was attacked simultaneously by 1,200 men in long boats and pinnaces under Captain Fenner and

Colonel Huntly; and by Colonels Brett and Umpton on one side, and Captains Richard Wingfield and Sampson on the other by escalade. The people in the upper town, either from panic or oversight, neglected to give the signal, and those below, thinking they had only to deal with an escalade on their walls by Captain Wingfield, fought desperately until they found two other forces had entered at other points, and then panic seized them, and, as Pricket (or Wingfield) describes it, " The towne was entered in three severall places; with an huge crie, the inhabitants betooke them to the high towne which they might with less perrill doo for that ours being strangers knew not the way to cut them off. The rest that were not put to the sword in furie fled to the rockes in the iland and hid themselves in chambers and sellers which were everie day found out in great numbers." A perfect saturnalia seems to have been thereupon indulged in by the English troops. Here was the fruition of all their golden dreams—a flying, panic-stricken foe, ample provisions to loot and to waste, and, above all, wine without limit. " Some others (*i.e.*, Spaniards) also found favour to bee taken prisoners but the rest falling into the hands of the common soldiers had their throates cut to the number of 500. . . . Everie seller was found full of wine whereupon our men by inordinate drinking both grewe senseless of the danger of the shot of the towne which hurt many of them, being druncke, and took the first ground of their sickness, for of such was our first and chiefest mortalitie."

Great stores of provisions were found in the lower town, and many were also captured as they were brought in by Spanish ships. These provisions were alleged by the English to have been collected for the purpose of a new attack on England, and it is quite probable that such was the case, although the evidence on the point is insufficient. At all events, the destruction of these stores is the only act which in any sense justified the expedition sent out by the adventurers.[1]

The next few days were spent by the invaders in desultory attacks on the upper town, burning a monastery and scouring the country round by Colonel Huntly, who "brought home verie great store of cowes and sheep to our great reliefe." A great crowd of country people, two thousand strong, came down with a run one day, armed with rough weapons, to see what manner of men were these who raided their cattle and burned their poor huts, but a discharge of musketry killed eighteen of them and sent the rest scampering away.[2] On "our side" we hear of an improvised gabion battery being shaken down by the first fire, and Master Spenser, the lieutenant of the ordnance, and many others killed by the enemy's guns as they stood all exposed. But brave Sir Edward Norris held his ground manfully

[1] The Venetian ambassador at Madrid, in his account to the Doge of the events at Corunna, says that Drake's booty from that place consisted of "6,000 salted oxen, fifteen thousand jars of biscuit, 6,000 barrels of powder and 3,000 hogsheads of wine ; all of it provision for the Armada which went so unsuccessfully last year, or else to furnish a new Armada according to the design which they entertain. This plunder will prove of the greatest service to the English . . . and here the news has caused much chagrin ; and it is hidden or minimised as much as possible."

[2] It was said in Madrid that these two thousand peasants had only six muskets amongst them.—*Venetian Calendar of State Papers.*

until his orders came to cease firing and retire. Captain Goodwin makes a mistake of a signal and prematurely attacks the upper town, getting shot through the mouth as a reward, and the "common sort" drop off by drink, pestilence, and bullet plentifully enough, but unrecorded. Norris and Drake sent home by Knollys flaming accounts of their success, and still asked for more provisions from England and more money; but Queen Bess was in a towering rage, and was not to be appeased. She could not forget or forgive the loss of her favourite. Raleigh and Blount were very well in their way, but she wanted Essex, and suspected Drake and Norris of being parties to his escape. On the 4th of May (O.S.) she wrote to them a remarkable letter, showing that she had tidings of Essex's being on board the *Swiftsure*, and demanding dire vengeance on Sir Roger Williams, who helped to hide him.[1]

[1] "She dowteth not but they have thoroughly weighed the heinousness of the offence lately committed by Sir Roger Williams in forsaking the army with one of her principal ships. If they have not already inflicted punishment of death upon him he is to be deprived of all command and kept in safe custody at their perils. If the Earl of Essex has joined the fleet they are to send him home instantly. If they do not they shall truly answer for the same at their smart, for as we have authority to rule so we look to be obeyed and these be no childish actions."—*State Papers* (*Domestic*), May 4, 1589.

The draft of this letter, deeply scored by the Queen's own hand, was submitted to Walsingham by Windebanke, the Secretary of the Signet, and the minister said that although the letter was as mild as could be expected "under the circumstances," he much feared that any proceedings against one so beloved as Sir Roger Williams would breed mutiny. And so apparently thought the generals, for they took no notice of the Queen's commands.

The Queen wrote another outspoken letter to the generals on the 20th of May, in which she says they were perverting the object of their expedition; which was to burn the King of

After four days of fruitless pottering the troops were presumably sober enough to attempt an attack upon the upper town, and the guns being pointed against it, the general sent a drummer to summon it to surrender before he opened fire. The summons was answered by a musket-shot that laid the poor drummer low, but immediately afterwards a pole was projected over the town wall, and from it there dangled a man hanged by the neck. This was the man who had fired the dastard shot. And then the Spaniards called a parley, and begged that the war might be fair on both sides, as it certainly should be on theirs. Considering that five hundred of their brethren had their throats cut ruthlessly, after they had submitted, this was magnanimous at least; "but as for surrendering the towne, they listened not greatly thereunto."

So Norris banged away with his cannon for three days to make a breach in the wall of the high town, and at the same time set men to work to bore a mine in the rock beneath the gate, and at the end of the time, all being in readiness, and his men, under the gallant brothers Wingfield, with Philpot, Sampson, and York, waiting to storm the two breaches, the mine turned out a dismal failure, and

---

Spain's navy and restore Dom Antonio, and then proceed to the Azores. Corunna, she says, is of little importance and the risk great, and she commands them to fulfil her orders at once. Do not, she says, suffer yourselves to be transported with an haviour of vainglory which will obfuscate the eyes of your judgment.

Secretary Windebanke, writing to Heneage at the same time, says the Queen is strangely set against the expedition, and is intensely incensed at the fruitless attack on Corunna. "She thinks they went to places for their own profit rather than for her service."—*State Papers (Domestic)*.

nothing was done. The next day they tried again, and this time with such success that one half of the gate tower was blown up, and the other half left tottering. On rushed the assailants. Some few got into the town, but as the officers and their immediate followers set foot on the breach and waved their men onward, down came the other half of the tower upon them, and crushed them beneath the ruins. Two standards were lost, but captured again, and scores of men were killed. In the dust and terror the unpractised soldiery thought they were the victims of some stratagem of the enemy and fled, leaving the officers and gentlemen volunteers to extricate themselves as best they could. Poor Captain Sydenham "was pitifully lost, who having three or foure great stones on his lower parts was held so fast, as neither himself could stirre, nor anie reasonable companie recover him. Notwithstanding the next day being found to be alive there was 10 or 12 lost in attempting to relieve him."

On the other side of the town the breach made in the walls by the culverins was too small, and when brave Yorke had led his men to push of pike with those who stood in the breach, the slope of rubbish on which they mounted suddenly slipped down, and left them six feet below the opening, and so they had to retreat too, through a narrow lane exposed to the full fire of the enemy, and thus the attack failed at both points.

In the meanwhile all Galicia was arming, and a prisoner brought in by the cattle raiders gave news that the Count de Andrada, with 8,000 men, was at Puente de Burgos, six miles off, which was said to be only the beginning of a great army being got together by the Count de Altamira. On the next day, May 6th, it was determined to attack them, and nine regiments of English marched out to the fray. The vanguard, under Sir Edward Norris, was divided into three bodies under Captains Middleton, Antony Wingfield, and Ethrington, respectively, and attacked the enemy in the centre and both flanks simultaneously, routing them at the first charge. They only stopped running when they came to a fortified bridge over a creek of the sea, on the other side of which was their entrenched camp. Sir Edward Norris, with Colonel Sidney, and Captains Fulford, Hinder and others, always in front, fought hand to hand over the bridge and into the trenches, under "an incredible volie of shot for that the shot of their armie flanked upon both sides of the bridge." But the earthworks were soon abandoned, and Sir Edward Norris, in his very eagerness to be first, tumbled over his pike and hurt his head grievously. The officers of the vanguard were nearly all more or less hurt, but when the enemy had fled the usual amusement of the "common sort" commenced. All round for miles the country was burnt and spoiled, and the flying countrymen were slaughtered without mercy or quarter. "So many as 2,000 men might kill in pursuit, so many fell before us that day"; and after that was over and the men were returning, hundreds of cowering peasants were found hidden in hedges and vineyards, and their "throates" were cut. Two hundred poor creatures took refuge in a "cloyster," which was burned and the men put to the sword as they tried to escape. "You might

## THE COUNTER-ARMADA OF 1589.

have seene the countrie more than three miles of compasse on fyre," says the English eye-witness, and he grows quite hysterical in his laudation of the English valour; but the Spanish accounts tell how the Netherlands wars, and the fears for Portugal and the French frontier, had denuded all northwestern Spain of soldiers, Count de Andrada's force only being a hasty levy of undrilled and practically unarmed countrymen, who were easily routed.

The next day the English began to ship their artillery and baggage and made ready to depart, after again unsuccessfully trying to fire the upper town. They managed indeed to burn down every house in the lower town, and they set sail on May 9 (O.S.), 1589.

In the meanwhile utter dismay reigned at Madrid. What was left of the fleet was acknowledged to be powerless for defence, and none knew for certain where the blow was to fall. The accounts from Corunna were intercepted by the Government, and were surmised to be worse than they really were; but still the general opinion was not far out in supposing that Drake could not do much permanent harm on the open places on the coast, but would eventually attack either Lisbon or Cadiz. Fernando de Toledo was appointed commander-in-chief, but soldiers could not be got together.[1] Pietro de Medici was hastily ordered to raise 6,000 mercenaries in Italy; and Contarini writes from Madrid to the Doge: "It is true that for want

---

[1] The bitter jest in Madrid at the time was that, whereas with the Armada the year before there went an army with no commander, there was now a commander with no army.

of soldiers they have adopted a plan which may prove more hurtful than helpful; they have enrolled Portuguese, and so have armed the very people whom they have cause to fear, but perhaps they think that as they have destroyed the leaders they have made themselves safe."

Norris was almost as much dreaded as Drake himself, and his skill and daring suggested to the terrified Court that he might intend to cut through the neck of land upon which Corunna stands, and entirely isolate the town, which he might then make into a great depôt for an English fleet. Philip, we are told, was in great anxiety, "not so much on account of the loss he suffers as for the insult which he feels that he has received in the fact that a woman, mistress of only half an island, with the help of a corsair and a common soldier, should have ventured on so arduous an enterprise, and dared to molest so powerful a sovereign."

The bitterest blow of all to Philip was the knowledge that Spain's impotence was now patent to the world, and that the mere presence of Drake was sufficient to paralyse all resistance. When the English force re-embarked at Corunna, says Contarini, they were not even molested, so glad were the besieged to be rid of him at any cost. "Whilst Drake was at Corunna he was so strongly entrenched that he suffered no loss at all. If he had remained a few days longer the place would have fallen for the reliefs were not as ready as was rumoured. Drake occupied the place called the fishmarket. He knocked down houses, seized cattle, killed soldiers, released officers on ransom, and by pillage of the suburbs and the burning of monasteries seemed to care more for plunder than for glory."[1] As we have seen, in fact, Drake's sole reason for going to Corunna at all against his mistress' orders was to satisfy with loot the mutinous rabble on board his ships, but of this the Spaniards were naturally ignorant.

The fleet sailed out of Corunna on the 9th of May, leaving smoking ruins behind them for many miles around; but contrary winds drove the ships back again and again. At last, on the 13th of May, the truant *Swiftsure* hove in sight, " to the great delight of us all," bringing the Earl of Essex, Sir Roger Williams, Master Walter Devereux ("the Earl's brother, a gentleman of wonderful great hope "), Sir Philip Butler ("who hath always been most inward with him "), and Sir Edward Wingfield.

However glad the men of lower rank may have been to see the dashing young nobleman, Drake and Norris can hardly have been overjoyed. They knew by this time that Elizabeth was in earnest about it, and that the purse-strings would be drawn tighter, and the censure be stricter, whilst her errant favourite was with the expedition; and some inkling of this even reached the writer of the English account of the expedition. " The Earle," he says, " having put himself into the journey against the opinion of the world, and as it seemed, to the hazard of his great fortune, though to the great advancement of his reputation (for as the honourable carriage of himself towards all men doth make him highlie esteemed at home, so did his exceeding forwardness in all services make him to be wondered

[1] Contarini to the Doge. Venetian Calendar of State Papers.

at amongst us) who I say put off . . . because he would avoide the importunity of messengers that were daily sent for his return and some other causes more secret to himself."

The earl's first request was that he should always be allowed to lead the vanguard of the army; "which was easilie granted unto him, being so desirous to satisfie him in all things": and thenceforward to the end of the expedition he marched at the head with Major-General Sir Roger Williams, who seemed, by the way, "not one penny the worse," for her Majesty's anathemas.

Early in the afternoon of May 16th (O.S.) the fleet cautiously approached the town of Peniche, in Portugal. Drake had learnt on his way that a great galleon from the Indies with a million crowns in gold had taken refuge under the guns of the fortress, and doubtless hoped to net so big a prize. But the Archduke Albert in Lisbon was also looking anxiously for the gold, and sent his galleys, under Bazan, to bring the galleon into the Tagus just before the arrival of the English at Peniche. The town of Peniche was held by Gonsalves de Ateide with a body of Portuguese who could not be trusted, and some Castilian reinforcements sent to him under Pedro de Guzman; but the fortress was commanded by a Captain Araujo, who was known to be secretly in favour of Dom Antonio. Here it was determined to land the force, and Ateide drew up his men at the landing-place before the fortress and opened fire upon the ships as they entered the bay. On the other side of the harbour, half a league off, the surf was running high, and a landing there was looked upon as impracticable, so that the shore was left undefended. Suddenly, when least expected by the Spaniards, Norris began to land his men on this side. Hot-headed Essex would not even wait for his boat to reach land, but jumped into the beating surf breast high with Sir Roger Williams and a band of gentlemen, and so struggled ashore to protect the landing of the rest. By the time Ateide and his 350 Castilians had reached the spot 2,000 English had landed on the beach of Consolation as it was called. Some slight show of resistance was made, and fifteen Spaniards fell at the push of the English pike; but the Castilians were out-numbered and nearly surrounded, and were forced to retire precipitately inland to a neighbouring hamlet to await reinforcements from Torres Vedras. When Norris had landed 12,000 or 13,000 men, with the loss of several boatloads in the surf, but without further molestation from the Spaniards, he summoned the Portuguese commandant of the fortress to surrender. He replied that he refused to surrender to the English, but would willingly do so to his lawful king, Dom Antonio. So the poor pretender, "bigger of spirit than of body," landed with his son Manoel, and his faithful bodyguard of a hundred Portuguese, to be received once more on his own land as a sovereign. He found all things ready for him: his canopy of state erected, plate for his table set out, and kneeling subjects seeking for his smiles. He spoke smoothly and fairly, we are told, to the country people, taking nothing from them, but giving, or at least promising, much, and assuring them all of his protection.

But if their new sovereign was chary of oppressing them, no such scruples afflicted their Castilian masters. My Portuguese diarist says that the Spaniards retaliated for Araujo's treachery in surrendering Peniche by stealing everything belonging to the Portuguese they could lay their hands upon, and he cites one case in which they took the large sum of two thousand crowns from one of the most influential friends of the Spanish cause. "But," he says, apologetically, "in confused times such as these soldiers *will* act so."

Dom Antonio's bodyguard was armed with muskets and pikes from the castle, and here the poor King kept his rough-and-ready Court for two days. He was tenacious of his regal dignity, and had many a little wrangle with the English about the scant ceremony with which they treated him. But greater disappointments were yet in store for him. The friars and peasants flocked in to salute their native king, but, alas, Antonio hoped and looked in vain for the coming of the lords and gentry from whom he expected so much. Wily Philip had been once more too cunning for his enemy At the first whisper of the expedition he had banished to distant places in his own dominions every Portuguese noble —seventy of them in all—who was not pledged hard and fast to the Castilian cause. One of Antonio's false friends, too, had escaped at Corunna, and had gone straight to Philip and divulged all the pretender's plans and the names of his supporters still in Portugal who were to help him into Lisbon. Their shrift, as may be supposed, was a short one, and when Antonio came to his kingdom he found none but monks and clowns to greet him. Such of the gentry as he approached were usually too panic-stricken to side with him, seeing the fate of others of their class, and my Portuguese scoffs at the insolence of the idea that Antonio and the English could hold Lisbon, even if they won it against all the might of Spain, or of the common Portuguese rising without the "fidalgos," and courting the ruin that would befall them if the "heretics" got the upper hand without the fidalgos to restrain them.

But Antonio put a brave face on matters, and was all eagerness to push on to his faithful capital of Lisbon, which he was confident awaited him with open arms. His confidence to a certain extent seems to have been shared by Norris, and here the second great mistake of the expedition was made. The first vital error was the fruitless waste of time at Corunna; the second was the resolution now arrived at by Norris, entirely against Drake's judgment, to march from Peniche overland forty-two miles to Lisbon. Drake, true to the sea and to the tactics by which he had so often beaten the Spaniards, was in favour of pushing on to Lisbon by sea, letting three or four fireships drift about the castle of São Gian, which commanded the entrance to the harbour, so that the smoke should spoil the aim of the guns, and then make a dash for the city—and doubtless, thought Drake, for the galleon, with its million gold crowns, lying in front of the India house. Dom Antonio, whose one idea was to keep foot on the land where he was king, sided with Norris. In vain Drake pointed out that they had no baggage train or proper provisions for a march through an enemy's country; that they had only one weak squadron of cavalry, of which the cattle was out of condition; that they had no fitting field artillery; and that once inland they would lose the support and protection of the fleet.

It was all of no avail; Dom Antonio and Norris had their way, and a single company was left to garrison Peniche,[1] supported by six ships, whilst the whole of the land forces were to march to Lisbon, and Drake undertook to bring the rest of the fleet to Cascaes, at the mouth of the river, when the weather would allow him to do so.

During the night after the landing, some cavalry under Captain Alarcon had joined the Spaniards, and a force of Portuguese militia had also been sent in by Don Luis Alencastro, but they soon deserted their colours and left their officers to shift for themselves. The next morning at four o'clock Captain Alarcon and a few of the Spanish cavalry reconnoitred the position at Peniche, but found the enemy too many for them, and could only scour back as hard as they could ride to Luis Alencastro, the Grand-Commander of

[1] A letter in the collection of the Marquis of Salisbury at Hatfield curiously illustrates the not altogether happy relations that existed between the English invaders and the pretender's friends. The letter is dated the 27th of May, and is from General Norris to Captain George (Burton ?), whom he had left in charge at Peniche, complaining that "the King is aggrieved that you do take upon you to give the word since he hath appointed a Governor. And in truth it is not reason but the Governor should have the pre-eminence and therefore henceforward fail not to let him have that honour." This is a sample of the frequent complaints that the English did not treat Antonio quite as a king expected to be treated in his own realm. The fact was that Antonio had been too long a suppliant and a fugitive dependent largely upon Elizabeth's caprices for the English to regard him otherwise than as a tool for their own ends.

the Order of Christ, who was endeavouring to reorganise a body of Portuguese a few miles off, on the road to Lisbon. But terrible tales of the strength of the English had already spread; and when Alarcon and Guzman reached the Grand-Commander they found his hasty levies in a panic at the story that Drake had brought with him nine hundred great Irish dogs as fierce as lions, and "capable of eating up a world of folks." So they flatly refused to stir; and the Grand-Commander could do no more than hasten back to Lisbon to inform the Cardinal-Archduke Albert of the state of affairs, whilst Guzman, with the troops, fell back upon Torres-Vedras, to hold if possible the road to Lisbon.

In the meanwhile the capital was in a state of intense excitement. The native inhabitants, with a lively recollection of the sacking of the city by Alba, flocked to the other side of the Tagus, notwithstanding the strict orders of the Cardinal-Archduke to the contrary. Provisions and munitions of war were hastily sent from Spain, and the Prior Fernando de Toledo was already on the move, slowly bringing such troops as he could muster for the relief of Lisbon, whilst the castles and walls of the city were put into a state of defence. The Castilians, few in number and intensely hated by the townsfolk, knew that in a fight the brunt would fall upon them, and that the Portuguese, even though they might not help the enemy, and this was by no means certain, would not raise a finger to support the dominion of Philip. The priests went from house to house, strong adherents of Dom Antonio almost to a man, whispering that the English were not, after all, such bad people; that there were many Catholics amongst them who were better Christians than the Castilians themselves, and, as the Spanish diarist says, other things of the sort which will not bear repeating. To the well-to-do they said that as soon as a native king was on the throne their wealth would enormously increase, whilst the poor were told that 'fishing in troubled waters was profitable to the fisherman."

On the other hand, the Archduke, knowing the people with whom he had to deal, established a veritable reign of terror, and sacrificed without mercy—often without evidence—any person who was even suspected of open sympathy with the invaders, although it was well known in Madrid that the populace of Lisbon had tacitly agreed to open the gates to Dom Antonio and to massacre the Spaniards on his approach. Some Portuguese nobles had left the Archduke on the first landing of Dom Antonio, but, finding that most of their order had been terrorised into quiescence, returned to Lisbon and tendered their submission. They were at once beheaded or imprisoned, and the rest became more slavish than ever in their professions of attachment to the Archduke. Terrible stories were spread at the same time of the "impious abominations" of the English heretics, and the dreadful fate that awaited all Catholics if the invader succeeded, until, as my Portuguese diarist says, " there was not even a loafer on the quay who did not know that he would be cast out or ruined if the English came." But it was all insufficient to make them willing to

## THE COUNTER-ARMADA OF 1589.

fight. The exodus still continued, and under cover of night the people stole across the river by thousands, and a boat whose usual freight was two ducats could not now be hired under fifty, whilst a bullock-cart and bullocks which could be bought right out in normal times for fifty ducats now charged sixty for a single journey to Aldea Gallega, on the other side of the Tagus. The people of the provinces, says my Portuguese diarist, oppressed the flying citizens more than the English, until the scandal became so great that the Archduke had to interfere and check their rapacity. Under some excuse or another every Portuguese was anxious to get away and leave the fighting to be done by some one else. The Portuguese diarist stoutly denies that his countrymen were cowards or traitors, but always explains that the common people *could not* have risen without the lead of the native nobles; and we have seen the methods by which they were terrorised and made powerless. The Spaniard, on the other hand, makes no secret of his contempt for the white-livered Lisbonenses, and uses much strong language about them. My Portuguese diarist greatly resents this feeling, and gives a little personal experience of his own to show how harsh were the words used by the Castilians towards the craven citizens. "On the morning," he says, "that the enemy fled I went up to the castle to get some things of mine out of my boxes which I had left there in the rooms of one of the officers, where I had determined to await my fate if things came to the worst. As I was on my way down to the palace again the rumour spread that the enemy was retreating, whereupon some soldiers ascended the watch tower to enjoy the sight. I asked them when they returned if the good news were true that the enemy was really flying, and one of them answered me roughly that they who were flying were not the enemy but those who still stay in Lisbon. To which I answered him not a word but God be with ye."

But by terrorism, energy, and promptness the Archduke at length got the city into a state for defence both against the enemy from without and the probable enemy within. The city water-tanks were locked and the supply brought from outside, so as to save the precious liquid for the coming siege. The resident Spaniards formed themselves into a bodyguard of 150 men, "very smart and well armed," and, as in duty bound, the Germans and Flemings offered two hundred harquebussiers in good order, whilst many Portuguese "fidalgos" slept in the corridors of the palace to protect the Archduke in the hour of need. Four colonels were appointed to organise bands of the inhabitants for the defence of the city, and Matias de Alburquerque, a famous sea-captain, took charge of the twelve war galleys in the Tagus and armed thirty merchant ships which were lying in the harbour. The defensive works round the city were divided into sections and apportioned to the command of officers of tried fidelity, whose names need not be recorded here, the river front being mainly entrusted to Portuguese, who evidently considered theirs the post of danger, as they had not the walls to protect them along the quay side. The Castilians, however, made no secret of the fact that they were placed there as no attack was expected from the river.

The parts most strongly guarded, almost entirely by Spaniards, were the quarters of St. Catalina, San Antonio, and San Roque, facing the north and west, from which quarters the English were expected to approach.

The English army, by all accounts twelve thousand strong, marched out of Peniche on the 17th of May, with the Earl of Essex and Sir Roger Williams leading; and Drake, accompanying them to the top of a hill at some distance off, greeted each regiment as it passed him with kindly words, and hopes of success, which he could hardly have anticipated.

Soon the English soldiery began to show their true metal. Strict orders had been given that the property and persons of Dom Antonio's faithful subjects were to be respected; but as soon as they got clear of Peniche housebreaking and pillage became rife, and Norris had to order his provost-marshal, Crisp, to hang a few of the malefactors before he could obtain obedience.

The Archduke had sent three squadrons of Spanish horsemen to reinforce Pedro de Guzman at Torres Vedras, block the road to Lisbon, and harass the English. They went out to reconnoitre the enemy at various points after he left Peniche, but they did not like the look of him, and fell back again to Torres Vedras, whilst messengers were hourly sent to the Archduke begging for more men, whom he could not send. At first it was rumoured amongst the English that a stand would be made at a village near Peniche, but when they arrived there the last Spanish horsemen were just scampering out of it. The next day it was said that certainly a great stand would be made at Torres Vedras, and this undoubtedly was the Archduke's intention; but even the almost impregnable Torres Vedras was untenable with a few hundred horse and a body of militia, who, if they fought at all, would fight on the other side; and the Spanish forces, for fear of being cut off from their base, hastily evacuated Torres Vedras and fell back gradually, harassing the flanks of the enemy as much as they could and cutting off stragglers.

And so the main body of Norris' force, with the Earl of Essex and Sir Roger Williams always leading, moved rapidly and peacefully towards Lisbon, whilst the panic in the capital grew greater as the English came nearer. Peaceably—but hungry—for the land was bare, and the English, we are told, "found our food dry and tasteless and hankered after their own fat meats and birds, comparing our barrenness with the abundance of their own land." There was little or no money in the host, and nothing was to be taken from the Portuguese without payment. There was in any case very little to take, for most of the people along the road had fled or had been stripped clean by the Castilian soldiers who had gone before. Drake's predictions of trouble in moving an army without a baggage train began to come true, and at last starvation was breeding open mutiny in the English host. Norris was then obliged to tell Antonio that unless food were forthcoming more plentifully the soldiers must be allowed to shift for themselves. The poor pretender could only beseech his controller, Campello, to scour the country far and wide for delicacies for the English, "who are naturally dainty and exquisite in their food"; but he could only pay in promises, and the land was bare, so the invaders still marched a hungry host towards the larders of Lisbon.

From day to day they were told that the Spaniards would certainly stand and fight to-morrow, but they were continually disappointed, as indeed was the stout-hearted Archduke in his palace, who received with dismay the constant news that his forces were falling further and further back towards the capital without fighting.

Whatever country people had remained on the road welcomed the invaders with cries of "Viva el Rei Dom Antonio!" but the poor King still looked in vain for the promised gentlemen. His desire to please his rustic adherents was almost pathetic. He condescended, we are told, to caress and embrace the "commonest little people"; and in order to make as brave a show as possible before the English, picked out any countryman who was decently fair-spoken to be paraded before them as some grand gentleman in disguise. But however hopeful he might show himself, he could not conceal the fact that not a dozen men-at-arms had joined him, and his only chance now was that Lisbon itself should declare in his favour. But the native citizens were distracted and divided. The judges and magistrates had abandoned their posts, the shopkeepers had deserted their stores, incendiary fires and pillage were of hourly occurrence, and the Archduke alone kept his head. Even he was not free from danger of attack, for more than one attempt was made to assassinate some of his chief officers.

On one occasion a large number of men were caught deserting their posts and escaping in a boat to the other side of the Tagus. When they were brought to the Archduke for punishment he said if they were too cowardly to fight in defence of their God and their fatherland they were useless to him and could go. This he knew, that even the Castilian women would mount the walls and fight with stones, if need be, in such a cause. Albert required all his firmness and nerve, for one sign of weakness from him and his handful of Spaniards, would have given heart to the craven Portuguese within and without the walls, who were thirsting for their blood.

Three-quarters of the Portuguese in Lisbon had fled or were in hiding, and the rest were in Spanish pay or watched day and night by jealous eyes. But watched as they were, and few in numbers, their hopes were still high, and amongst themselves their speech grew bolder. They got news daily from English prisoners and others of the approach of their king, and plotted together how they would serve the hated Castilians when the English deliverers came.

The rumour ran that the city would be surrendered to the invader on Corpus Christi day, and not a Spaniard was to be left alive, and much more to the same effect. But, alas! on one occasion when a few English prisoners were being brought in a panic-cry arose that the invaders had entered the city, and then each man fled to hiding to save his own skin rather than to his post, and the few Spanish guards that remained had to drag them out of cellars and lofts by main force, kicking

## THE COUNTER-ARMADA OF 1589.

and cuffing them for a set of cowards for not helping the defenders. The Count de Fuentes, once on a false alarm, was sent out of the city with every man who could be spared to Orlas, three leagues off on the road to Cascaes, where it was expected the enemy would pass; but the English went by Torres Vedras, and Fuentes had to hurry back into Lisbon again the same day, to avoid being cut off and the gates being shut against him.

On the 19th of May Norris and his troops marched into Torres Vedras, where Dom Antonio was received with regal honours, and the oath of allegiance taken to him. He was desirous of making a detour to Santarem, through, as he said, a rich country favourable to him, but Norris knew the danger of delay, and insisted upon pushing forward to Lisbon.

Guzman and his Spanish horsemen had fallen back during the previous night to Jara, nearer Lisbon, but he had left Captain Alarcon, with two companies of horse, to hang on the skirts of the enemy. The next day Captain Yorke, who commanded Norris' cavalry, determined to try their metal, and sent a corporal with eight men who rode through forty of the enemy, whilst Yorke himself, with forty English horse, put to precipitous flight Alarcon's two hundred. On the following day, May 21st, the English, disappointed again of a fight, were lodged in the village of Louvres, not far from Lisbon, which Guzman had hurriedly evacuated after being very nearly surprised by Norris. The village was small and the accommodation poor, so Drake's regiment, thinking to better their quarters, went to sleep at a little hamlet a mile off. In the early dawn a cry was raised of "Viva el Rei Dom Antonio!" which was the usual friendly salutation of the country folk. The young English sentries fraternised with those who approached, and admitted them into the sleeping-camp. It was an ambuscade, and many of the English were slain, but the enemy was finally driven off by two companies of Englishmen who were lodged near. The next day, at a village near Lisbon, a large number were treacherously poisoned by the bad water from a well, or, as some said, by the honey which they found in the houses. This was three miles from Lisbon, at a place called Alvelade, and at eleven o'clock at night Essex left the camp with Sir Roger Williams and 1,000 men to lie in ambuscade near the town. When they had approached almost to the walls a few of them began banging at the gates and otherwise trying to alarm those within and provoke a sally. But the device was too transparent, and a few men shot and a sleepless night were the only result. When the English had arrived at Alvelade, Count de Fuentes, with the main body of Spaniards, was at Alcantara, a mile or so nearer Lisbon. Thither Albert hastily summoned a council of war, and urged his officers at last to make a stand at once before the English could co-operate with their friends within the walls of Lisbon. Fuentes and the other Spanish commanders were of the same opinion, but the Portuguese Colonel, Fernando de Castro, made a speech pointing out that the English were short of stores, cut off from their base, and weakened by sickness and short commons. "Let us," he said, "fall back into the

## THE COUNTER-ARMADA OF 1589. 57

city and conquer them by hunger and delay. Behind our walls they will be powerless to injure us, whilst we can draw abundant supplies from across the river, and they cannot blockade us even by land with less than 40,000 men." This exactly suited the other Portuguese, who were never comfortable unless they had a good thick wall between themselves and their enemies. The opinion of the Spaniards was overborne, and the defending force entered the gates of Lisbon on Corpus Christi day, midst the ringing of bells and the more or less sincere rejoicing of the populace. Lisbon feasted and welcomed its defenders, whilst poor Dom Antonio, we are told, at Alvelade just outside, had not a fowl or even a loaf of rye bread to eat. "You may guess how he is hated by the Portuguese," says my Portuguese diarist, "that he being so near his native Lisbon not even a costermonger or a clown dared to send him a meal, whilst we in the city had plenty."

Most of the houses adjoining the walls had been blown up, but the monastery of the Trinidade, down the hill towards the river, still remained. The prior was understood to be in favour of Dom Antonio, as were nearly all churchmen, and Ruy Diaz de Lobo, one of the few nobles with Dom Antonio, undertook to negotiate with him to admit the English to the city through the monastery garden. By the aid of two sympathetic monks he obtained access to the prior. But the latter had been gained over by the Spaniards, and a few hours afterwards the pale heads of Ruy Diaz de Lobo and the two monks were grinning with half-closed, lustreless eyes from the top of three poles on the great quay, whilst Sir

Roger Williams and his men, when they approached the monastery in expectation of a friendly reception, were received with a shower of harquebuss balls, and fell back. The rest of the day, now that the main body of English had come up, was spent in quartering the men in the suburbs of the city, entrenched camps being formed, protected by breastworks of wine-pipes filled with earth. Tired with their six days' march and their labour in the trenches, Norris' little army were glad to pass their first night before Lisbon in such peace as the besieged would allow them.

If the enterprise was ever to succeed this was the moment. The English were more numerous as regards men bearing arms, but they had come upon their wild-goose chase against a fortified city without any battering artillery or proper appliances for a siege, whilst the Spaniards were behind strong walls, with unlimited sources of supply from the river front across the Tagus. Norris, on the other hand, was short of supplies, with fifteen miles of defensible country between him and Cascaes, the point where the fleet was to await him. The advantage, therefore, was clearly on the side of the besieged, but for the one element of the disaffection of Lisbon itself from within, and in this lay Dom Antonio's last chance. A letter written by Don Francisco Odonte, adjutant-general in Lisbon, on the day following the arrival of the English forces before the walls, gives a vivid description of the state of affairs there at the time.[1]

"Dom Antonio," he says, "spent the night in the house of the Duke d'Aveiro, and then early in the

[1] Venetian Calender of State Papers.

morning completed the investment of the city and continued his search for some secret gate by which he might enter. But the garrison harassed him as much as they could. Don Sancho Bravo and Captain Alarcon have been skirmishing all day outside the city, and have sent in 25 or 30 English prisoners who have been consigned to the galleys; and if they could only do the same by all those who are really fighting us, whilst feigning to be our friends, they might man more galleys than are to be found in all christendom this day, for those who have shown their colours during the last three days, and that without a blush, are simply infinite, nor is there any wonder that Dom Antonio has attempted this enterprise, owing to the promises held out to him; for from the moment he disembarked, he has been supplied with abundance of provisions,[1] whilst not a man has offered us his services. All the aldermen of the city are against us but two, the rest are all in hiding, and some even have supplied Dom Antonio's troops, with as little shamefacedness as if they had come from England with him. In this quarter of the city there is not a man left. Some have fled across the river, some are hidden, some have joined Dom Antonio. The troops under the four colonels publicly declare they will not fight. Dom Antonio was certain the moment he appeared the city would rise, and on this account we are in great alarm and have passed a very bad night. God help us!"

But the English did not sleep tranquilly either. In the first hours of the morning of the 25th of May

[1] This is more likely to be true than the assertion of my Portuguese that Antonio could get nothing to eat. The great body of the people were unquestionably in his favour, but had no leaders and would not fight.

Don Garcia Bravo, with 500 Spanish troops from Oporto, arrived in Lisbon. They were hungry, ragged, and weary, but they were eager to meet the foe, and barely gave themselves time to snatch a hurried meal before sallying from the gate of San Anton and up the hill to the quarters of Colonel Brett in the farm of Andres Soares. Another force at the same time came from the gate of Santa Catalina and forced Brett's trenches from that side. The long rows of windows of the monastery of San Roque on the hill were lined by Spanish musketeers, who kept up a deadly fire on the English, whilst two of the great guns of the castle were brought to bear upon one exposed side of the invaders' camp. The attack was made before dawn, and Brett had hardly time to muster his men in the darkness and confusion, when a cannon-shot from the walls laid him low. Captain Carsey and Captain Carr were mortally wounded, and 200 other officers and men slain. The rest of the English forces were aroused, and came to the rescue under Colonel Lane and Colonel Medkirk, and "put them to a sodain fowle retreate, insomuch as the Earle of Essex had the chase of them even to the gates of the High towne, wherein they left behind them many of their best commanders." A body of Spanish horse, sallying from the gates of San Anton to support their comrades, met the latter in full retreat in a narrow lane, and unwillingly trampled them down; thus adding to the confusion, which was completed by a flank charge upon the struggling mass by Yorke's cavalry. The English chronicler claims that the Spanish loss tripled ours, but my diarists say that they had only twenty-five killed and forty wounded, and the

Portuguese tries to account for the heavy loss of wounded by accusing the English of using poisoned bullets. The next day the English tried to get in through the monastery, but they found the city forewarned and on the alert, although the monks had done their best for them. The day after they bribed a Portuguese captain in charge of the wall at the nearest point to the river to let them pass round at low tide, but the spies told the Archduke, and the English found their ally replaced by a Spaniard with a strong force, who sent them flying back again. And so three days passed in constant skirmishes, whilst Norris was chafing and helpless without. The fatal mistake he had made in leaving the fleet was now apparent. The time, too, they had lost at Corunna was irreparable. Fernando de Toledo was approaching with relief, and the first dismay in Spain had now given way to desperate energy. The loss of men in the English camp from sickness and wounds was terrible, supplies and munitions were desperately short, there was no medical aid or transport for the sick and disabled, whilst the Portuguese in Lisbon, from whom everything had been hoped, still made no sign.

Dom Antonio still put a brave face on the matter, but his heart was sinking. For the first two days he had lodged in the rear of the English camp, outside Santa Catalina, but on the third, says my Portuguese diarist, he began to fear for his safety, and, wearied of low fare and the sound of musketry, sought refuge in the house of a Portuguese gentleman on the road to Cascaes. But he was repulsed and barely escaped capture, and thereafter could but cling desperately to the English force. In vain he looked now for the general rising in his favour, for the promised nobles who never came, and hour by hour the prospect darkened. The Earl of Essex, young, inexperienced, hot-headed, was for assaulting all sorts of impossible places with pike and musket, but Norris knew better, and sadly acknowledged to himself that the expedition had failed.

Drake, with the fleet, had in the meanwhile reached Cascaes with everything he could lay hands on in the form of prizes. He had cast anchor on the very day twelvemonth that the great Armada had first sailed out of Lisbon, and the townspeople of the capital were full of portents which they saw in this coincidence. Every one in Lisbon by this time feared that he would sail up the river and enter the harbour; and such was the dread of his name that if he had done so he might have turned the tide of victory. But his advice had been rejected, and he would not venture under the guns of the forts with an under-manned fleet and no soldiers. So he remained at Cascaes and left Norris to get out of the hobble as best he could. When he arrived he found the town almost abandoned, for the citizens had fled in terror at his very name. My Portuguese says that Cardenas, the commander of the fortress, "a great gentleman," was deceived by a monk (or, as he says, the devil in disguise of one) into the belief that Lisbon had fallen, and he accordingly gave up the fortress, and himself took to flight. The Castilian and the Englishman tell the story somewhat differently, and say that Cardenas was an adherent of Dom Antonio, and stipulated that a show of compulsion should be used before he surrendered the fortress. The

# THE COUNTER-ARMADA OF 1589.

result in any case was the same to him, for the "great gentleman's" head soon afterwards adorned one of the Archduke's poles on the quay at Lisbon.

Drake had therefore established himself without difficulty at Cascaes, and patiently awaited the result of the land attack on Lisbon.

If the English outside the walls of the capital were in a bad way, the small force of steadfast Spaniards inside were not much better. They knew that the Portuguese citizens around them were hourly watching for an opportunity to cut their throats and let in the native pretender. Panics of treason and treachery were of hourly occurrence, and on several occasions only the coolness of the Cardinal-Archduke averted disaster. Every day men of the best blood of Portugal, often taken from the immediate surrounding of the Archduke, were seized for assumed treason, the policy being to deprive the disaffected populace of native leaders. To further terrorise the citizens, and prevent them from plucking up heart to open the gates, a great review of all the Spanish troops was held in an open space where the enemy could see as well as the wavering townfolk. My Spanish diarist says, "With the sun flashing on shining morions and the brave show of arms and men all were convinced, friends and enemies alike that the success of our cause was certain."

Boldness and firmness won the day. The next morning Norris called his colonels together to seek their advice and consult with Dom Antonio. He said that as the besieged stood firm and the populace made no move, the English force must have artillery and munitions if they were to succeed, and asked their opinion as to whether he should wait for Dom Antonio's forces, which came not, and meanwhile send a detachment to Cascaes for munitions, or raise the siege altogether. Many were for sending 3,000 men to Cascaes at once. They had given the enemy a good drubbing, they said, and they would sally no more; but Norris had lost hope in Portuguese promises, and was not quite so contemptuous of the enemy as some of them, and he decided that he would wait only one day more for Dom Antonio's levies. If 3,000 came in that night he would send a like number of English to Cascaes for the munitions, otherwise he would raise the siege and leave before daybreak. In vain Antonio prayed for a few days' longer grace. In nine days all Portugal would acclaim him. Lisbon was wavering already, and would turn the scale. But all his prayers were in vain; and before dawn the English army was mustered and ready for the march. Essex was disgusted at the turn things had taken, and went up to the principal gate (he and Williams being the last men to leave) and broke his lance against it, crying out that if there was any within who would come out and have a bout with him in honour of his mistress let him come, and he gave them all the lie to their teeth. And then he turned away and followed the army, no doubt much relieved in his mind.

During the day that Norris was awaiting the arrival of Dom Antonio's troops the English had not left their trenches, and the defenders feared that some deep design lay behind this. Were they mining, or was Drake sending up some heavy guns? they thought. So when the dawn of the 27th of May showed that the main body of the English was already on its way to Cascaes, Count de Fuentes still doubted whether it was not all a feint to draw him out from the shelter of his walls, and peremptorily refused permission to Count Villa Dorta to follow them up and engage them. The way of the retreating force lay along the shore, but to avoid the fire of the galleys which followed their movements they chose the rough by-paths where possible. And so, all undisciplined, sick, and starving, they wandered and struggled on as best they could, four hundred at least of stragglers and sick being killed or captured by Villa Dorta, who hung upon the rear, notwithstanding his chief's prohibition. Later in the day Fuentes so far conquered his suspicion as to lead his army out to Viera, half-way to Cascaes, but he had barely sighted the enemy than some rumour or suspicion reached him of an intended rising in Lisbon during his absence, and he hurried back again to the city. My Portuguese diarist ridicules the suggestion of such a danger as unworthy of any sensible man; but the utter futility of the English and Portuguese proceedings from the first was such as well might excuse Fuentes for thinking that some deeper design must surely lay behind. The suspicion of the Portuguese on the part of the Spaniards at this time is illustrated by an anecdote given by the Portuguese diarist. Alvaro Souza, the captain of Philip's Portuguese guard, with five companions, accompanied Sancho Bravo, who took out a force to harry the English on their way to Cascaes. Souza straggled and was captured by Spanish soldiers, who did not know him. They were near the castle of São Gian at the mouth of Lisbon harbour and knowing that Pero Venegas, the commandant, was a friend of his father, Souza sent a messenger to him begging him to answer for his loyalty. Venegas declined to reply, and Souza was lead off under arrest. On the way he met the famous Alvaro de Bazan going to his galleys. He was a friend, and Souza appealed to him to stand by him and his companions, "but he answered coldly that he knew him not, nor was this a time to recognise any one." He had, he said, recently answered for some Portuguese fidalgos in the palace, and a few hours afterwards they were arrested for treason.

Fifteen weary miles over rough ground, and with Villa Dorta's troops harassing their flank and rear, the English managed to cover during the day, and at last, late in the evening, they marched into Cascaes.[1] We may well imagine that the meeting between Drake and Norris was not very cordial. The officers threw the whole blame for failure upon Drake for not coming up the river to support them before Lisbon; the sailors, on the other hand, saying that the march overland was against Drake's advice, and that his ships, without men-at-arms to defend them and work the guns, would have been at the mercy of the enemy. At all events, it was

[1] If the Earl of Essex was rash and headstrong, he was also chivalrous. Pricket (or Wingfield) says: "Hee for money hired men to carrie sick and hurt upon pikes (for want of waggons) and hee (whose true virtue and nobilitie, as it dooth in all other his actions appear so did it very much in this) threw his owne stuffe, I mean apparell and necessaries from his owne carriages, and let them be left by the way, to put hurt and sick men upon them in this march."

clear they had failed in two of the objects of the voyage—namely, to burn the King of Spain's ships and restore Dom Antonio; and one other only remained to be attempted, which was to take the Azores.

I have already said that the raising of the siege of Lisbon took the defenders by surprise. They fully believed it to be an attempt to draw the Spanish troops out of the town in order that the citizens might rise and massacre the few Spaniards left. So certain were they of this that an unfortunate Portuguese noble—Count Redondo—who arrived that day and went to pay his respects to the Archduke, was immediately seized and beheaded *pour encourager les autres.* As soon as they saw the English had really gone, Count de Fuentes with his six or seven thousand men again made a reconnaissance almost to the English position at Cascaes, and finding the invaders well entrenched, with the fleet behind them, decided that it would be too risky to attack them, and hastened back again to Lisbon. News of the nearness of the Spaniards was brought in by some friars, of whom great numbers hung about Dom Antonio's quarters, and Norris and Essex each promised the messengers a hundred crowns if they found the enemy in the place reported, as they were spoiling for a fight in the open before embarking. But Fuentes had gone to Lisbon, and the friars lost their reward. Norris, however, still eager, sent a page who spoke French, and a trumpeter, post-haste to Lisbon, with a challenge to Fuentes and his army to come into the open and fight. The opportunity was too good for Essex to miss, so he too sent a cartel by the page on his own account, giving every one the lie in a general way and offering to fight anybody in single combat. The messenger came back again without an answer, only that the Spaniards had threatened to hang him for bringing such vapouring insolence to them; but the Spaniard tells the story in another way, less honourably for himself. He says, whilst the messengers were being entertained "as if they were great gentlemen" at breakfast by some of the captains who spoke French, the letters (which they had said could only be opened by the Archduke's permission) were surreptitiously steamed, read, and re-sealed, and handed back again as if unopened, with the reply that his Highness would not allow them to be opened. So Norris and Essex had their bravado for nothing, and went without their fight.

In Lisbon the common people were as disturbed as ever, doubtless feeling that their chance of freedom was slipping away from them, and alarms were constantly raised that the English were returning. But Spanish reinforcements were arriving now. The Duke of Braganza, head of the Portuguese nobility, arrived in royal state with a great body of retainers to help the Archduke, and all hope for Dom Antonio gradually ebbed away.

The English commanders in Cascaes began now to think it high time to put themselves right with the angry Queen, who continued to send furious messages about their disobedience and about Essex and Sir Roger Williams. On the 2nd of June they wrote from Cascaes a full account of all that had happened in the best light they could devise, and saying they knew not what to do unless supplies came at once from England. Everybody was terribly seasick, they said, and well-nigh starving. Seeing that no more provisions could be expected, they wrote, on the 5th of June, that they had decided to go to St. Michaels; and then, for the first time, they confessed that Essex was with them. They had met him, they said, to their great surprise, off Cape Finisterra, but could not send him home before, as they could not spare the *Swiftsure;* but still no word about Sir Roger Williams.[1]

If Drake could not or would not burn the Spanish fleet on this occasion, he was always a splendid hand at plundering merchantmen, and during the six days that his fleet lay before Cascaes he scoured the sea for miles round in search of prizes, taking as many as forty German hulks loaded with Spanish merchandise. Into these prizes the men from the Dutch flyboats were transhipped, and the Dutch captains sent off without being paid their freights, glad, no doubt, to get away from such company on any terms.

In the meanwhile Lisbon was gradually settling down. People who had been hiding in churches and cellars for the last ten days crept out, nearly all under the impression that the Spaniards had all been murdered, and that King Antonio had come to his own again. Dire was their disappoint-

---

[1] Essex started for England on the 16th of June, two days after his brother, on receipt of letters direct from the Queen, brought by a ship with stores from England. Williams was very desirous of accompanying him, but the generals refused to let him go, as they doubtless wished him to have the benefit of the favourite's mollifying influence with the Queen for some weeks before he arrived in England.

ment when they found that they were not the only people who had skulked in hiding, and that none of all the city had dared to strike the blow that would have made Portugal free again. So they patiently bent their neck to the yoke and cheered his Highness the Archduke at the top of their voices as he went in state to the cathedral to hear a solemn *Te Deum* of victory.

The Spaniards did their best to follow up the enemy. The ships in the Tagus were fitted out to watch Cascaes and follow the English fleet, doing all the damage they could, and Don Pedro de Guzman was sent to cut off the English garrison left at Peniche. They urged the horses, says the Spanish diarist, until they were ready to drop, but arrived too late to stop the embarkation, except of about 200 men, who were put to death.

On the 8th of June the English fleet set sail, pursued and harassed by the galleys from Lisbon in nearly a dead calm. Three of our ships were taken or sunk and one burned, by her captain, Minshaw, after a desperate resistance. A wind sprang up, however, and the Spanish galleys were left behind; but soon the fleet got scattered, the men died, and were thrown overboard by the hundred from scurvy, starvation, and wounds; but, notwithstanding all, after sailing ostensibly for the Azores, Drake turned back again and, picking up twenty-five of his ships which had been separated from him, sailed up the bay and attacked Vigo. He had only 2,000 men fit to fight: sickness and privation had thinned them down to that, but with those few men, finding Vigo deserted, the English burnt and wasted the town and all the villages around.

"A verie pleasant rich valley but wee burnt it all, houses and corne, so as the countrey was spoyled seven or eight miles in length." Then they decided to drop down to the isle of Bayona, and there put the pick of the men and stores on twenty of the best ships for Drake to take to the Azores, whilst the rest returned to England. But for some reason Drake broke the agreement and passed Bayona without even calling, and the thirty ships that were awaiting him there were left to their fate. Beset with tempest and pestilence, without a commander, it was decided by those on board to make the best of their way to England, in terrible distress as they were for provisions and water. After ten days' voyage they arrived at Plymouth on the 2nd of July, and found that Drake had already arrived there with the Queen's ships, having abandoned his voyage to the Azores. Most of the remaining ships had sought other ports in preference, in order to sell their prizes without having to share the proceeds with others.

Such of the soldiers as came to Plymouth were sent grumbling home with five shillings each for their wages and the arms they bore. The English chronicler thinks that this was "verie good pay, considering they were victualled all the time." Such, however, was not the opinion of the unfortunate men themselves, who had not been allowed to loot as much as they thought fit in Portugal. They said that if they had been permitted to march as through an enemy's country, they would have come back the richest army that ever returned to England. Not more than 5,000 of them ever came home; but their story was so dismal a one that all England rang with reprobation of the bad management and parsimony that had brought the expedition to so inglorious a conclusion.

The first and third objects of the expedition—namely, the burning of the Spanish fleet and the capture of St. Michaels—were never even attempted, but the second object was very nearly being attained, and the restoration of Dom Antonio, practically as a vassal of England, might have been effected a dozen times over if the Portuguese in Lisbon had not been an utterly terrified set of poltroons. On various occasions, when Count de Fuentes and his troops were outside, a few dozen daring men might have seized the gates and have turned the tide in Antonio's favour. It was not to be, however, and the poor King wandered a poverty-stricken fugitive yet for a few years before he died, but his desperate struggle for sovereignty ended with the ignominious failure of the English attempt to avenge a great national injury by a joint-stock enterprise.

*JULIAN ROMERO—SWASHBUCKLER.*

## JULIAN ROMERO—SWASHBUCKLER.

In a slumberous street in old Madrid, called anciently the Calle de Cantaranas, but now inappropriately named after Lope de Vega, there stands a venerable convent of barefooted Trinitarian nuns. The fortress-like red walls with the tiny grated windows looking upon the street, the quaint, sad tranquillity which hangs around the place, are only such as mark hundreds of other like retreats in Madrid and elsewhere; and yet to this particular convent many reverent steps are bent from all quarters of the earth, for here lie the bones of the "maimed one of Lepanto," the author of "Don Quixote." He died only a few yards away, in his house in the Calle de Leon, and was quietly laid to rest in the convent, where one of his own daughters was a nun. The very fact of his burial there was almost forgotten—was indeed for many years disputed, until proved beyond possibility of doubt not long since—and when the fury for destroying religious foundations seized the rulers of Madrid after the revolution of 1868, the convent was marked down for destruction like so many others of its kind. And destroyed it would have been but for the pious zeal of the good "setenton," Mesonero Romanos, most beloved of Madrid antiquarians, who woke up the Academy of History, and brought such pressure to bear upon the Government as to save the sepulchre of Cervantes from profanation for all future time, and thus enabled the great author, after he had lain in his grave for two and a half centuries, to repay his debt to the Trinitarian fathers who rescued him from his galling slavery in the hands of the infidel. A stone tablet is now fixed in the wall of the convent setting forth the fact of his sepulture there in 1616, and the foundation of the community a few years previously by Doña Juana Gaitan, daughter of General Julian Romero. The name of the latter awakens no responsive echoes in Spanish minds. I have before me, indeed, a recently published Spanish historical work which ascribes his very existence to a wrong period. With the exception of a few particulars of his later life given in a local history of Cuenca by Father Muñoz, no Spanish writer has ever been at the trouble of tracing what little may be known of his stirring career. And yet the man in his day was the very prototype of those indomitable adventurers, lusting for blood and gold, who, the sword in one hand and the cross in the other, hunted down to death the Indians of one hemisphere and the "heretics" of the other. Keen, cruel, Alba had no more ruthless instrument for his fell work than "Captain Julian," upon whom and Sancho de Avila the hatred of the persecuted Flemings was mainly concentrated. In the course of my somewhat out-of-the-track studies I have found the name of Julian Romero constantly cropping up, and so many personal traits of him have appeared, that by carefully piecing them together a more complete account may be formed of the life and character of this typical swashbuckler than of, perhaps, any of his fellows. His life, too, offers some interest to Englishmen, for he swaggered and ruffled in London many a time and oft, and was one of those Spanish mercenaries who, in the reigns of Henry VIII. and Edward VI., fought so bravely against the French and Scots and quelled by their ferocity the risings of Kett in Norfolk and Arundell in the West Country. Practically nothing whatever was known of the lives—hardly indeed the existence—of the Spanish mercenaries in England until the recent publication of the anonymous "Spanish Chronicle of Henry VIII.,"[1] which I now attribute to Antonio de Guaras, a leading Spanish merchant in London, whom I know to have been on close terms of intimacy with the Spanish soldiers, and particularly with Julian Romero, whose early adventures in England are evidently related at first hand in the Chronicle.

Of all the turbulent soldiers of fortune who quarrelled, intrigued, and triumphed in England, and whose adventures are so minutely told in the Chronicle, only one was heard of in after life. The general, Sir Peter Gamboa, was murdered with Captain Sir Alonso de Villa Sirga in St. Sepulchre's churchyard, hard by Newgate, one wet winter's night in 1551, by Captain Guevara, who was incontinently hanged in Smithfield. Sir

[1] "Chronicle of Henry VIII.," Edited by Martin A. S. Hume. London, 1889.

Pero Negro died of the sweating sickness in one of the crowded lanes of old London city. Juan de Haro was killed by the English for attempted desertion with his company to the French enemy before Boulogne; others fell in the Flemish wars, and only the rash and boastful "Captain Julian" lived to become Alba's trusted henchman, and to hand his name down to the execration of generations of Flemings as one of the prime movers of the "Spanish Fury" in Antwerp. So great was the fame of his ferocity that the panic mongers, who were for ever sending to Elizabeth and Cecil intelligence of the dreadful vengeance which was to fall upon England at the hands of King Philip, could invent nothing more terror-striking than their constantly repeated dread that Julian Romero was to swoop down upon the coast and serve English Protestants in the same way as he had treated those of the Netherlands. He had, indeed, as will be shown in his own words at various periods of his life—now for the first time brought together—all the vices and virtues of his class and time. Vain and boastful, bigoted and cruel, he was nevertheless true to his salt, faithful, brave, and steadfast; of that stern, self-sacrificing stuff by which alone empires may be won or despotism defended. He was born at Huelamo, in the province of Cuenca, of very humble folk, for even when he was in high command and on terms of close intimacy with nobles and ministers, he was never given the nobiliary address of Don, which was enjoyed by the most remote and out-at-elbows representative of the hidalgo class. He was not much of a scholar either, for his signature which exists at Simancas is the only part of his letters in his own hand, and is painfully traced in great bold straight lines, like a row of halberds.

In the winter of 1534 every village in Spain resounded with the drum-beat of the recruiters, who were seeking soldiers for the Emperor's great expedition against the Moors, which was to start from Barcelona in the spring. Spanish hearts were all aflame with wondrous stories of fortune and adventure. The excitement, the freedom, the idleness, and the possible gains of a soldier's life had seized upon the imagination of Spanish youth; and the turbulent spirit of warlike adventure in far countries was, for the next century at least, to be the dominant note of the national character. Julian must have been a mere boy, but he joined the standard, so he wrote forty years afterwards, at Christmas, 1534, as a foot-soldier, and, with a pike on his shoulder, started on his life of adventure. There was no one to record the doings and sufferings of the humble man-at-arms in those stirring days, and beyond the fact that he drifted from Spain to Tunis, from Tunis to Italy, and thence to Flanders and France, always in the midst of the fighting in the Emperor's wars, nothing is known for the next ten years of Julian Romero's service. In the beginning of 1544 Henry VIII. had arranged to enter into alliance with the Emperor to jointly attack the King of France, and the probability is that if they had together marched upon Paris promptly, they would have had France at their mercy. But other counsels prevailed, and, whilst Charles operated in Picardy and French Flanders, Henry sent the Duke of Norfolk and his brilliant son, Surrey, with an army of 15,000 men, to besiege Montreuil. The King's brother-in-law, Charles Brandon, Duke of Suffolk, at the same time with a large force "sat down before" Boulogne, and, on the 14th of July, great Harry himself landed at his good town of Calais to take the supreme command of his army before Boulogne. He was accompanied by a brilliant train of courtiers and soldiers, and took with him as his chief military adviser a great Spanish noble, Beltran de la Cueva, third Duke of Alburquerque, whose important share in the reduction of the town has been almost entirely ignored by English historians. Besides the 200 Spanish soldiers who followed the Duke, there were already three Spanish captains in Henry's service, each with a company of his countrymen, to the aggregate number of about 260 men, all of them seasoned veterans in the Continental wars; and these, together with the less experienced English levies, succeeded in capturing the town of Boulogne on the 15th of September. It appears that a breach had been made in the walls three weeks before, and the Spaniards begged Henry to let them take the place by assault. He told them that he would rather waste 10,000 pounds of powder than that a single one of his Spaniards should be sacrificed, "whereupon they blushed for mere shame." But as usual Henry had his own way, and the town surrendered; "*the Frenchmen,*" says Wriothesley, "*departing out of the towne with as much goodes as they might carye, both men and women, besyde that the waggons caryed; and the King his Majestie entered the said towne the 18th September with greate tryumphe, and the 20th day a solempne procession was kept with Te Deum songe for the Victory of the King his Majestie and many fyers made in the citye and in every part of the realme. The last day of September the King his Majestie landed at Dover at midnight."* The reason for Henry's hurried return was his desire to retain all the credit for his victory without waiting for the probable reverse. Charles V. had come to terms with the French, and when he had sent word to his English ally that he was negotiating, Henry arrogantly said that the Emperor might make peace if he pleased, but he, Henry, would suit himself in the matter. But when he found the whole French army turned against him he hurriedly raised the siege of Montreuil, put all his forces into Boulogne under Lord Grey, and got back to England as fast as he could, whilst his laurels were yet green. All through the next year the French siege of Boulogne went on, the three companies of Spanish mercenaries, steady old soldiers as they were, being the mainstay of the defence. They complained bitterly of the raw Englishmen's habit of killing the prisoners instead of holding them to ransom, and on one occasion were near mutiny because their prisoners were murdered. "How now," said Captain Salablanca to Lord Grey, "do you think we are in the King's service for the wretched four ducats a month we earn? Not so my lord; we serve with the hope of taking prisoners and getting ransom. Your men have even now killed a gentleman of mine for whom I should have got at least five or six thousand crowns ransom." Whatever their object may have been in serving the schismatic king, Henry thought very highly of them, and when in the year 1545 he was about to send Warwick to attack the Scots, an opportunity occurred for him to engage some more, he gladly seized it. Charles V. had disbanded a large proportion of his army after the peace of Crespi was concluded, and had embarked them for Spain with orders that, under pain of death, they were to take service with no other sovereign. A ship with 800 or 1,000 of these disbanded soldiers on their way home anchored in the Downs, and the warriors being, we are told, "already tired of the sea," they sent an offer of their services to the King of England. The captain of the vessel, however, would not wait for the answer to reach them, but on his putting into Plymouth the whole of them landed and entered the English service. They were promptly sent off to Warwick's army in Scotland under an experienced old soldier of their number called Pedro Gamboa, who was made colonel, with power to create his own captains. Julian Romero landed with this force in some subordinate capacity, but on his arrival in Scotland received his first English commission as captain, from Gamboa. This was in the summer of 1545, and when the winter came the troops were put into quarters, whilst Gamboa and his newly fledged captains came to London to air their finery at Henry's Court. The King made much of them, and in the early spring of 1546, a temporary peace having been patched up with Scotland, ordered them to take their companies to the French coast between Calais and Boulogne, where the English were erecting a fort. Whilst Gamboa, Julian Romero, and the other new captains, had been ruffling at Court, receiving grants and attentions from the King, the three or four old Spanish commanders with their companies, who had been long in Henry's service, had been enduring hard fare and rough service, and obtaining but little loot at Boulogne ; so that on the arrival in France of the new men, straight from Court favour, a very bitter feeling was shown towards them. One of the old captains, Cristobal Mora, deserted bodily with his men to the enemy, and another one, Juan de Haro, was killed in attempting to do so. It may therefore well be supposed that when peace was made in June, 1546, and the compatriots met again on neutral ground, there was a good deal of thumb-biting and recrimination. Mora was flouted in the streets by his fellow-countrymen for having disgraced the mercenary creed by deserting his paymaster before the enemy ; whilst he retorted by accusing Gamboa and his friends of disobeying their natural sovereign the Emperor in taking service under an excommunicated heretic. Events came to a head at last by the deserting captain, Cristobal de Mora, sending a challenge from Montreuil to Colonel Gamboa in Calais in July. Either for some reason of disparity of age or rank between the two, or else out of mere hot-headed combativeness on the part of Julian Romero, the latter accepted the challenge for his chief, and has left upon record an extremely minute description of the fight. Sir Henry Knyvett went off to obtain the King of England's permission, which was gladly given, and "a thousand broad angels sent to Julian to put himself in order withal." The King of France ordered the erection of lists at Montreuil, where the wage of battle should be decided, and when all was ready Julian Romero, in the full pomp of war, started on his road from Calais to Montreuil, attended by a great company of English and Spanish gentlemen to see the fun. The following is the account given by Julian's friend.

"Well when they arrived in France and the day being come the seconds and umpires saw that each one had equal arms. They were to fight on horseback and each one had a sword, and both rapiers and daggers, and their corselets were open at the back with great holes big enough for two fists to go in on both pieces. This scheme was invented by the French because Mora had one of the best and quickest horses in France, and as they were not to fight with the lance, Mora thought, with the fleetness of his horse, he would be able to wound Julian in the back with his rapier, and so vanquish him.

"When the umpires had seen the arms were equal they gave the signal for the trumpets to sound, and the opponents at once closed with one another, and, at the first blows with the swords, Julian's sword fell from his hands and he seized his rapier. Mora was not backward and threw away his sword for his rapier; and, as he had such an active horse, he went circling round Julian so as to wound him in the back. But Julian was no sluggard, and when Mora saw he could not do this, he decided to kill Julian's horse, which he did with a thrust in the chest; and a few moments afterwards it fell to the ground. At that moment Julian, thinking to do the same for Mora, attacked him with that object; but Mora was too quick with his horse for Julian to wound it, and the rapier fell from Julian's hand, almost at the moment that his horse dropped under him; and as he felt his horse was going to fall he leapt quickly off his back and Mora had not time to ride him down, thanks to the horse which was on the ground. Julian to escape being ridden down, and finding himself armed only with his dagger, was forced to shield himself behind his fallen horse, whilst Mora went round and round and Julian dodged behind the horse. This went on for more than three hours, and at last Mora cried out, 'Surrender, Julian! I do not want to kill thee!' but Julian did not answer a word. There was hardly an hour of daylight left, and Julian would be vanquished at sunset. And, as he saw that Mora was strutting about waiting for the sun to go down, Julian kept wide awake and, watching his opportunity, dropped on one knee behind his prostrate horse and with his dagger cut the straps of his spurs, which he threw away. Seeing his rapier not far from him he made a dash to regain it, and succeeded before Mora could ride him down.

"The gentleman who was acting as Julian's second, seeing how things were going, was very downcast and wished he never had come and said to the Spanish captains: 'Gentlemen, our man is losing.' Then said Captain Cristobal Diaz, 'What, sir! the day is not yet done and I still hope to God that Julian will come off the victor.' 'Do you not see, sir,' said the other, 'that Mora is only flourishing about waiting for sundown?' As they were chatting thus, they saw how Julian had snatched up his rapier again, and how Mora was attacking him. Julian had just time to deal a thrust at Mora's horse, which, feeling itself wounded began to prance, and its rider, fearing that it would fall with him underneath it, determined to get a short distance away and dismount. Julian, however, being on foot and light, without his spurs, went running after him, and when he was trying to dismount, embraced him in such a manner as to bring him to the ground, and with his dagger cut the ties of his helmet. Mora then surrendered at once, and Julian took his arm, and with the sword of his enemy in his hand, led him three times round the field that all might see how he had surrendered."

For this not very chivalrous victory Julian was overwhelmed with honours, the French king, we are told, casting a gold chain round his neck worth more than 700 crowns, whilst the Dauphin gave him a surcoat stamped with gold, worth more than the King's chain; and King Henry of England, when the Spanish officers returned to England, extended special favour to Julian Romero, upon whom he settled a life pension of 600 ducats, which was a larger sum than any of his fellows, except Colonel Gamboa, who got a thousand. In any case it was only paid for a few years.

If the behaviour of the combatants in the duel lacked the chivalry we are apt to expect, still less magnanimous was the treatment of the Spanish officers towards their companies. When the peace was concluded and Julian's duel fought, orders came from England that the troops were to be dismissed, and the mercenary captains were to repair to London. The latter portion of this order was concealed from the soldiers, who were told by Colonel Gamboa that, as they were all dismissed from the English service, they would march together and offer their services elsewhere. He thereupon led them across the frontier into the Emperor's Flemish dominions, and then with the captains gave the men the slip, and left them to shift for themselves. The captains hung about the Court in London all the summer and autumn (1546), quarrelling, gaming, and swaggering, and Julian Romero, less refined and more hot-headed than the rest, well nigh got into serious trouble. His friend who tells the story, evidently at first hand, says that he had been "showing off" very much more than his means or his pay would warrant, and he had borrowed money to such an extent that he hardly dared to walk out publicly. One of his pressing creditors was a Milanese called Baptist Baron, who after much trouble managed to get him arrested for a debt of 200 ducats. Julian was furious with rage at the idea of being haled off to jail, and persuaded the catchpole who had him in custody to take him to Colonel Gamboa's house, in hope that he would pay the money.

"No sooner had he arrived there, than he launched into loud complaints and began to say unreasonable things, amongst others, that anybody who would serve heretics must be a great big knave; and he swore that he would have no more of it, but would go with only a pike on his shoulder and four ducats (a month) pay to serve elsewhere; and he said a good many other things that had much better have been omitted, for certainly no good came of them."

Gamboa made himself responsible for the money, but Julian's loose talk about heretics was dangerous, and the colonel, whose subsequent behaviour to the other captains shows him to have been a bad-hearted man, seems to have done nothing to shield his subordinate from the consequences of his indiscretion. Gamboa was himself accused at first of treason by the Privy Council, for allowing such talk in his house without punishment. He declared that he was deaf, and did not hear what Julian had said, "which," says the narrator (almost certainly the "merchant" Guaras), "was the truth, as he was in his chamber at the time." "The Council presently sent for Julian and rated him soundly, to which Julian replied: 'Gentlemen, I have said nothing for which I should be so maltreated.' 'Well,' they answered, 'you said this, that, and the other, and there are witnesses who heard you.' But Julian denied it, and they called a merchant who was present in the house of the colonel and had heard everything that had passed. Before this merchant went before the Council, Gamboa spoke to him and begged him to accuse Julian as much as he could, so that they should take away his pay from him; but the merchant, seeing the malice of Gamboa, said, 'Señor Gamboa, I am no mischief-maker to do harm where I can do good,' and he would not speak to Gamboa any more. The lords then sent for the merchant; all the captains as well as Julian being present, and, as the merchant was going in, Gamboa said to him aloud, so that all should hear, 'Señor, I beseech you to favour Julian as much as you can; for good or evil to him depends upon what you say.' Good God! how artfully Gamboa said that, when not three hours before he had begged him earnestly to accuse him and get his income taken away. But Julian and the other captains thought that Gamboa was favourable to him." The "merchant's" evidence does not seem to have palliated the case against Julian, but that perhaps was because "they made him place his hands upon the Gospels, and he swore to tell the truth." He said that Julian was in a rage at being arrested, and shouted out some coarse expressions about the King and Council not caring much for him, and that he would rather serve elsewhere for four ducats than here for a mint of money. "Then," said the lords, "didst thou not hear him say that he would come with a pike on his shoulder to fight against such heretics?" To which the merchant replied that the soldiers were making so much noise that he did not hear well what was said. The end of the matter was that, just as the Council were going to sentence Julian to punishment and dismissal, Paget put in a good word for him, and got him off with a severe wigging and a threat to punish him severely if he let his tongue run too loosely again; "whereupon Julian made no answer but made a very low bow, and then they told him to go, and if any one was sorry he was not dismissed it was Gamboa."

A few weeks after this the trouble with Scotland broke out again, and the captains were ordered to raise a fresh force of Spanish men-at-arms. This was not easily done at short notice, and Julian and his fellow Spanish officers frankly said that they could not get together men who would do them credit in the time specified, and they had no confidence in Burgundians and others who could be quickly recruited. Gamboa, however, made no difficulty about it; but to the great disgust of the Spaniards raised a regiment of Burgundians, whom he led to Scotland to take part in the siege of

Haddington. On Gamboa's coming south for the winter this regiment, under its ensign, Perez, deserted *en masse* to the enemy, for which desertion Perez was hanged when the place was captured; but in the meanwhile the circumstance still further widened the breach between Gamboa and the other Spanish officers. The King died at the beginning of the year 1547, and by the time Somerset was leaving London for his short and triumphant campaign in Scotland, plenty of Spanish and Italian mercenaries had joined the standards of our captains. They confessedly turned the tide of victory to the English side at the battle of Pinkie by a dashing flank charge under Gamboa, and a few days afterwards, at the burning of Leith, they again greatly distinguished themselves. Julian, of course, was in the thick of it, and his friend asserts that he was made an English knight after Pinkie. I can find no confirmation of this, although the English authorities show that after the burning of Leith the Protector knighted, amongst others, on the 28th of September, 1547, Sir Peter Gamboa, Pero Negro, Alonso de Villa Sirga, and Cristobal Diaz.

Julian remained in Scotland during the campaigns of 1548-9, and took part in the relief of Haddington; but Gamboa in the latter year was dismissed in consequence of his unpopularity with the other Spaniards and an accusation of peculation made against him. Of Julian Romero we hear in all parts. He and Pero Negro were in charge at Broughty Ferry, near Dundee, and a few of their men made a dash one day at a French general who was strolling a short distance from his lines, and captured him in the face of his own troops before he could be rescued. The French complained especially of Julian's and Pero Negro's celerity of movement, by which they were able to give them the slip, encumbered as the French were by the unscientific methods of their Scotch allies.[1] Warwick had the help of a considerable body of Spaniards, and almost certainly of Julian Romero, in his defeat of Kett's rebellion in the autumn of 1549; certainly in the winter of that year when Warwick, with the prestige of his victories upon him, thought he was strong enough to strike a final blow at the Protector, Julian was one of the foreign captains he took with him to overawe Somerset at his *levée*, and to demand of him in their name rich rewards for their services in Scotland and elsewhere. As soon as Warwick had got rid of Somerset he changed his tone. England was no longer a fit place for Catholics. The King, Edward VI., was known to be dying, and the next heiress was a papist and half a Spaniard, against whom the Spanish officers could not be trusted to fight in favour of Northumberland's Protestant *protegée*. So they were dismissed, those that were left of them, and are thenceforward swallowed up in the unfathomable abyss of the dead past; all except Julian Romero, who was reserved for greater things.

There was no lack of demand for the services of such men, for the Emperor, his natural sovereign, was at war with the French once more, and less than two years after he left England we hear of Romero again. Sir John Mason, writing to

[1] Jean de Beaugé, "Histoire de la guerre d'Ecosse," 1548-9. Maitland Club.

the English Council on the 7th of July, 1554,[1] reports that Julian with five standards of Spaniards and others was holding out against the French in the castle of Dinant. He is, Sir John says, unlikely to be taken; but if he be, all the Liege country must soon follow. A week afterwards Dr. Wotton writes to Queen Mary[2] an account of the fall of Dinant, and says: "The town and castle of Dinant have been taken, the former surrendered by composition without loss of goods, the latter, wherein were some Spaniards with Captain Julian, who formerly served in England, made a gallant resistance, but at last held parliament and yielded, the soldiers departing with their swords by their side."

The Spanish historian Sandoval blames Romero for his capture and the loss of Dinant, which he attributes to his want of prudence in going out to parley, "but rarely indeed do both valour and prudence reside in one person, although this captain afterwards proved that he possessed both qualities; for he became one of the most famous soldiers of our time." Romero seems first to have attracted general public notice by his bravery and dash at the great battle of St. Quintin in 1557, and in the contemporary poem called "La Araucana" he is mentioned as one of the most conspicuous heroes of the storming of the town, in command of a regiment of Spaniards, Germans, and Walloons. For the ten years that followed the peace of 1558 the centre of war was changed, and the almost constant struggles between Philip II. and the Turks kept Italy and Sicily full of Spanish soldiers. Romero

[1] Calendar of State Papers (Foreign).
[2] Ibid.

during most of the time was quartered in the Milanese, whilst not before the enemy; and in the meanwhile had been promoted to the rank of Maestre de Campo (colonel), but in 1567 Philip took the fatal decision of grappling in a duel to the death with a closer and more dangerous power than the Turk—namely, that of Protestantism and national freedom in his own Netherlands dominions. The humble remonstrance of the Flemish nobles and Egmont's visit to Madrid had convinced the stealthy bigot that, if he insisted upon ruling his Flemish dominions according to Spanish methods, he could only do it by the ruthless power of the sword. His kindly and popular sister, Margaret of Parma, Flemish to the heart as she was, had already shown signs of sympathy with the demands of her countrymen, and was an unfit instrument for Philip's new plans. There was no one but hard-hearted old Alba who could be trusted to carry them out to the bitter end with the needful catlike cruelty. So early in 1567 the Spanish troops from Milan and Naples, the Italians from Savoy and Parma, the veterans who for years had been fighting the infidel in the Mediterranean, were set in motion to join the Duke of Alba. Julian Romero was at the time in command of the regiment of Sicily stationed in Milan under the fourth Duke of Alburquerque, the son of Henry VIII's military dry-nurse at Boulogne; and he, like the rest of them, led his men to Brussels. The Flemish nobles were lulled into a feeling of false security. Kindly messages came from Philip in Madrid. He himself would come and set all things right. Alba and his son flattered the shallow Egmont, and courted the distrustful Horn, whose brother Montigny was kept at Madrid by specious excuses, and the smiling mask was kept over Alba's grim face till all was ready.

Egmont had readily accepted that fateful invitation to dinner for the 9th of September, and even Horn had been persuaded to leave the security of his own country for the same purpose, when late on the night of the 8th a Spanish officer of apparently high rank came secretly to his (Egmont's) house in disguise and significantly warned him to escape at once, whilst there was yet time. To the last day of her life the Countess of Egmont was confident that this officer was Julian Romero;[1] but, whoever he was, Egmont neglected the warning and went to the feast next day. Sancho de Avila posted troops in all the streets leading to the house, to the wonder of the townsfolk, and on the stairs of the Hotel itself were stationed 200 stalwart harquebussiers under Colonel Julian Romero, who himself stood at the door of the room in which the treacherous arrest was to be effected.[2] At the given moment Sancho de Avila laid hands on Egmont, whilst Romero stood by and overawed any attempt of the Flemings at resistance.

At 11 o'clock in the morning of the 6th of June of the following year, the day that the Counts were to die, Julian it was who went to Egmont's chamber to conduct him to the scaffold on the great square in Brussels. He wished to tie

---

[1] Motley.
[2] "Documentos ineditos para la historia de España," vol. lxxv.

the Count's hands, but the noble refused to be thus degraded. During Egmont's last few moments he turned in bitter anguish to Julian Romero and asked him earnestly whether the sentence was irrevocable, and whether a pardon might not, even now, be granted to him. Romero appeared to think that the Count's courage was failing him, and only answered by a contemptuous shrug of his shoulders and a negative sign; whereupon Egmont gnashed his teeth in silent rage and went to his death.[1]

Alba's severity for the moment paralysed all resistance on land, and only those "sea beggars," who afterwards secured the independence of the Netherlands, kept alive the tradition of Flemish patriotism. Some of the Spanish troops could therefore be dispensed with, particularly as Philip's treasury was empty of money to pay them, and many found their way back to Spain again. Amongst these was Julian Romero, who had married a wife of his own province a few years before (1565), and yearned for a spell of family joys far from war's alarms. His time of rest was but a short one. He was marked out now conspicuously as one of the most unscrupulous of Alba's officers, who could be depended upon in any emergency, and who was fanatically loyal to his sovereign and the faith for which he was fighting. An instance of this is given by Don Bernardino de Mendoza.[2] Certain soldiers under that officer were in treaty to enter into the service of the King of France—not a very great offence, one would think, in the eyes of Julian, who had himself served the King of England

[1] Motley.
[2] "Comentarios de las Guerras de los paises bajos." Mendoza.

—and Alba, desirous of appearing impartial, had decided that the three ringleaders should be tried by their own comrades, appointing Julian as president of the tribunal. He sentenced them all to be shot, and on the decision being submitted to Alba, the latter made a long speech in praise of such severity, and highly commended Romero for his inflexibility. Philip was contemplating a job that called for such a man as this. He had been driven to desperation by Elizabeth's protection of the rebel Flemish privateers, and her seizure of his treasure, and had effusively welcomed Thomas Stukeley when he arrived in Madrid in 1570 with proposals for the invasion of Ireland and the raising of the country in favour of Philip. This would, at all events, keep Elizabeth's hands full, and Philip, being misled as to Stukeley's standing and influence, treated him with great honour. He had a large pension granted to him and a palace to reside in; he was made a Spanish knight, and Julian Romero, amongst others, was invited to confer with him as to the plans for the subjugation of Ireland. It was decided that Romero should take command of the expedition, if it were sent, and English spies soon got hold of the news and communicated it to the Queen. Philip was not long in finding out that Stukeley was a mere windbag, and very coolly got rid of him as soon as possible; but for many months after the Spanish king had abandoned the idea, when indeed he was in such straits as hardly to be able to hold his own, the dreaded name of Julian Romero was in everybody's mouth as the coming avenger of Philip's grievances against the English queen and her ministers.

One zealous spy named Reynolds Digby writes to Cecil from St. Jean de Luz on December 28, 1570, telling him of "the subtle and devilish practices against his country," and saying that the Duke of Medina Celi and Julian Romero had already embarked "a great store of ordnance for battery and field, great numbers of copper ovens, baskets, mattocks, and other stores, with 100 mule loads of money, the object being to go to Flanders, ship Alba and his army, and sail to Scotland for the purpose of attacking it and seizing the King."[1] There was no truth in it, but on the 25th of January, 1571, another spy named Hogan, living in Madrid, wrote saying that Romero was going to Ireland with 6,000 soldiers.[2] Walsingham, in Paris, reports the same news as being brought by French agents from Madrid, and the Spanish ambassador in England, evidently believed it, although he pretended not to do so, in his interviews with the English ministers.[3] Elizabeth herself was much alarmed, and wrote to Walsingham,[4] telling him to see the Spanish ambassador in Paris (Francés de Alava), and say "that she cannot believe the news sent her that there is an intention of sending Julian Romero or such like with a number of soldiers to Ireland to follow some vain device of these rebels, and she much wonders that the King should give credit to such a man as Stukeley, about whom no good can be said." The haughty Don Francés ("the proudest man I ever

[1] Calendar of State Papers (Foreign).
[2] Ibid.
[3] Calendar of State Papers (Elizabeth), Spanish, vol. ii.
[4] Calendar of State Papers (Foreign).

met," says Walsingham) told him that he had never heard of Stukeley, "and as for any attempts by Julian Romero to be done in Ireland, they were no Spaniards who had that enterprise in hand"—which was quite true, for Philip never intended to send a Spanish force, and indeed when, years after, he did aid an expedition, he ordered that all the commanders should be Italians.[1]

Philip wanted Romero for more important work than aiding Stukeley's hairbrained schemes. Alba was now face to face with a people in arms in Holland and Zealand, under one of the greatest men of his age, the Prince of Orange. Cruel severity had only goaded the Netherlanders to desperation, and Alba, old and ill, felt that his method had failed. He was begging to be relieved from the conduct of the war, and the Duke of Medina Celi was sent to replace him, with Julian Romero in command of the reinforcements which accompanied him. Medina Celi himself never took possession of his viceroyalty, for Alba was too jealous to give it up, now that his health was somewhat better, and the fresh troops sent enabled him to act more vigorously; but Julian Romero got to work as soon as he set foot on shore. He had been partially disabled by a severe wound in the leg, but landed his men at the Sluys and at once joined Don Fadrique, Alba's son, before Mons; and on the 17th of July, 1572, only a few weeks after he landed, he led the first charge of the battle in which Fadrique beat the French Huguenot force who were trying to relieve Mons. Fadrique wrote to his father from the battlefield in enthusiastic praise of Julian, whom

[1] Calendar of State Papers (Elizabeth), Spanish, vol. ii.

he coupled with the famous Italian General Chapin Vitelli, who, although severely wounded, behaved with great bravery. Unfortunately most of Genlis' troops that were captured were murdered in cold blood afterwards, it is to be feared with Julian Romero's full acquiescence, if nothing worse. He was now an important personage since his sojourn at Philip's Court, and in a letter to the King's secretary, Zayas, dated before Mons, August 23, 1572,[1] writes a full account of the state of affairs, in the wording of which there are now and again signs that he was still a bluff soldier.

"Holland," he says, "looks as ugly as ever, Friesland no better, and Zealand much worse, but I look upon it all as nothing by the side of this Mons business, upon which I have set my heart. If we can only stop up this hole in the frontier the rest is only so much air; although we shall sweat if we are to camp before Mons all the winter, for we shall have to fight on skates." Julian's fears were groundless. The grim news of St. Bartholomew convinced the citizens of Mons that no help could reach them from the French Protestants, and only a month afterwards—the 22nd of September, 1572—Romero wrote a long account to Zayas of the surrender of the devoted town, which "he says we were very fortunate to get by surrender, for no troops but Spaniards could have taken it, so strong is it, and of Spaniards we have very few."

Then, swift and relentless as a thunderbolt, came Alba's vengeance on the southern provinces of Flanders, hopeless of succour now either from Orange or the French. Every town was to

[1] "Simancas Documentos ineditos," vol. lxxv.

support a Spanish garrison or be put to the sword, and of all the cruel instruments for the work none were so much in tune with the mastermind as was Julian Romero. The rebel garrisons of most of the little towns had fled, there was but slight resistance, and Fadrique, on his march from Zutphen to Amsterdam in November, summoned the town of Naarden to admit the Spanish troops into the place. Some demur was made to this, but a few days afterwards the principal men of the town were sent after Fadrique, afraid of their own boldness, to discuss terms for submission. They were refused an interview, and told that a force had already been ordered to Naarden to compel compliance. The citizens, panic-stricken at the news, sent a deputation to offer complete unconditional submission, but before they could reach Fadrique's headquarters at Bussem they met Julian Romero on his way to Naarden, who told them that he had full authority to treat. Arrived at the town, he demanded the keys, which were surrendered to him on his solemn promise that the lives and properties of the townsfolk should be respected. He gave (says Hoofd, the historian) his hand thrice as a pledge of this, and no written pledge was exacted of him. From what we know of Julian Romero's temper we can well imagine this. Romero and his 600 harquebussiers entered the town and were hospitably received. A great feast was spread to do them honour at Burgomaster Gerrit's house. When the banquet was finished Romero collected his men in the great square and summoned the citizens to a conference in the town hall. The bell rang, and the citizens came, all unsuspecting, to hear the conditions imposed upon them; but when they were met, to the number of about six hundred, in the hall, Romero gave a signal at the door and his Spaniards fired a volley upon the closely packed crowd of unarmed men. Thenceforward the little town was a shambles; men, women, and children were all murdered amidst scenes of the most heartrending atrocity, and even infants were made sport of, being cast by the pikemen from spear to spear. The Burgomaster was roasted until he gave up all his fortune as ransom, and was then hanged at his own doorpost in the presence of Romero and Don Fadrique, who had arrived the day after the massacre. Motley, who takes his account from Hoofd, has not added anything to the horror of the story, and it is confirmed by Alba himself in a letter to the King, saying, "They cut the throats of them all, soldiers and townspeople alike, without leaving a single soul alive." Strada says that this massacre had an entirely opposite effect to that expected. It aroused such fury and hate all over Flanders and Holland as to double the difficulty of Alba's task. Strada makes as light of it as possible, but even he says, "It really seems as if the vengeance wrought exceeded the fault. All the inhabitants alike, innocent and guilty, were killed, the houses burnt, the walls razed, and it looked more like a crime than a punishment." [1]

But Holland and Zealand were made of different stuff to South Flanders, and the massacre of Naarden only caused Haarlem to be more obstinate in its determination to hold out at any cost. Fadrique

[1] Strada, "De Bello Belgico."

and his army were before it in the bitter winter of 1572, and it became necessary for him to ensure an open passage between him and Utrecht, whence he drew his supplies. This was interfered with by a rebel fort on the outskirts of Haarlem, near the opposite bank of the Sparen to that upon which the road lay. This fort was flanked on two sides by water—on the one side, where the river was narrow, the defences were impregnable; whilst on the other flank, where the stream opened out and was considered impassable, the fort was otherwise undefended. Early in December spies reported to Fadrique that at certain states of the tide the broad water might be forded and the fort attacked by surprise on its undefended side. His letter to his father detailing how this was done is still at Simancas.[1] He says that at daybreak he sent Julian Romero with 400 picked harquebussiers to attempt the task. Count Bossu and other experienced soldiers had said that it was impossible, but Romero insisted upon attempting it. The water reached above the knees of the men, and the ice had to be broken at every step; the ford was very narrow, and a false step precipitated the armed men into deep water. The men in the fort discovered them and opened fire, and for a full hour they thus skirmished in the frozen river, when they found that a rebel force from the town, equal to their own, had crossed the river on the ice higher up, and were attacking them from their own bank, so that they were between two fires. Romero drew his men out of the river, charged the new force and drove

[1] "Documentos ineditos," vol. lxxv.

them back over the ice again. But in their flight they showed him the way across the ice as well, and how by that road the undefended side of the fort might be reached. With incredible dash he crossed after them and stormed the fort on that side, carried it with pike and musket only, and, as Fadrique tells the Duke, cut the throat of every man who did not escape by flight. Fadrique is quite enthusiastic about Romero's share in the affair. The "heretics," he says, showed surprising bravery, and the fort was of enormous strength— "the best I ever saw." "I thought we were fighting beasts, but I find we have to do with men." "Colonel Julian has carried himself in this action as splendidly as he always does and is as eager as ever to serve his Majesty. He marched for a good league and half with the water over his knees, skirmishing with the fort, before the Haarlem force came. Just think of it, your Excellency; marching like this with such a leg as Julian's! I can assure you that a better soldier than he for dash and enterprise never came from our country. Pray thank him warmly for he richly deserves it." Only a few days later Julian was once more to the fore. Lumay, Count de la Mark, made an attempt to relieve Haarlem with a large force, but was beaten by the Spaniards, "Julian with his regiment," we are told by an anonymous eyewitness,[1] "leading the attack in front of every one." Encouraged by this victory, the Spaniards a week afterwards—the 20th of December, 1572—attempted to take the place by storm, but were unsuccessful. Julian was standing on a trench directing operations when a

[1] "Documentos ineditos," vol. lxxv.

musket-shot destroyed one of his eyes, but even that did not put him *hors de combat* for long, for he writes to the Duke's secretary, Albernoz, on the 13th of the next month (January, 1573) from Amsterdam: "I have been impatiently expecting Illan's arrival, in order that I might go to the front, but if he comes not I am determined I will wait no longer, but will set out to-morrow; for I see that things are now going to begin in real earnest. I am pretty well, but not so well as I want to be to serve Don Fadrique; but I will do so with all my poor strength, standing or falling. He has sent me word that I must go and lodge in his quarters or he will burn mine down over my head. I will obey him in this as in all things, and although I know full well I shall not lack for dainties there, I will not spare you from sending me the other box of marmalade you promised me, as the one you sent is half gone already."

For the next six months each step in the terrible siege of Haarlem is related in the letters from Don Fadrique, Gaspar de Robles, and Romero himself. Wherever fighting was going on Colonel Julian was always in the front rank, and we hear of him creeping forward from month to month nearer to the devoted city as death and famine make it weaker. Romero's own letter to Alba of the 25th of May, 1573,[1] gives the best account I have read of the incidents of the siege from the Spanish point of view, although neither that nor any other of the series I have mentioned appears ever to have been utilised by historians. When at last, in July, 1575, the famished heroes in the city surrendered, Julian

[1] "Documentos ineditos," vol. lxxv.

Romero was deputed to accompany Count Bossu to the wood where the submission was to be arranged, and himself to hold the town gate that no soul should issue therefrom without due warrant.

Of the cruel massacre of the starving people which followed Julian Romero does not boast, but it may be not uncharitably assumed that he played his usual sympathetic part in it. Certain it is that no sooner was it over than Colonel Julian, with an army of 4,000 men, commenced his fell march over Holland. Mendoza[1] says: "Julian entered by the Dunes as far as the Hague, taking Catwyk, Walkemburg, Wassenaer, Naeldwyk, St. Geradique, Squelpewyk Noortwyk, Vlaerdingen, the fort of Mansendus, where he cut the throats of St. Aldegonde and 600 men, Münster, Gravesande, &c." And then he went towards Leyden, which was being besieged by Valdes. Morgan, writing to Lord Burleigh from Delft[2] on the 12th of November, 1575, represents the Dutch burghers as completely cowed for the moment by Romero's ferocity. He says: "Julian with his 4,000 men is entrenched half-way between the Hague and Delft, cutting off all communication between the latter place and Leyden."

But by this time Alba felt that cruelty had failed to crush Orange and the Zealanders, supported as they were by England and helped by the German princes; and sated as even he was of blood, he determined to give up the struggle and allow another policy to be tried. Romero was tired of it too, and wished to retire with his chief. Alba

---

[1] "Comentario de las Guerras de los paises bajos."
[2] Calendar of State Papers (Foreign).

himself wrote to the King from Brussels on the 15th of December, 1573.[1] "Colonel Julian Romero has served here in the way your Majesty has been informed. He had returned here from Holland, determined to go to Spain and beseech your Majesty to allow him to rest at home, seeing that he has served for 40 years. When your Majesty's letter for him had been handed to him and I had myself impressed upon him how much he would be missed here at the present juncture, he consented to send Captain Illan to Spain on his private affairs, whilst he still remains in the service here. I pray your Majesty to take such measures for rewarding Julian's many services as they deserve. I can assure you that what he has done in this campaign alone places your Majesty under a deep obligation to him. He is one of the most useful men of his quality that I have ever known, and I shall warmly welcome any mark of favour your Majesty may confer upon him."

Romero's own letter to the King to accompany this plainly tells how much the hard old soldier yearned for rest. "I have been," he says, "in your Majesty's service now in this guise for well-nigh forty years, without leaving it for a single hour; my work in this campaign has been, as your Majesty knows, extremely hard, and as I have lost the full use of my legs, arms, and eyes, I besought the Duke to give me leave to go home, which he did. When I went to Brussels to take leave of him a letter was handed to me from your Majesty ordering me not to leave these States. I obey your Majesty's orders, but the Duke and the

[1] "Documentos ineditos," vol. lxxv.

Grand Commander (Requesens) have given me leave to send Captain Illan to beg your Majesty personally to let me go and see my home again. I need greatly to go, as is proved by my asking to do so now, for otherwise I would not even go if I had leave.

Philip was the most ungenerous and ungrateful of employers, and for reasons which presently will be stated it is doubtful whether Julian's devotion was rewarded as Alba recommended that it should be, notwithstanding a letter in the Record Office [1] from one of the many false Englishmen then in Spanish Flanders, written to a Captain Windebanke in Elizabeth's service. The writer was trying to get Windebanke to play the traitor, and deplores that so good a captain should be so scurvily rewarded by the Queen, whose penuriousness he compares with Philip's (entirely imaginary) liberality. "Captain Julian Romero," he says, "whom I knew a poor captain in Ireland, is now worth £2,000, and has a pension of a thousand ducats." The writer was probably false in his facts as he was in his patriotism, for I can find no record of Julian's ever having been in Ireland, and only a few months after the date of the letter we have his own word that he was almost in indigence.

The new Viceroy, Requesens, was to try to do by conciliation what Alba had failed to effect by severity. It was time to adopt a new policy, for Southern Flanders was now nearly as disaffected as Holland, and Zealand was entirely in the hands of the Gueux. Its capital, Middleburg, was held by Mondragon and his Spaniards, but

[1] Calendar of State Papers (Foreign).

he was closely beleaguered by the rebels and in the direst straits. Mondragon was one of the best and bravest of the commanders on the Spanish side, whose heroic relief of Tergoes still remains one of the brightest feats of war ever performed, he had informed Requesens that, unless he were relieved with food and stores, he should be forced to lay down his sword and give up Middleburg to the despised "beggars of the sea"; so the new Viceroy's first duty was to send aid to Middleburg and Ramua. Two fleets were fitted out for the purpose in January, 1574, one consisting of large ships under the famous Sancho de Avila was to go by the main Scheldt and the Hundt, rather for the purpose of diverting the rebel force than for any other action, whilst nine standards of soldiers under Romero, and a great quantity of stores, were to go in a fleet of seventy-two canal boats, barges, galliots, and crookstems, through the narrow channels by way of Bergen-op-Zoom to the besieged town. The naval commander was to have been De Beauvoir, with Glimes as second in command. The former fell ill, and the Viceroy gave the chief control to Romero, who protested that he was a soldier and not a sailor, but at last consented to take the command.

The expedition began badly. Requesens came to the quay of Antwerp to see it depart; Romero's flagship led the way, and as a salvo of honour was fired, a gun on one of the boats burst, and the craft sank with all hands. Then the leader looked behind and found several of his vessels lagging. Antwerp itself was riddled with disaffection, and the Flemish sailors had given him the slip, so the boats had to be left behind. Then Romero and his fleet dropped down the river and anchored near Bergen, opposite Romerswald, to await another tide, Requesens, the Viceroy, proceeding to the same place by road to witness the final departure of the expedition from Bergen. At daybreak on the 21st the rebel fleet, under Boisot, Admiral of Flanders, was seen to be approaching them from the open water opposite. Romero's fleet was surrounded by shallows and sand-banks, and largely manned by Flemish sailors whose loyalty, to say the least of it, was doubtful, and de Glimes, seeing the danger, begged his chief not to fight. Cardinal Bentivoglio[1] says: "The Vice-Admiral would not have fought, knowing the great disadvantage on his side. The enemy's ships were many more in number, but Romero, either because his valour blinded his judgment, or from his want of knowledge of maritime affairs, or perhaps because the risk was forced upon him by Mondragon's urgent need, insisted upon fighting." The disaster that followed is ascribed by Bentivoglio to treachery of Romero's Flemish sailors, but, be that as it may, de Glimes' ship first stranded, and others immediately followed, and, thus helpless, were exposed to a galling musketry fire. Captain Osorio with other ships went to the aid of de Glimes and immediately met with the same fate. Greek fire was thrown into the Spanish vessels, and many of them were burnt to the water's edge, the Viceroy the while standing on the dyke helplessly witnessing the destruction of his force. When de Glimes, the Vice-Admiral, had been killed, and his part of the fleet destroyed, the rebels, acquainted

[1] "Guerra di Fiandra."

as they were with the intricate passages, came alongside of Romero's flagship, grappling with it and with its consorts. Boisot's decks towered high over the canal boats, and the crews shot down from their superior position until nearly all the Spaniards were killed, when at last a round shot crashed through the timbers of the flagship, and Romero, fearing she was foundering, jumped overboard on the land side with his few surviving comrades. He came up spluttering and floundering within a few feet of the Viceroy, who stood upon the bank. As he dragged himself up the dyke he blurted out with a voice as vigorous as when he was giving the command to charge, "I told your Excellency how it would be! You knew I was no sailor but a foot soldier and nothing else. No more fleets for me; if you gave me a hundred I should probably lose them all." Requesens gave a graceful and generous answer, but the blow was a heavy one for the Spanish power, for Middleburg and Ramua surrendered to the rebels, and henceforward for ever Zealand was lost to King Philip.[1] Seven hundred of the Spanish force were killed, as was Boisot, the Flemish admiral, and Romero's ship, with all his papers and instructions, fell into the hands of the enemy.

Romero was sick at heart. Requesens' mild temporising looked to Alba's iron lieutenant like lamentable weakness. There was only one way for Julian to meet heresy and the assertion of inde-

---

[1] The account of this disaster is taken from three contemporary accounts—Mendoza's "Comentarios de la Guerra de los paises bajos"; Strada's "De Bello Belgico," and Bentivoglio's "Guerra di Fiandra."

pendence, and that was by extermination. Philip apparently had sent him no rewards, or even thanks, for his staying after Alba left, and had simply ignored his prayer for leave to return home. This was nothing new, for the King always treated his most faithful servants thus, but bluff Julian probably did not know this at the time, and was bitterly disappointed. After his defeat at Bergen he busied himself for some months in planning fortifications and re-organising the forces, which Requesens had found in a state of almost open mutiny for want of pay. By the end of June his task was done, and affairs in South Flanders were looking much more tranquil. No answer came from Madrid to Julian, who, sick and mortified, counted the hours for the time when he might see his home again. In June he wrote an interesting letter to the Viceroy, which deserves to be repeated nearly in full. After recommending the names of five officers for the future command of the forces he says:[1] "I must now address you with my customary frankness and clearness, and disabuse your mind, for once and for all, of the idea that any offers or promises from his Majesty, or any one else, will make me waver in my determination to return home next September. Nothing but my own death shall stand in the way of this, so urgent is my need to go; since my soul's health and the welfare of my wife and children depend upon it, and the least of these reasons would be sufficient to make me firm in my resolve. I have long wished to go but have deferred it because my services here were so much required. I very unwillingly consented to stay when the Duke of Alba

[1] "Documentos ineditos," vol. lxxv.

left ; with the sole object of being by your Excellency's side whilst you were new to your position. I have been well repaid by the pleasure of knowing you and would still serve you with all love and zeal, but the moment now has arrived beyond which I cannot, and will not, stay. You may judge whether I need go when I say that I have served his Majesty 40 years next Christmas without once resting from the wars and my duty. I have lost in the service an arm, a leg, an eye, and an ear ; and the rest of my person is so seared with wounds that I suffer incessantly. I have now just lost a dear son upon whom I built all my hopes—and with good reason as the whole army will bear witness. You will judge whether such troubles as these are not enough to break down my health and spirits. Moreover I married nine years ago, thinking that I might have some rest, but since then I have never been an entire year at home. I have spent during my service nearly all the money I had with my wife, and although I have a daughter at home, and one here of marriageable age, I can do nothing to help them ; except with the trifle still left of my wife's money. I can, moreover, see plainly that this is being exhausted by me at such a rate, that unless I can get home at once, both my wife and myself will have to end our days in the poor-house. You are so christian a prince that I feel sure you will not try to hinder my resolution, for, believe me, it is not for the purpose of exalting or selling myself at a higher price that I urge it. If when I have been home the King still thinks I may be useful, I will try with all my heart, but it must be in some place where I may set up my home and have my wife by my side, for without her, all the world shall not make me stir. I think I have already well deserved by my sufferings and long service any favours his Majesty has conferred upon me."

To this affecting and dignified letter the Viceroy replied saying that he would no longer stand in the way. He had written four or five times already to the King, urging him to fitly reward Julian's great services, and had reason to believe that something would shortly be done, but he had again written in the most pressing terms begging the King not to neglect so good and true a servant. A day or two afterwards Romero again wrote to the Viceroy another manly letter, which shows how bitterly he felt the King's indifference to him. He says: "With reference to your Excellency's kindness in begging his Majesty to reward me, I am constrained to beseech that no further great effort should be made. I will endeavour to pass the few years left to me as decently as I can, and if I cannot have everything I desire I am already as reconciled to leave it all as one who has the candle in his hand. God is my witness that I have never served the King for lucre; no, that has never been my target! True it is that I am cut to the heart to see his Majesty extend his favours to others, who were suckling at the breast when I was already a veteran, whilst he forgets me, but this I lay to my ill luck and to God's will that I should remain a poor man. But naked I was born; I have lived honourably and I care for naught else. Pray therefore, trouble yourself no further on my account. I trust before my departure hence God will settle the affairs of these States. At this season of the year there is little stirring, and if when I have been home and set my house in order, your Excellency should remain in your present straits; I pledge my word as a Christian to come and serve again with all my strength. If I were a batchelor and as hale as I used to be, you should see what I would do. Worcum, June 27, 1574."

If Romero's desire of seeing his home again was fulfilled, as it probably was, his visit must have been of short duration, for in October of the next year he was commanding thirty standards of troops before Zerusee, and endeavoured to capture an island near Dortrecht, but was beaten by the Prince of Orange himself with the loss of 800 men.[1]

Early in the following year things had reached an acute stage. Requesens was dead, and Don Juan of Austria, his successor, had not arrived. The mercenaries in the Spanish service, unpaid and chafing at inaction, were in open mutiny, and were plundering and maltreating friends and foes indifferently to indemnify themselves. The Council of State, mostly Flemish and Walloon nobles, were profoundly divided, and already were doing their best to hold their own against the savage Spanish soldiery. Brussels was held by Walloon troops in the interests of the Council of State, the Spanish troops in the neighbourhood being under the command of Romero. By the middle of March the Council were obliged to meet and devise some means of pacifying the mutineers by raising money to pay them, "without which many strange seditions must happen."

[1] Calendar of State Papers (Foreign).

They agreed with Romero to pay certain soldiers forty crowns each, to satisfy them until the arrival of the new Governor, and then sent him to parley with the mutineers. Strada says they would not listen to him, but in any case most of his men fraternised with and joined them. On his return to Brussels he was again sent by the Council against the rebel Spaniards who had gone towards Maestricht. English agents in Flanders[1] report that he had arranged a plot to be carried out in his absence. He had left 200 of his men in Brussels, and the plan was for Count Barlemont, one of the Council, to deliver the keys of the city to them, in order that the mutineers, and probably Romero with them, should enter the city and sack it. The plot was discovered, and Barlemont deprived of the keys, and after Romero had fruitlessly been to Maestricht, he found on his return to Brussels the citizens in a frenzy of rage against the Spaniards in consequence of the massacres at Alost and elsewhere by the mutineers. The infuriated Flemings tore to pieces a servant of Jerome Rodas, the leading Spanish councillor, and the latter, with Romero and Vargas, had to fly for their lives to the stronghold in the palace. Henceforward the Flemish Council and the Spaniards were completely estranged. The Council proclaimed the mutineers rebels against the King, whilst Rodas assumed to be Philip's sole representative.

Philip was in deep distress at the news.[2] Romero was to be warmly thanked, the Council must dis-

---
[1] Herll to Burleigh, Rogers to Walsingham, and Harise to Burleigh. Calendar of State Papers (Foreign).
[2] Philip to Rodas. Calendar of State Papers (Foreign).

band their forces, money would be sent, Don Juan would soon arrive, and all would be settled. In the meantime, however, the forces of the Council were attacking the mutineers at Ghent, Maestricht, Alost, and elsewhere, and the Spanish commanders, Sancho de Avila, Romero, Vargas, &c., whilst ostensibly condemning them, were constrained daily to side more with their fellow-countrymen. Romero at last escaped from Brussels and fortified himself at Lierre, where a considerable force gradually joined him. The Council sent word that they would attack him if he did not submit to their authority, but when they attempted to do so his force, with that of Vargas, routed the States troops. The massacre which followed is explained by Mendoza by the fact that the Spaniards were hot-headed youngsters, which they were not, but he is evidently ashamed of it. A large number of spectators, students from Louvain and others, had come out to see the fight. They were all slaughtered, as were soldiers and civilians, armed and unarmed, men and women, without quarter and without mercy, up to the very gates of Louvain. Thenceforward all hope of restraint was lost. The Spanish soldiery were so many bloodthirsty wild beasts, making no distinction between Flemish friends or foes, and it was war to the knife on both sides. Romero's headquarters were still at Lierre, although he kept up a close connection with the mutineers at Alost, and his men seem to have outdistanced others in their savagery, no attempt to moderate which appears to have been made by their chief. Savage Rodas himself got frightened in October, and wrote to the King that the Spanish soldiers were pillaging on all sides, and if some remedy were not sent soon from Spain, all would go to perdition.[1]

Wherever Romero had a chance of fighting the States forces he did so, and Mendoza gives particulars of many brilliant skirmishes in which the Spaniards were successful, but which usually ended in an indiscriminate massacre of Flemings. Sancho de Avila in the Antwerp citadel the while was keeping up a close communication with the mutineers at Alost, Ghent, and other places, whilst the citizens were collecting such forces of Walloons and German mercenaries as they could. Sancho at last was informed that unless he ceased to send aid to Alost he himself would be held as a rebel to the King. This was a signal that he must either submit to the dictation of the despised Flemish Council or fight, and he chose the latter alternative. He sent out messengers on all sides for the Spaniards to concentrate in Antwerp, and soon Romero started out from Lierre with all his men. On his way he met the main body of malcontents from Alost and greeted them with effusion. Vargas with his men joined them also, and on the 4th of November they all entered the citadel of Antwerp together. The townsmen and their troops had already begun to run up earthworks to defend themselves against the bloodthirsty marauders who had made a shambles of Alost, Maestricht, and wherever else they had gained the upper hand. The rich booty of Antwerp, and the thirst for blood, they knew would launch the greedy hawks from the citadel upon the panting quarry

[1] Rodas to Philip (intercepted). Calendar of State Papers (Foreign).

below, and they determined to sell their lives and property dearly. Hungry and tired as the Alost men were on their arrival at daybreak, no meal would they consume until, as they said, they could break their fast in Antwerp. Slaking their thirst and firing their brains only with wine, by eleven o'clock before noon they were ready for the struggle. Then with solemn prayer and blessing of banners as a preparation for their fell work, they swept down in three bodies to the town to the aggregate number of about 6,000 men. The scene that followed has often been described, and need not be repeated here. In a few hours the richest city in Christendom was a ravished corpse of its former self. Romero, with his stalwarts of Spaniards and Almains, entered the city by the St. George's gate and swept along the street of St. Michael, driving weak young Egmont before him into a church at the end, where the Count was taken.

Everywhere the Walloons turned and fled before the Spaniards. The brave Champigny, Granvelle's brother, did his best heroically; the townsmen, unused to arms, made what resistance they could, but the States troops were worse than useless, and butchery was the only order of the day. In the great square every house was occupied by Sancho de Avila's men, who kept up a fusilade upon the frightened crowds of unarmed people huddled together in the doorways. Soon the curling smoke showed that the rich stores of merchandise, the noble palaces of the merchant princes, and the lowly cottages of the artisans were alike doomed to wanton destruction. The Spaniards, drunk with blood, blind with rage, spared neither age, sex, nor faith; and with one great gust of fury swept like a blight over the doomed city. When the blood-lust was partly sated, it was found that 6,000 unarmed people at least had been slaughtered, and 6,000,000 ducats worth of property stolen, with as much again burnt. The States infantry had all fled or been killed. The Catholic Flemish nobles were scattered and lost, and the Spaniards had Antwerp beneath their talons. Strada says that the massacre and plunder were as much the work of the Walloons and Germans as of the Spaniards, and bears testimony to the efforts of the Spanish leaders to restrain the fury of their men, mentioning Sancho de Avila, Mondragon, and others as having exerted their influence to that end, but markedly omits the name of Romero. Rodas, writing to the King a day after the fight, says the town was sacked against orders, and that Avila, Romero, and Vargas, used great diligence to stop plunder. "They deserve," he says, "well of his Majesty for the services they have rendered in this great victory." Dr. Wilson, who certainly was not prejudiced in favour of the Spaniards, says, on the other hand, in a letter to Walsingham of the 13th of November,[1] that he fears the Spaniards much less than the English refugees, "who are said to have done the greatest murders and most horrible above all others, and all Englishmen are hated for their sake."

Flemings of every faith were welded together now against the wreckers of their homes, and even those nobles who, through all the evil past had stood by Spain, the Perennots, the Croys, the Montmorencis, the Zweveghems, were at one with

[1] State Papers (Domestic).

the Protestants of the North. Don Juan found himself, when he arrived, in face of a united people glowing with indignation, and determined to prevent the destruction of its liberties, strong enough now to force terms upon him. The first demand of the Flemings was that all Spaniards should withdraw from Flanders, and the second that Rodas, Avila, and Romero should lose their heads for their share in the massacres. To the first demand the Prince was forced to accede, with the second he fenced diplomatically; and soon Romero was on the march at the head of his men going from Flanders to Italy with the curses of all Flemings following him.

Don Juan could not brook for long the dictation and exactions of the Council, he took the bit between his teeth, seized the citadel of Namur, defied them all to do their worst, and made up his mind to fight it out in spite of the King's orders. Then the veteran forces, by which Alba had crushed the Low Countries, the bloodthirsty savages who had ravished them before, were once more recalled from Italy, late in 1577. Romero was designated for the chief command of an army of 6,000 men who were to act subsequently under Alexander Farnese in Flanders. He was starting on his march from Cremona at the head of his force, when the war-worn old soldier, without a moment's warning, fell from his horse, dead. He breathed his last as he had lived, full-armed and harnessed for the fray, surrounded by the fierce soldiery he had led so often. Strada says his death caused the deepest grief, as he was looked upon as the mainstay of the new attempt to dominate the Flemings. Another contemporary historian, Cabrera de Cordova, wrote of him, "his loss caused profound sorrow by reason of the urgent need for his valour and experience, which had enabled him to rise from a common soldier to be a general, whilst his prowess and knowledge of war well deserved the last promotion to the rank in which he died, namely, that of commander-in-chief of great enterprises."

For some years even after his death his name was used to threaten England with, and the presence of another younger Captain Julian with the Spanish auxiliaries to the Irish rebellion of 1579–80 gave rise to many trembling rumours that the terrible Romero himself was there.

But he is forgotten now, even in his own country; the cause he fought for, the supremacy of Catholicism, has been beaten everywhere but in Spain, where stern intolerance, and indifference to personal suffering still linger as things to be proud of. It has seemed to me, however, that the devotion, the valour, and the self-sacrifice of the rough soldier who rose to be "commander-in-chief of great enterprises," dimmed though they be by cruel ferocity, might well be rescued in this gentler age from the oblivion in which they lay so long.

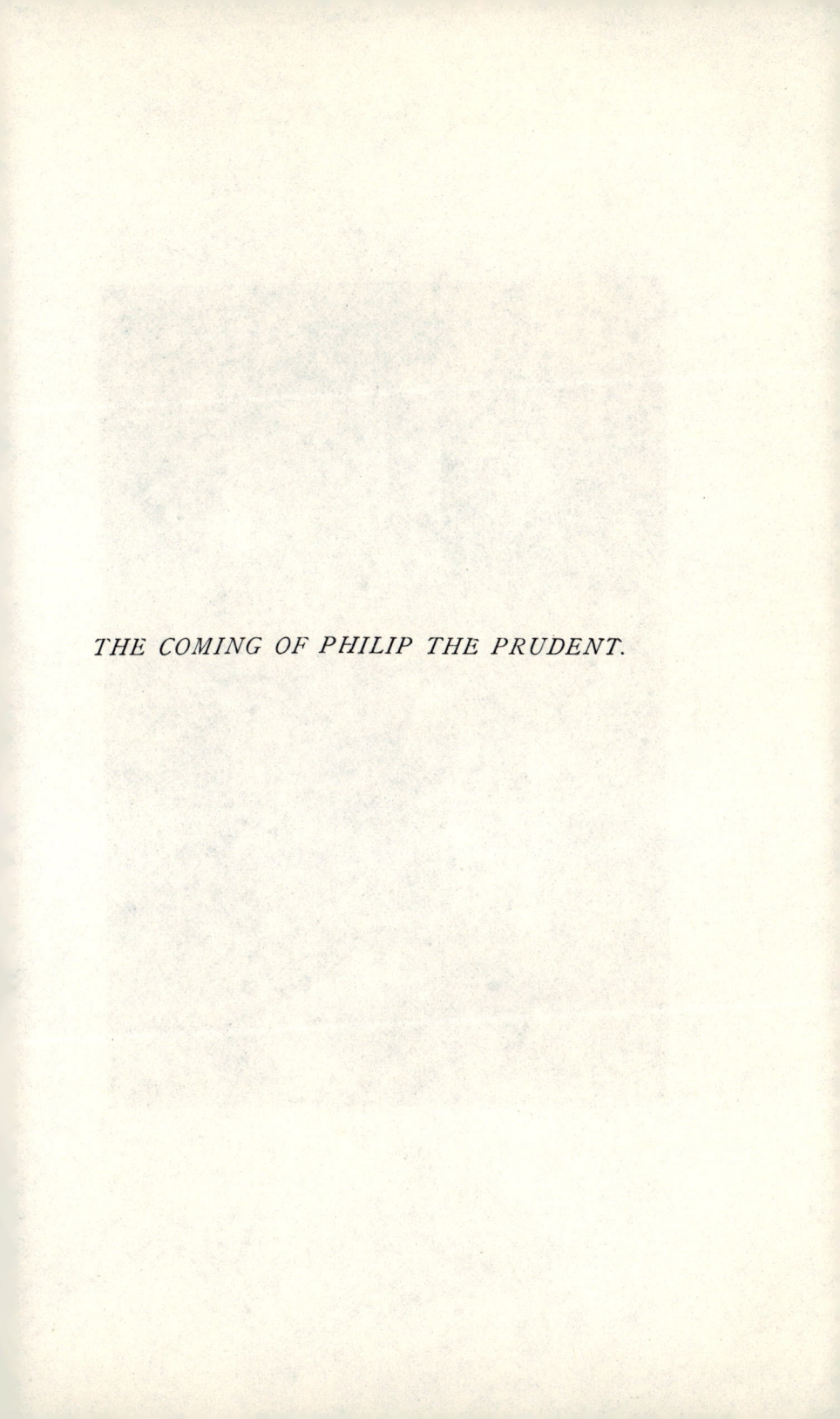

*THE COMING OF PHILIP THE PRUDENT.*

PHILIP AND MARY.
*(After the painting by Antonio Mor.)*

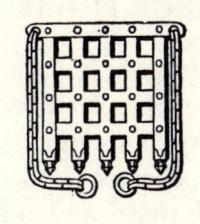

## THE COMING OF PHILIP THE PRUDENT.[1]

IT is somewhat curious that English historians, in describing an event fraught with such tremendous possibilities to Christianity as the coming of the Spanish prince to wed Mary of England, should have entirely overlooked a source of information which was more likely than any other to abound in interesting and trustworthy details of the voyage—I mean the contemporary narratives of Spaniards who accompanied Philip hither. So far as regards the splendid pageantry that marked the new consort's entrance into London the English records themselves leave nothing to be desired. Darnley's tutor, John Elder, in his letter to his pupil's uncle, the Bishop of Caithness,[2] descends to the minutest particulars, and is amply confirmed by the anonymous Chronicle of Queen Mary in the Harleian manuscripts, whence John Stow derived his informa-

[1] *The English Historical Review*, April, 1892.
[2] This curious and rare tract was reprinted by the Camden Society, 1849, and is the groundwork of Foxe's and Hollingshed's accounts of the events related therein.

tion; by Edward Underhyll, "the hot-gospeller";[1] and the letters of the French ambassador, Antoine de Noailles.[2] The gorgeous ceremonies that attended the marriage in Winchester Cathedral are also sufficiently described by these and other authorities, as well as in the official account of the English heralds of the time, copied from the Book of Precedents of Ralph Brooke, York herald, and printed in Leland's "Collectanea," edit. 1774, and by the Camden Society, 1849;[3] but the accounts given by English historians of Philip's voyage and reception at Southampton appear to rest entirely upon a narrative of the Venetian, Baoardo, published in Venice in 1558, four years after the event, and the letters of Noailles to the King of France. Miss Strickland and the late Mr. Froude, both of whom draw upon Baoardo to a large extent for their local colour, quote him as an eyewitness of the scenes he describes. Whether he was so or not I do not know, although I have been unable to discover any evidence of his presence, but in any case the bitter animus against Philip shown in his narrative is so clear that it is unfair to accept his statements without ample confirmation.

Such confirmation seems to have been sought,

[1] Edward Underhyll was one of the gentlemen pensioners, and his quaint narrative of the accession of Mary and the subsequent events, now amongst the Harleian manuscripts, was largely used by Strype and others.
[2] Ambassades de Noailles. Leyden, 1763.
[3] To these may be added the slight but interesting narrative existing in manuscript at Louvain, and printed by Tytler in his "Edward VI and Mary," and the letters of the Venetian ambassador in Flanders to the Doge and Senate, for which see Calendar of State Papers (Venetian) of the date in question.

by Mr. Froude at all events, in the letters of the French ambassador, and from this material, coupled with the fact that certain prudent measures of precaution were suggested by Simon Renard, the Emperor's ambassador, in his letters to his master, the historian paints his highly coloured picture of Philip as a sulky, seasick craven trembling at his very shadow, in momentary fear of poison, consummating a sacrifice from which his soul revolts. To justify this view Professor Froude depended mainly upon Noailles. It must, however, be remembered, first, that the French ambassador was not in a position to know the exact details of Philip's voyage and reception; secondly, that he was the last person in the world to give a fair account of them; thirdly, that the historian has gone beyond his authority, even such as it was; and fourthly, that several witnesses of the events described, whose evidence has hitherto been ignored, entirely fail to confirm the view taken by Mr. Froude from Noailles and Baoardo.

Throughout the whole negotiations that had preceded the arrangement of the marriage Noailles had been absurdly ill-informed and wide of the mark.[1] His letters to the King of France and the Constable teem with predictions and assertions which subsequent events proved to be quite wrong, and it is easy to see that for months

[1] He was equally at sea at the beginning of Mary's reign, when he vigorously aided Northumberland's conspiracy to place Lady Jane Grey on the throne, and repeatedly told his master that Mary's cause was an absolutely hopeless one. On the ignominious collapse of Dudley, Noailles excused his own want of prescience by saying that nothing but a direct miracle from heaven could have brought about such a change.

previous to the marriage he was entirely hoodwinked, and out of touch with trustworthy sources of information. In a letter to the French adviser of Mary of Lorraine in Scotland, M. d'Oysel, dated 29th of March, 1554, for instance, he speaks of the Earl of Bedford's departure for Spain as an accomplished fact, and has no doubt that he had already sailed from Plymouth to fetch the Prince. On May 18th, after ringing the changes upon this for nearly two months, he tells the King that the rumour runs that Bedford is to go shortly to Spain, but that the Prince will not come until the winter, whereas Philip had already left Valladolid at the time on his way to England. On the 31st of March Noailles is quite persuaded that Wyatt's life will be spared, and less than a fortnight later he describes his execution. On the 29th of March, again, he says that the Bishop of Norwich, the Queen's ambassador to the Emperor, had been summoned to perform the marriage, and was to be created Archbishop of York for the purpose. Gardiner, Bishop of Winchester, really performed the ceremony. Noailles again is quite sure that other Wyatts will arise, and that 50,000 men will be in arms to receive the Prince, and in April, after writing for weeks of the preparations for the arrival of Philip on the south coast and marriage at Winchester, he believes it all to be a feint and that the Prince will suddenly appear and be married in London. On the 29th of the same month he is strongly of opinion that Sir James Crofts will be executed on the following Monday, whereas that distinguished old soldier lived and fought and sold himself for many years afterwards. Hardly a letter, indeed, from

Noailles at this period fails to show that the man, having been completely outwitted by Renard's keen diplomacy, was entirely at sea, and badly served by his informers.

But I go beyond this. Philip had anchored in Southampton Water on the afternoon of the 19th of July, 1554, and landed on that of the 20th. On the night of the 20th, after the Prince had landed, Noailles learnt in London, by an imperial messenger, for the first time of his arrival, and communicated the news to the King of France immediately by letter; and on the 23rd he writes:—

"J'ai envoyé ung des miens á Hamptonne et a Winchestre et despescheray demain encores ung aultre pour estre mieulx par mesme informé de tout ce qui se fera tant a la terre que sur la mer . . . affin de tenir advertye vostre majeste."

It is clear, therefore, that Noailles had no trustworthy person to give an exact account of the reception of the Prince until the arrival of the latter at Winchester; and the description in his letters of Philip's voyage and doings at Southampton was merely current gossip dressed up to suit the palate of the writer and his master.[1] How much impartiality could be expected from Noailles under the

[1] I am of course aware that the ambassador had previously sent his brother François de Noailles to request the Queen to stand godmother to his newly born son, but François only arrived at Winchester from London on the day the Queen received news of the arrival of the Prince off the Isle of Wight, which could not have been earlier than the 19th, and was back in London again in time for the child to be christened, with the Countess of Surrey as the Queen's proxy, on the 22nd, which would certainly leave him no time to go to Southampton to witness the landing. See "Ambassades de Noailles," iii. 282.

circumstances may well be imagined. He had been thoroughly outmanœuvred, and French diplomacy had received a greater blow than it had sustained for many years in seeing England drift apparently for good into the arms of Spain. His country was at the very moment engaged in a long and costly war with the Emperor, and he himself had just been detected and exposed for the second time in his attempts to suborn and support rebellion in England, and was in high dudgeon at being pointedly excluded from participation in the marriage festivities. What wonder, then, that after slandering the Queen for months past he should do as much as possible to darken the shadows of the picture of Philip sent for the delectation of Philip's enemy? It were expecting too much to suppose that the outwitted diplomatist and supple courtier would do otherwise.

Ill-natured, however, as are Noailles' references to Philip, even they do not, in my opinion, warrant the distorted picture inferentially derived from them. To instance a small matter of which much is made by Froude—namely, the vivid scene of the seasick Prince gulping down beer on the night of his arrival at Southampton, to please the English spectators at his public repast—Noailles says not a word about Philip's being ill or seasick, nor do any other chroniclers of the time, that I am aware of. The only foundation for the story seems to be a remark contained in a letter from the Earl of Bedford and Lord Fitzwalter from Santiago (Calendar of State Papers, Foreign) to the effect that, "as the Prince suffers much at sea, it will be well to make preparations for him to land at Plymouth, or other port on the south coast if necessary."

The voyage was a beautifully calm one, and the Prince had remained on board the *Espiritu Santo*, at anchor in Southampton Water, for twenty hours at least before he landed; and, instead of the dramatic scene at his public supper described by Froude, his repast was a private one; and according even to Noailles, who is alone responsible for the story, *after supper*, in the presence chamber, Philip told his Spanish courtiers that in future they must forget the customs of their country and live like Englishmen, and " when, according to the English fashion, a quantity of wine, beer, and ale was brought in silver flagons, he took some beer and drank it "—a very simple and appropriate compliment to his new country; but even Noailles tells the story without a hint of the loathing of unwilling sacrifice with which Froude invested the perfectly natural scene.

Having thus far spoken of the authorities upon which English historians have hitherto based their descriptions of the coming of Philip the Prudent, and pointed out a few of what I venture to think their obvious shortcomings, I will mention some other contemporary narratives which may well, it is true, sin just as much on the score of partiality, but at any rate afford a view of the events recorded that has hitherto been almost entirely ignored—namely, the view taken by those Spaniards who accompanied their Prince in his voyage to England in quest of his eager but elderly bride.[1]

[1] Mr. Prescott is the only historian writing in the English language who refers to Spanish accounts at all, and his reference is confined to a single mention of Cabrera's bald and stolid history and one or two quotations from Sepulveda, who appears to have derived what little information he gives from

Amongst the five hundred courtiers and servants, besides soldiers, who accompanied Philip to England, several would naturally be able and disposed to put upon record, for transmission to their friends in Spain, full narratives of the great events they witnessed—events, be it said, which had deeply stirred the public imagination of Spaniards, who had been taught to believe that the marriage of their prince in England would mean not only the mastery of their country over France, but the restoration of all Christendom to the true faith. These letters, in a period when newspapers were not, would frequently be printed and circulated by enterprising booksellers, and no doubt many of such news-letters, both in print and manuscript, are still hidden in bundles and volumes of miscellaneous papers in the public and private libraries in the Peninsula. One curious manuscript letter, written from Winchester by Juan de Barahona to Antonio de Barahona, was found in the library of the Escorial fifty years ago, and published in the first volume of the "Documentos ineditos para la Historia de España" in 1842. The manuscript had belonged to the contemporary chronicler Florian de Ocampo, and gives an extremely full account of the voyage, reception, and marriage, abounding in curious details of the life, dress, and manners of the time. In referring to this narrative in the following pages I shall distinguish it as narrative No. 1.

one of the narratives now before me. Simon Renard's letters to the Emperor in the Granvelle papers are naturally also referred to by most historians of the period in question, but, important as they are from many points of view, they only give a purely official and diplomatic account, and are Flemish and imperial rather than Spanish and personal in their interest.

## THE COMING OF PHILIP THE PRUDENT. 133

Many years later there was discovered in the Biblioteca Nacional a record which, to Spaniards at least, was much more valuable and interesting. It was a printed tract entitled "Summary and Veracious Relation of the Happy Voyage made by the Unconquered Prince of the Spains, Don Felipe, to England, and his Reception in Vinchester, where he was married, with his Departure for London; in which are contained the great and marvellous things that happened at that time. Dedicated to the Most Illustrious Lady Donna Luisa Enriquez de Giron, Countess of Benavente, by Andres Muñoz, Servant to his Serene Highness the Infante Don Carlos. Imprinted in Çaragoca, in the house of Esteban de Najera, 1554, at the cost of Miguel de Çapila, bookseller." The author was a lackey to the unhappy Don Carlos, then a child, and his own personal observation is confined to the elaborate preparations for Philip's voyage made in the city of Valladolid and the journey of the little prince to Benavente, in Castile, to take leave of his father. What he saw and heard he relates with a trivial minuteness of detail, particularly as to the persons who were to accompany Philip and the clothes they took with them, which to an ordinary reader would be tedious in the extreme. But although his own share in the voyage ended at Benavente, whence Don Carlos returned to Valladolid, Muñoz apparently made arrangements with some member of the suite—no doubt of similar rank to himself—to send him particulars from England, and his account is therefore carried down to the departure of Philip and Mary for London after their marriage. This is by far the fullest account known, especially as to the events prior to Philip's embarkation; but the writer's position naturally caused him to dwell mainly upon the sartorial aspect of things which came under his observation, and he describes the splendour and pageantry rather as a spectator than as an actor. I shall call Muñoz's narrative No. 2.

About the same time as the discovery of Muñoz's letter three other letters, which in my opinion are even more valuable, because of the position of the supposed author, were found in the Escorial library. The first is a printed tract in the form of a diary and is entitled "Transcript of a Letter sent from England to this City of Seville, in which is given a Relation of the Events of the Voyage of our Lord the Prince Don Philip, from his Embarkation in the Coruña, a Port of Spain, to his Marriage to the Serene Queen of England. 1554." The book bears the well-known device, although not the name, of the celebrated Sevillian printer Andres de Burgos. In the same library was found a manuscript letter taking up the narrative where the last-mentioned tract ended—namely, after the marriage at Winchester at the end of July—and carrying it to August 19th, when the Court was at Richmond. No printed copy of this continuation is known to exist, but it is almost certainly written by the same hand, and contains many remarks and opinions which would probably have been suppressed if the letter had been published. A continuation of this, again, was also found in the Escorial, written apparently by the same person, bringing the narrative down to October 2nd, and is dated from London, where the King and Queen then were. These three letters, which I shall distinguish by the numbers 3,

4, and 5, were published, together with Muñoz's narrative (No. 2), by the Society of Bibliophilists of Madrid in 1877, under the editorship of Don Pascual de Gayangos.

In inquiring into the probable authorship of these three extremely valuable and interesting letters Señor de Gayangos gives good reason for supposing that they were written by a young courtier named Pedro Enriquez, one of Philip's stewards. He is known to have had a perfect mania for writing relations of what he saw and heard, and has been called the Spanish Tacitus.[1] He was a brother of the Marquis of Villanueva and a relative both of the Duke and Duchess of Alba, of whose movements he gives a very minute account in the above letters. He also identifies himself as a steward of the King in one of his complaints of the exclusive service of Philip by Englishmen, and is known to have been one of the very few Spanish noblemen who remained with Philip in London. His style, moreover, is peculiar, and I have had a former opportunity of commenting upon it in connection with a rapid and industrious piece of historical transcription of his, executed in the following year in Ghent;[2] and I have no doubt that Don Pedro Enriquez was the author of the three letters I am speaking of. Few people could have had better opportunities of observation than he. He accompanied Philip everywhere; his rank and his relationship to the all-powerful Alba brought him within the inner circle of the Court, and the

[1] Cabrera, "Relaciones," and Nicolas Antonio, "Biblioteca Nova."

[2] "Chronicle of King Henry VIII. of England." London: Bell and Sons. 1889.

feelings he expresses are those of the nobles who surrounded the King and not the gossip of the servants' hall or a valet's list of his master's finery. With these four letters the Society for Bibliophilists printed another by a different author, addressed from London at the end of December, 1554, giving a very full account of the reception of Cardinal Pole; but as this does not touch the subject in hand I omit any further reference to it.

In the British Museum there is a small tract in Italian, apparently printed in Milan in 1554, called " The Departure of the Serene Prince with the Spanish Fleet, and his Arrival in England, with the Order observed by the Queen in his Highness's Reception, and the most Happy Wedding ; with the Names of the English, Spanish, and other Lords and Gentlemen who were present, and the Liveries, Festivities, and other Things done at the Wedding." It is signed " Giovanni Paulo Car," and the writer was a servant of the Marquis of Pescara. A paraphrase or adaptation of the letter also exists in the Museum, and appears to have been published in Rome in the same year, but it is not signed, and contains many additional particulars. The contents of these two tracts, again, appear to have been blended into a narrative published in the following year, probably in Rome, in which the person to whom the letter is addressed is described as the "illustrious Signor Francesco Taverna Cracanz," and although it is not signed by Car it evidently is by him, as he speaks of the Marquis of Pescara all through the narrative as his master. I propose in referring to this narrative to call it No. 6. We have thus a mass of contemporary evidence from persons

## THE COMING OF PHILIP THE PRUDENT.

who were certainly attached to Philip's suite, by the aid of which and the authorities already known a more minute and trustworthy account than any hitherto presented of the events in question may be constructed.

Renard had first broached the subject of the marriage to Mary in August, 1553, and all the attempts of Noailles to inspire fear and hatred of the match in the breasts of the Queen and her people had only made her more determined to carry out the wishes of her heart, and, as she no doubt herself thought, to enhance the happiness and prosperity of her people. Egmont and his glittering train had been snowballed by the London 'prentices when he came formally to offer Philip's hand to the Queen in January, 1554. A whirlwind of passion and panic had passed over southern England at the thought of a Spanish consort ruling in the land, and at about the time that gallant Wyatt and his dwindling troop of "draggle-tayles" were wearily toiling up Fleet Street, only to find that the Queen's courage and their leader's irresolution had wrecked their enterprise, a dusty courier clattered into Valladolid with the premature news that Lord Privy Seal, the Earl of Bedford, and another English lord had started for Spain with the contract that was to make Philip king of England. His Highness was hunting at umbrageous Aranjuez, a hundred miles off, and the messenger, just alighting to kiss the hand of poor lame little Prince Carlos, went scouring over the tawny plains again, bearing his pregnant tidings.

The courting had all been done by the Emperor through clever Renard; and the Prince, dutiful son as he was, bent to his father's will without even knowing the terms of the bargain by which he was to be bound for life. The conditions imposed by the patriotism of Mary and her Council were hard for the most powerful monarch on earth to brook for his son. Philip's power was so fenced round by limitations and safeguards that it was plain to see the English nobles meant his sceptre to be a shadowy one, and the sombre, sensitive pride of the Prince was wounded to the quick at the light esteem in which they seemed to hold him; but, as Sandoval says, "he, like a second Isaac, was ready to sacrifice himself to his father's will and the good of the Church." And he did so gracefully and with dignity. No sooner had the courier delivered his message at Aranjuez than Philip set off on his return to Valladolid with his gaudy escort of horsemen in their red and yellow doublets. In hot haste the old Castilian capital put on its holiday garb to celebrate the event; the great square, standing much as it stands to-day, was bravely adorned, and costly hangings covered all one side of it where the Prince sat to see the jousts, tourneys, cane-play, and fireworks, and where he sat, alas! the next time he saw Valladolid, on his return five years afterwards, to watch unmoved the hellish fireworks of the great *auto de fé*.

The wedding rejoicings had hardly begun when they were changed to mourning by the news of the death of Don Juan of Portugal, the husband of Philip's sister Juana; and the narrator, Muñoz, breaks off in the midst of his rapture over the splendour of Valladolid's joy to relate the pompous grandeur of its sorrow—how between the screen and the altar of St. Paul's there were 3,000 candles of white and yellow wax, and how all the solemnity of previous exequies paled before these. In the meantime Philip had sent one of his stewards, Don Gutierre Lope de Padilla, to receive the English envoys at Laredo. After waiting there for a month with the Prince's guard to pay them due honour, he found that the news sent had been premature, and that the marriage treaty had not yet even been ratified, and was not, indeed, until Egmont's second visit to England in March. So Padilla found his way back again to Valladolid by the end of March, and they decided to take the matter in more leisurely fashion in future. But in a few weeks came news from the Emperor himself that the contract was ratified, and then the Marquis de las Navas was ordered to take the Prince's first present to his bride. We are told that the Marquis fitted himself out for his mission regardless of cost, and his splendour appears to have been equalled by the princely gifts of which he was the bearer, and the noble hospitality extended to him in England.[1] Philip's offering to Mary consisted of "a great table diamond, mounted as a rose in a superb gold setting, valued at 50,000 ducats; a collar or necklace of 18 brilliants, exquisitely worked and set with dainty grace, valued at 32,000 ducats; a great diamond with a fine large pearl pendant from it (this was Mary's favourite jewel, and may be seen on her breast in most portraits). They were (says narrative No. 2) the most lovely pair of gems ever seen in the world, and were worth 25,000 ducats. Then comes

[1] See letter from Lord Edmund Dudley to the Council, quoted in Tytler, " Edward VI. and Mary."

a list of pearls, diamonds, emeralds, and rubies of inestimable value, and other presents without number for the Queen and her ladies. Eighty fine horses and fifty hackneys were sent on to Corunna to await the Prince's coming, and all Castile and Aragon, not to speak of Leon, were alive with artificers of the gorgeous garb and trappings to fit out the proud nobles who were to follow their Prince, each, with true Spanish ostentation, bent upon outstripping the others in the richness and splendour of themselves and their train.[1] Muñoz, in narrative No. 2, gives a list of the clothes made for each of the principal grandees, which it would be tedious and unnecessary to repeat here.

The Prince, great as he was, was only first among his peers, and if he could be magnificent so could his train, and Alba and Medina-Celi, Egmont and Aguilar, Pescara and Feria vied with their master in their finery. Each great noble—and there were twenty of them—took his train of servants in new liveries, and the Prince had a Spanish guard of 100 gentlemen in red and yellow, 100 Germans in the same uniform, but with silk facings, "as their custom is to go bravely dressed," 100 archers on horseback, and 300 servants in the same gaudy colours of Aragon. All this splendid apparatus was a comparatively new thing for Spaniards at the time; the homely, unceremonious relations between sovereign and people had only been put aside for the pompous etiquette

[1] This was in despite of Renard's recommendation to Philip: "Seulement sera requis que les Espaignolez qui suyvront vostre Alteze comportent les façons de faire des Angloys et soient modestes, confians que vostre Alteze les aicarassera par son humanité costumiere."

of the house of Burgundy, on the coming of Philip's grandfather from Flanders with his Spanish bride to take up the sceptre dropped by the dead hand of Isabel the Catholic, and the gold of the Indies had since that time poured into Spain and spread a thirst for showy pomp even amongst the frank, honest, homely gentlemen who had formed a majority of the Spanish hidalgo class. The changed taste, however, was new enough still to attract the attention of the crowd who had not yet become accustomed to so much splendour.

All these elaborate preparations being completed, Philip, with nearly 1,000 horsemen, glittering and flashing in the pitiless Castilian sun, left Valladolid on the 14th of May—not for England yet, but far down on the Portuguese frontier, at Alcantara, to meet his widowed sister, who had been forced to come out of her bitter grief to govern her father's kingdom during Philip's absence. He accompanied her five days on her journey to Valladolid, and then turning aside to take a last leave of his mad grandmother, Juana la Loca, bent his course towards Benavente, on the high road to Santiago, arriving there on the 3rd of June, covered with dust of travel, but gracious, as he could be, to those who had entertained his boy Carlos, who had preceded him.

Next day there was a grand bull-fight in the plaza, which Philip and Carlos saw from Pero Hernandez's flower-decked house. The return of the Princes to Count Benavente's castle was not quite so dignified as it might have been, as one bull was so "devilish" that it refused to be killed, and held the plaza victoriously against all comers until the next morning, whereupon Philip and his son had to slip out by Pero Hernandez's back door and reach the castle by a roundabout way. The day after there was a hunt and a tourney, and then after supper the Princes mounted on a high scaffold, richly dight, to see "a procession of beautiful and strange inventions." Torches blazed all round them, and each device was led by one of the neighbouring squires with twenty pikemen and drummers and fifers, each detachment in a separate livery. Elephants manufactured out of horses and pasteboard, castles with savages inside, a green tabernacle with a lovely maiden borne by savages, a model of a ship dressed with English and Spanish flags, and, strangest of all, a girl in a coffin complaining of Cupid, who came behind on horseback. When the device reached the middle of the plaza the god of love was suddenly hoisted on high by a rope round his middle, and let off fireworks, to the delectation of the crowd. As a relief to this foolery the great Lope de Rueda then represented "a sacred play with comic interludes," which, no doubt, was better worth seeing than the "conceits and fireworks" that pleased the narrator so much. The next day, after bidding good-bye to the son who was afterwards to hate him so bitterly, the Prince started in the cool of the summer night on his way to the sea.

At Astorga a splendid reception had been prepared for him, but he could not stay, and pushed on with all possible speed, news having reached him that the Earl of Bedford and Lord Fitzwalter were already awaiting him at Santiago. There he arrived on the vigil of St. John, the 23rd of June, and there as usual golden keys were offered by kneeling citizens; silks and satins, velvets and brocades.

flaunted in the sun, and in the upper window of a house on the line of route sat the two English lords, their mantles before their faces, watching the progress of their future king to worship at the shrine of the Spanish patron saint, St. James. The next morning Philip sent a party of his highest nobles to bring Bedford and Fitzwalter to him, and "being advised of their coming, his Highness came out of his chamber into a great hall, strangely hung with rich tapestries, and on the lords half-kneeling and doffing their bonnets the Prince received them graciously, with his hat in his hand. The principal ambassador (*i.e.*, Bedford), a grandee and a good Christian, produced the marriage contract, the conditions of which his Highness accepted before all present. As the contents were only known to the Prince and his Council, we were unable to learn them. The English nobles then kissed hands in turn, and as they went out one said to the other in his own tongue, 'Oh! God be praised for sending us so good a king as this.' The remark was made so quietly that it would not have been noticed, only that a Spanish gentleman who understood their language stood close to them and happened to hear it."

The envoys had some reason to be pleased with their Queen's future consort, for after accompanying him to the cathedral the next day Bedford received as a gift what is described as being one of the finest pieces of gold ever seen, of exquisite and elaborate workmanship, chased with grotesque figures, and standing a yard and a half high, of solid gold. The narrator (No. 2) says that 6,000 ducats' worth of gold was employed in the making of it, and the handiwork cost more than 1,000. The twenty

English gentlemen who accompanied the envoys all received splendid gifts, although their appearance was already sufficiently rich with their "thick gold chains and great copiousness of buttons," which last characteristic of English fashion at the time seems to have attracted most of the Spanish observers. Four days were spent in rest and rejoicing at Santiago, and then a three days' ride brought them to Corunna, where there were more rejoicings. Kneeling aldermen at the gate presented golden keys as usual; a marvellous canopy was held over the Prince's head; triumphal arches spanned the way; and the local poet had contrived to evolve the following couplet, which was held aloft by five nymphs—

"No basta fuerza ni maña
Contra el principe de España,

which may be rendered—

"Force and cunning both in vain
Strive against the Prince of Spain."

The narrator (No. 2) airs his historical knowledge in describing an allegorical group containing a figure of Hercules, whom he speaks of as having been "a King of Spain before Christ, and having built many great edifices in the country, such as the Pillars of Hercules at Cadiz and the tower at the entrance to the port of Corunna, where there is a marvellous mirror showing ships that are far off at sea."

With all pomp, and with a naked sword of justice borne before him by his master of the horse, the Prince was conducted to the shore to see the gallant fleet riding at anchor awaiting him. Drawn up on the beach were 600 Guipuzcoan sea warriors armed with lances, and as the fleet and castle thundered out their salutations the townsfolk, we are told, feared their dwellings would all be shaken down, and "for an hour and a half neither heaven nor earth was visible." Thence the Prince went round by the castle to the little dock, where forty Biscay fisher boats were ready with their glistening cargoes of fine fish to cast at the feet of their beloved Philip. The English ambassadors begged as a favour that the new consort would make the voyage in one of the British ships that had brought them over, but this was not considered prudent by Philip's cautious councillors, and as a compromise the English envoys were allowed to choose from amongst all the Spanish ships the one that was to convey the Prince. Their choice fell upon a fine merchant vessel commanded by the bravest and best of those bold Biscay mariners who are the pride of Spain, Martin de Bertondona, and the next morning Philip and his Court went to inspect it. A splendid sight it must have been with its towering carved and gilded poop and forecastle. It was hung, we are told, from stem to stern with fine scarlet cloth, and aloft on every available spot were coloured silk pennons. The forecastle was hung with crimson brocade painted with golden flames. A royal standard, thirty yards long, of crimson damask, with the Prince's arms painted on it, hung from the mainmast, and a similar flag from the mizzenmast. The foremast had ten pointed silk flags painted with the royal arms, and there were thirty other similar flags on the stays and shrouds. Three hundred sailors in red uniforms formed the crew, and we are assured that the effect of the ship was that of a lovely flower-garden, as well it might be, and the cost of the decorations was 10,000 ducats. The English ships were then inspected and admired, and the ship that had carried the Marquis de las Navas over to England with the jewels was visited, and its captain related how the good Queen was anxious for her consort's arrival, and how she had ordered 1,000 gentlemen to await him with as many horses, as she thought no horses would be brought from Spain. All next day is spent in hunting, and the favourite, Ruy Gomez, preceding his master on his return into the town, is saluted by the fleet instead of the Prince by mistake, much to the latter's amusement. The next day heralds announced that every one was to be examined by the Prince's alcalde before embarking, and that no woman was to go without her husband. Muñoz says that 12,000 soldiers were shipped in the hundred ships (some of which carried 300 bronze pieces) and thirty sloops that formed the fleet, but this seems to be an exaggeration, as narrative No. 6 gives 6,000 soldiers and as many sailors as going in the main squadron that conveyed Philip (consisting of about 100 sail); and Noailles, who would minimise it as much as possible, says 4,000. Don Luis de Carvajal remained behind with about thirty sail to take the troops that had not arrived (Noailles says 2,000) and bring up the rear.

On the 12th of July Philip and his Court embarked in a sumptuous galley of twenty-four oars, manned by sailors in scarlet and gold, with plumed hats of scarlet silk, and, amidst music, singing, and daring gymnastic feats of the mariners, went on board Martin de Bertondona's ship the *Espiritu Santo*. The next day, Friday, at three in the afternoon they set sail, the dense crowd on shore crying to God to send the travellers a safe voyage, and in the same breath hurling defiance to the French. There was a slight swell and wind until next day at dinner, when the weather fell dead calm, "which looked as if it might last a month, but raised the spirits of those who were depressed by "marine vomitings." The next day a delightful fair breeze sprang up, and on a smooth sea the splendid fleet ran across the bay, sighting Ushant on Sunday. On Wednesday a Flemish fleet of eighteen galleons, which was cruising in the Channel, hove in sight, and convoyed them past the Needles with some ships of the English navy, and into Southampton Water, where on Thursday, the 19th of July, at four o'clock, the combined fleet anchored amid the royal salute from the English and Flemish fleets of thirty sail that were assembled to receive them. The English and Flemish sailors had not got on particularly well together during the time the two fleets had awaited the arrival of Philip. Renard had complained to the Emperor that the Flemish sailors were hustled and insulted whenever they set foot on shore, and Howard, the lord admiral, had mocked at their ships and called them cockle shells;[1] but I can find no contemporary authority for the extremely unlikely story of the English admiral having thrown a shot across the bows of the Prince's fleet to compel it to salute the English flag.

[1] Renard to the Emperor, quoted in Tytler, "Edward VI. and Mary."

Philip, however, was determined to gain over the jealous hearts of his new subjects by his courtesy and graciousness. Renard's recommendations and the Emperor's instructions had been very definite on the point, and every account, Spanish, English, and Italian, with the sole exception of Baoardo's, quoted by Froude, agrees that the Prince's demeanour was kindly, courteous, and frank. Damula, the Venetian ambassador to the Emperor, writes to the Doge,[1] saying that on disembarking the Prince treated everybody with great graciousness and affability, without any pomp or royal ceremony, mixing with people as a comrade; and Cabrera, speaking of his arrival, says: "Some of the English were inclined to be sulky, but the King won them over with his prudence and affability, and with gifts and favours, together with his family courtesy." (Our narrative No. 6 specially mentions the Prince's *cortesia e gentilezza di parlare*.[2])

As soon as the anchors were down the English and Flemish admirals went on board the *Espiritu Santo* to salute the Prince, and the Marquis de las Navas put off from Southampton with the six young

[1] July, Calendar of State Papers, Venetian.
[2] Soriano, the Venetian ambassador in Madrid, says that the gentle courtesy he adopted in England was continued after his return to Spain, and that, whilst maintaining his natural gravity and dignity, his kindness and graciousness were remarkable to all persons. Michaeli, the Venetian ambassador in London, who had sided with Noailles in his opposition to the match, is emphatic in his testimony of Philip's affability whilst in England, and says that his conduct towards his wife was enough to make any woman love him, "for in truth no one else in the world could have been a better or more loving husband." These and many other similar contemporary assurances prove that Philip acted all through the business like an honest, high-minded gentleman.

## THE COMING OF PHILIP THE PRUDENT.

noblemen who were to be the new King's lords-in-waiting. The Prince dined and slept on board, and the next day there came off to him the Emperor's ambassador, the Marquis de las Navas, Figueroa ("the ancient ambassador with the long white beard"), Pescara, and the Earls of Arundel, Derby, Shrewsbury, and Pembroke (?). Noailles was probably wrong as regards the last-named nobleman, as the Spanish narratives agree that he arrived at Southampton from the Queen next day, with a splendid escort for the new sovereign. He was also wrong in asserting that the King was invested with the Garter on board his vessel, for it appears to have been given to him in the barge before he stepped on shore by Arundel, probably assisted by Sir John Williams—Lord Williams of Thame [1]—to whom one of our narratives says the Prince gave the wand of chamberlain, whilst the other narratives say the office was conferred on "the man who brought him the Garter." The future consort received these high personages on board the *Espiritu Santo* cap in hand, and after presenting them to his principal courtiers went on board the splendid barge awaiting him, accompanied by the English nobles and by Alba, Feria, Ruy Gomez and four chamberlains, Olivares, Pedro de Cordoba, Gutierre Lopez de Padilla, Diego de Acevedo, Egmont, Horn, and Bergues. No sign was made to the rest of the fleet, and the mass of courtiers only obtained leave to land after the royal party had approached the shore. No soldier or man-at-arms, however, was

---

[1] He died in 1559, and a magnificent alabaster monument, with the recumbent figures of himself and his wife, exists in fine preservation in the chancel of Thame church, of which he was a liberal benefactor.

to land, on pain of death, for not only had Philip learnt from Renard the agony of distrust of the Spanish arms felt by the English people, but he had received news of his father's reverse in the Netherlands and urgent orders to send him all the troops and money he had or could obtain. The Spanish fleet were not even allowed to enter the port of Southampton, but after some delay, and great discontent of the Spaniards at what they considered such churlish treatment, were sent to Portsmouth to revictual for their voyage to Flanders.

After the presentation of the chain and badge of the Garter Philip stepped on English soil, and the first to greet him was Sir Anthony Browne, who announced in a Latin speech that the Queen had chosen him for her consort's master of the horse, by whom her Majesty had sent him the beautiful white charger housed in crimson velvet and gold that was champing the bit hard by. The Prince thanked his new grand equerry, but said he would walk to the house prepared for him; but Browne and the lords of the household told him this was unusual, and the former "took him up in his arms and put him on the saddle," and then kissing the stirrups walked bare-headed by the side of his master. All the English and Spanish courtiers preceded them, and amidst apparent rejoicing they slowly passed through the curious crowd to the Church of the Holy Rood. The Prince must have looked an impressive figure with his dapper, erect bearing, his yellow beard and close-cropped yellow head, dressed as he was in black velvet and silver, his massive gold chains and priceless gems glittering in his velvet bonnet and at his neck and wrists.

Browne was no unworthy pendant to his prince. He was dressed in a suit of black velvet entirely covered with gold embroidery and a surcoat of the same with long hanging sleeves.[1] When the Prince had returned thanks for his safe voyage he was conducted to the lodgings prepared for him, which we are told were beautifully adorned, particularly two rooms, a bedroom and presence chamber hung with gold-worked damask with the name of King Henry on it; but none of our narrators say anything about Baoardo's story of the dismay caused by the words *Fidei defensor* on the hangings. All the English archers and the guard and porters about the Prince wore the flaming colours of Aragon, and the Spanish attendants and courtiers looked on with jealous rage at the attendance on him of English servants. The dinner and supper were private, but the meals were ostentatious, ceremonious, and too abundant for the Spanish taste. On Saturday, the next day, the same programme was gone through: to Mass in the same order as before, the Spanish courtiers being obliged to leave before the service was over, in order to banish the idea that they were in official attendance on the Prince, who came out surrounded by Englishmen only. It rained so hard that his Highness, who had no hat or cape, had to borrow them of an Englishman near him, although the church was just opposite his lodging.

Southampton is described in glowing terms. It is said to be a beautiful port with 300 houses, which were filled to their utmost capacity by the courtiers

[1] Probably the dress in which he is represented in the magnificent painting of him belonging to the Marquis of Exeter at Burghley (No. 236, Tudor Exhibition).

and the 400 Spanish servants who landed the day after the Prince. The Queen at Winchester had learnt post-haste of the landing of her future husband, and an active interchange of messengers were soon scouring backwards and forwards through the pitiless rain of the next three days. Early on Saturday morning the Earl of Pembroke arrived from the Queen with an escort for the Prince of 200 gentlemen dressed in black velvet with gold chains and medals, and 300 others in scarlet cloth with velvet facings, all splendidly mounted. Then Egmont posts off to kiss the Queen's hand, and meets Gardiner coming to Philip with a costly diamond ring from her Majesty. The next day twelve beautiful hackneys come from the bride to her affianced husband, and after that the well-beloved Ruy Gomez is dispatched with a ring to thank her, and this interchange of courtesy and compliment is thus kept up until all things are arranged for the journey to Winchester.

Before Philip left Southampton, however, better news came from Flanders. The French had not followed up their victory at Marienberg, and the Imperialists could breathe again. The 600 jennets that came from Spain were therefore disembarked and remained in England, as well as Philip's own horses, "which," says Pedro Enriquez (No. 3), "the master of the horse took to his own stable; not a bad beginning to try and keep them altogether in the long run." On Sunday, the day before he left Southampton, Philip dined in public for the only time there. He was served with great ceremony by the English, but Alba, although he took no wand of office in his hand, insisted on handing his master the napkin, and the Spanish courtiers looked

# THE COMING OF PHILIP THE PRUDENT. 153

on with ill-disguised contempt at what they considered the clumsy service of their successors. The courtier who wrote narrative No. 3 bursts out at this point with his complaint: "My lady Doña Maria de Mendoza was quite right when she said we should be no more good. We are all quite vagabonds now and of no use to any one. We had far better go and serve the Emperor in the war. They make us pay twenty times the value of everything we buy."

The next morning in the pouring rain the royal cavalcade set out for Winchester, 3,000 strong. The nobles and gentry had been flocking in for days with their retainers in new liveries; Pembroke's escort, with 200 halberdiers of the guard and as many light-horse archers, dressed much as are the beefeaters of to-day, guarded the Prince's person, the Spanish guard, to their chagrin, being still on board the ships. On the road 600 more gentlemen, dressed in black velvet with gold chains, met his Highness, and when nearing Winchester six of the Queen's pages, beautifully dressed in crimson brocade with gold sashes, with as many superb steeds, were encountered, who told his Highness the Queen had sent the horses to him as a present. But not a word anywhere of Baoardo's sensational story, embellished by Froude, of the breathless messenger from the Queen, the terror-stricken Prince, and the gloomy resolve to consummate his sacrifice even if he got wet in doing it.

Philip was surrounded by the English nobles Winchester, Arundel, Derby, Worcester, Bedford, Rutland, Pembroke, Surrey, Clinton, Cobham, Willoughby, Darcy, Maltravers, Talbot, Strange, Fitzwalter, and North, and by about fifteen Spanish grandees, whose names will have less interest for English readers. He was dressed, when he started, in a black velvet surcoat adorned with diamonds, leather boots, and trunks and doublet of white satin embroidered with gold; but this delicate finery had to be covered by a red felt cloak to protect it from the rain. Notwithstanding this it was too wet for him to enter Winchester without a change, so he stayed at a "hospital that had been a monastery one mile from the city,' and there donned a black velvet surcoat covered with gold bugles and a suit of white velvet trimmed in the same way, and thus he entered, passing the usual red-clothed kneeling aldermen with gold keys on cushions, and then to the grand cathedral, which impressed the Spaniards with wonder, and above all to find that " Mass was as solemnly sung there as at Toledo.'

A little crowd of mitred bishops stood at the great west door, crosses raised and censers swinging, and in solemn procession to the high altar, under a velvet canopy, they led the man whom they looked upon as God's chosen instrument to permanently restore their faith in England. Then, after admiring the cathedral, Philip and his Court went to the dean's house, which had been prepared for his reception, in order to allay the maiden scruples of the Queen with regard to his sleeping under the same roof with her at the bishop's palace before the solemnisation of the marriage. After Philip had supped, and presumably was thinking more of going to bed than anything else, the Lord Chamberlain [1] and the Lord Steward [2] came to him, it being ten o'clock at night,

[1] Sir John Gage.
[2] The Earl of Arundel.

and said the Queen was waiting for him in her closet, and wished him to visit her secretly with very few followers. He at once put on another gorgeous suit, consisting of a French surcoat embroidered in silver and gold, and a doublet and trunks of white kid embroidered in gold, "and very gallant he looked," says Muñoz's informant (No. 2). The party traversed a narrow lane between the two gardens, and on reaching a door in the wall the Lord Steward told the Prince he could take with him such courtiers as he chose. Philip did not seem disposed to run any risks, and construed the invitation in a liberal spirit, taking into the garden Alba, Medina-Celi, Pescara, Feria, Aguilar, Chinchon, Horn, Egmont, Lopez-Acevedo, Mendoza, Carillo, and others. They found themselves in a beautiful garden with rippling fountains and arbours, which reminded them, they say, of the books of chivalry. Indeed, nothing is more curious than the grave seriousness with which all the Spanish narrators refer to England as the land of Amadis and of Arthur and his knights, and their attempts to identify localities and characteristics of England with the descriptions they have read of the land of romance, which they firmly believe to be England and not Brittany.

The Prince and his party entered by a little back door, and ascended a narrow, winding staircase to the Queen's closet. She was in a "long narrow room or corridor where they divert themselves," surrounded by four or five aged nobles and as many old ladies, the Bishop of Winchester being also with her, and the whole party, we are told, was marvellously richly dressed, the Queen herself wearing a black velvet gown cut high in the English style without any trimming, a petticoat of frosted silver, a wimple of black velvet trimmed with gold, and a girdle and collar of wonderful gems. She was walking up and down when the Prince entered, and as soon as she saw him went quickly towards him and kissed her hand before taking his. In return he kissed her on the mouth "in the English fashion," and she led him by the hand to a chair placed by the side of her own under a canopy. The Queen spoke in French and her future husband in Spanish, and they thus made themselves well understood. Whilst they were in animated converse the Lord Admiral (Lord William Howard), "who is a great talker and very jocose," risked some rather highly flavoured jokes, which the free manners of the time apparently permitted. The two lovers sat under their brocade canopy chatting for a long time; but this probably seemed somewhat slow to the bridegroom, who, after asking the Queen to give her hand for all his Spaniards to kiss, as they loved her well, begged to be allowed to see her ladies, who were in another room. The Queen went with him, and as the ladies approached two by two he kissed them all "in his way" with his plumed cap in his hand, "so as not to break the custom of the country, which is a very good one." Whether the Queen thought it good on this occasion is not clear; but when her lover wanted to leave directly the extensive osculation was over she would not let him go, but carried him off for another long talk with her. "No wonder," says the narrator (No. 2), "she is so glad to get him and to see what a gallant swain he is." When he had to leave her she playfully taught him to say "Good-night," and he made this the excuse for going to the ladies again to say it to them; but when he reached them he had forgotten the outlandish words, and had to come back to the Queen to ask her, "whereat she was much pleased," but probably less so when he found it necessary to go back once more to the ladies to salute them with "God ni hit," Car, the Marquis of Pescara's servant (narrator No. 6), in describing this interview says that the Queen's governess told the Prince she thanked God for letting her live to see the day, but asked his pardon for not having reared a more beautiful bride for him. According to one of the Italian variants of the same narrative the Queen is still less complimentary to herself, and in reply to Philip's thanks to her after the marriage says it is she who is grateful to him for taking an old and ugly wife [1] (*brutta e vecchia*). The courtier's narrative (No. 4) speaks of the Queen in somewhat less unfavourable terms and says: "Although she is not at all handsome, being of short stature and rather thin than fat, she has a very clear red and white complexion. She has no eyebrows, is a perfect saint, but dresses very badly."

This narrator is very critical about the ladies' dresses and is quite shocked at some of the English fashions. He says:—

"They wear farthingales of coloured cloth without silk; the gowns they wear over them are of

---

[1] In the narrative signed by Car (British Museum) the Queen is described in this interview as "chatting gaily, and although she is a little elderly she displays the grace befitting a queen."

damask, satin, or velvet of various colours, but very badly made. Some of them have velvet shoes slashed like men's, and some wear leather. Their stockings are black, and they show their legs even up to the knees, at least when they are travelling, as their skirts are so short. They really look quite indelicate when they are seated or riding. They are not at all handsome, nor do they dance gracefully, as all their dancing only consists of ambling and trotting. Not a single Spanish gentleman is in love with any of them [1] . . . and they are not women for whom the Spaniards need put themselves out of the way in entertaining or spending money on them, which is a good thing for the Spaniards."

When the same narrator reaches London he speaks with somewhat more experience, but his opinion is not much modified. He says, when speaking of the vast numbers of ladies that served the Queen :—

"Those I have seen in the palace have not struck me as being handsome; indeed, they are downright ugly. I do not know how this is, because outside I have seen some very beautiful and attractive women. In this country women do not often wear clogs and wraps, as they do in Spain, but go about the city and even travel in their bodices. Some of them walk in London with veils and masks before their faces, which makes them look like nuns, who do not wish to be known. Women here wear their skirts

---

[1] Don Pedro Enriquez was wrong here. One of the greatest of the Spanish nobles, Count de Feria, had fallen madly in love with Jane Dormer, one of the Queen's maids of honour, and soon afterwards privately married her.

very short, and their black stockings are trim and tightly gartered; the shoes are neat, but are slashed like men's, which does not look well to Spanish eyes."

Philip, we are told, slept late next morning, and as soon as he was up the Queen's tailor brought him two superb dresses, one made of very rich brocade profusely embroidered with gold bugles and pearls, with splendid diamonds for buttons, and the other of crimson brocade. His Highness went to Mass in a purple velvet surcoat with silver fringe and white satin doublet, and then after his private dinner went in great state to see the Queen. She received him in the great hall of the palace, with the courtiers ranged on a raised platform on each side. The great officers of state preceded her, and she was followed by fifty ladies splendidly dressed in purple velvet, " but none of them pretty," and having met her consort in the middle of the hall she led him to the daïs, where he stood in sweet converse with her for some time. But fickle Philip " went, as usual, to talk to the ladies, and we, about twelve of us, kissed the Queen's hand." " We " also seem to have been talking to the ladies before that, but do not appear to have got on very well, as " we could hardly understand each other." Then Philip went to Vespers and the Queen to her chapel, and after supper they met again, and Figueroa privately read the Emperor's abdication, which made Philip king of Naples, and all the ambassadors, except Noailles, paid homage to the new sovereign, who received them bareheaded.[1]

[1] Baoardo, quoted by Mr. Froude, says " he raised his hat to nobody," but these narratives often mention his being uncovered.

The wedding ceremony next day is fully described by the English authorities already mentioned, and the narratives before us, although extremely minute in detail, do not vary much from the accepted accounts. The ancient cathedral was all aflame with splendid colour, and the world has rarely seen so gorgeous and so rich a company as was there assembled. All the pomp that regal expenditure could buy in an age of ostentation was there. All the impressive solemnity that the Roman Church could give to its ceremonies was lavished upon this. The Queen, we are told, blazed with jewels to such an extent that the eye was blinded as it looked upon her; her dress was of black velvet flashing with gems, and a splendid mantle of cloth of gold fell from her shoulders; but through the Mass that followed the marriage service she never took her eyes off the crucifix upon which they were devoutly fixed. Her fifty ladies were dressed in cloth of gold and silver, and "looked more like celestial angels than mortal creatures." Philip matched his bride in splendour. He too wore a mantle of cloth of gold embroidered with precious stones, and the rest of his dress was the white satin suit the Queen had sent him the day before, and he too was a blaze of jewels. The Earl of Derby, who preceded the Queen with a sword of state, appears to have greatly impressed the imaginations of the Spaniards, as several references are made to his power and splendour. He is spoken of as the "king of Mongara (Man), who wears a leaden crown," and it is easy to see that much of the interest in him is caused by the supposed identification of his kingdom with scenes of the romances of chivalry.

After the ceremony the King and the Queen walked through an immense crowd to the palace side by side, and entered the great hall,[1] which the narrator (No. 2) calls the "hall of Poncia," for the wedding banquet. A high table, eight yards long, was placed on a daïs, and at it sat the King and Queen, the latter being on the right and in a finer chair than her husband. Gardiner sat at the end of the high table, and on the floor were four other tables, where the nobles, to the number of 158, partook of the feast. Before the King and Queen stood Lords Pembroke and Strange with the sword and staff of state, and all the courtly ceremony of saluting the dishes as they are brought in, and doffing bonnets to the throne, even in the absence of the Queen, is set forth with admiring iteration by the form-loving Spaniards. Their jealous eyes, too, do not fail to notice that the Queen takes precedence in everything. Not only has she the best chair, but she eats from gold plate, whilst her consort eats from silver. This, they say, is no doubt because he is not yet a crowned king, and it will be altered later. All the tables are served with silver, except some large dishes; and great sideboards of plate stand at each end of the hall. The buffet behind the high table had over a hundred great pieces of gold and silver plate, with a "great gilt clock half as high as a man," and a fountain of precious marble with a gold rim. There were four services of meat and fish, each service consisting of thirty dishes,[2]

[1] Narrator No. 6 says, "The hall, which is beautifully hung with cloth of gold and silk, measures forty of my paces long and twenty wide."
[2] Underhyll (Harleian Manuscript, 425, f. 97) gives a very quaint account of his share in this banquet. "On the

and minstrels played during the feast, whilst the solid splendour and pompous ceremony appear to have impressed all the Spaniards with wonder not unmixed with envy. It is, indeed, here that the jealousy of the courtier narrator (Nos. 3, 4, and 5) first bursts out. The only Spaniard who was allowed to serve the King was Don Inigo de Mendoza, son of the Duke of Infantado, who was cupbearer, and four yeomen of the mouth, who helped; but "as for any of the Prince's own stewards doing anything, such a thing was never thought of, and not one of us took a wand in our hands, nor does it seem likely we ever shall, neither the controller nor any one else, and they had better turn us all out as vagabonds." The Earl of Arundel presented the ewer with water for the King's hands, and the Marquis of Winchester the napkin. The ewer, we are

maryage daye the kynge and quene dyned in the halle in the bushop's palice sittynge under the cloth of estate and none eles att that table. The nobillitie satte att the syde tables. Wee (*i.e.*, the gentlemen pensioners) weare the cheffe sarueters to cary the meate and the yearle of Sussex ower captayne was the shewer. The seconde course att the maryage off a kynge is gevyne unto the bearers; I meane the meate butt nott the dishes for they were off golde. It was my chaunce to carye a greate pastie of a redde dere in a great charger uery delicately baked; which for the weyght thereoff dyuers refused; the wyche pastie I sentt unto London to my wyffe and her brother who cherede therewith many off ther frends. I wyll not take uppon me to wryte the maner of the maryage, off the feaste nor of the daunssyngs of the Spanyards thatt day who weare greatly owte off countenaunce specyally King Phelip dauncynge when they dide see me lorde Braye, Mr. Carowe and others so farre excede them; but wyll leve it unto the learned as it behovithe hym to be thatt shall wryte a story off so greate a tryoumffe." The Louvian Chronicle (Tytler) says :—" The dinner lasted till six in the evening, after which there was store of music, and before nine all had retired."

## THE COMING OF PHILIP THE PRUDENT. 163

told (narrative No. 6), contained "not water, but white wine, as is the custom here."

Then, after the Queen had pledged all her guests in a cup of wine, and a herald had proclaimed the titles of Philip as King of England, France, Naples, and Jerusalem, Prince of Spain, and Count of Flanders, the royal party retired to another chamber, with the English and Spanish nobles, where the time passed in pleasant converse, the Spaniards talking with the English ladies, "although we had great trouble to make out their meaning, except of those who spoke Latin, so we have all resolved not to give them any presents of gloves until we can understand them. The gentlemen who speak the language are mostly very glad to find that the Spaniards cannot do so."

When all was ready the ball began, but as the English ladies only danced in their own fashion and the Spanish courtiers in theirs, the latter were rather left out in the cold, until the King and Queen danced a measure together in the German style, which was known to both. After dancing until nightfall, supper was served with the same ceremony as dinner, and then more talk and gallant compliment, and so to bed.

The next day the King only was visible, and dined alone in public, and on the succeeding day the same; but on the third day (Saturday) the Queen heard Mass in her private pew and received the Duchess of Alba, who had arrived from Southampton after the marriage. The reception of this proud dame was ceremonious enough for anything; but from the bitter complaints of her kinsman, who probably wrote three of the letters before us, it is clear that she, in common with the rest of the Spanish nobles, was deeply dissatisfied with her position in this country, so different from what they expected. The Duchess was conducted to the palace by the Earls of Kildare and Pembroke and all the Court, and when she entered the presence the Queen came almost to the door to meet her. The Duchess knelt, and the Queen, failing to raise her, courtesied almost as low and kissed her on the mouth, "which she usually does only to certain ladies of her own family." She led the Duchess to the daïs and seated herself on the floor, inviting her guest to do likewise, but the latter begged her Majesty to sit on the chair before she (the Duchess) would sit on the floor. The Queen refused to do so, and sent for two stools, upon one of which she sat, whereupon the Duchess, instead of accepting the other, sat beside it on the floor. The Queen then left her stool and took her place on the floor also, and finally, after much friendly wrangling, both ladies settled on their respective stools side by side. The Queen understood Spanish, but spoke in French, and the Marquis de las Navas interpreted to the Duchess, who only understood Spanish. When the Earl of Derby was presented to the Duchess, he greatly shocked her by offering to kiss her on the mouth, according to the universal English fashion, and she drew back to avoid the salute, but not quite in time, although she assured the Spaniards that the earl had only managed to kiss her cheek.

But the chagrin of the proud, dissatisfied Spaniards was growing deeper as they saw their hopes of domination in England disappear. The men-at-arms and bodyguard, cooped up in their ships at Portsmouth and Southampton, forbidden to land under pain of death, were becoming restive; the courtiers and their followers, scoffed at and insulted in the streets, and waylaid and robbed if they ventured into the country, were forced to put up with everything silently, by order of the King; but they could relieve their minds by writing to their friends in Spain an account of their sorrows. Writing from Winchester, narrator No. 2 says:—

"After all this weary voyage, these people wish to subject us to a certain extent to their laws, because it is a new thing for them to have Spaniards in their country, and they want to feel safe. The Spaniards here are not comfortable, nor are they so well off as in Castile. Some even say they would rather be in the worst stubble-field in the kingdom of Toledo than in the groves of Amadis."

The courtier who wrote No. 3 is even more emphatic. He says:—

"Great rogues infest the roads and have robbed some of our people, amongst others the chamberlain of Don Juan de Pacheco, from whom they took 400 crowns and all his plate and jewelry. Not a trace has been found of them, nor of the four or five boxes missing from the King's lodgings, although the Council is sending out on all sides. The friars have had to be lodged in the college for safety and bitterly repent having come."

But dissatisfied as the Spaniards were, there was still sufficient novelty in their surroundings during their stay at Winchester in the last days of July to keep them amused. The wonderful round table of King Arthur in the castle, where the twelve peers are still enchanted, and their names written round in the places where they sat, claims the wondering attention of the visitors. The curious beer made with barley and a herb, instead of wheat, as in Flanders, is discussed; and the strange habit the ladies, and even some gentlemen, have of putting sugar in their wine, and the never-ending dancing going on amongst the ladies of the palace excite remark. On the last day of July most of the English lords and squires had gone home for the present; the Spaniards were distributed about Winchester and Southampton; the admiral of Spain was under orders to take a part of the fleet back again; and the bulk of the Spanish troops were only awaiting a fair wind to take them to Flanders, and the King and Queen, with a small suite, set out for Basing, the Lord Treasurer's[1] house, fifteen miles off. Most of the accounts before us end at this point but the two interesting letters to which I have given the numbers 4 and 5, written respectively from Richmond and London, show clearly the gradual exacerbation of the dislike between the Spanish and English as time went on, in spite of the diplomatic attempts to connect Philip's name at every opportunity with acts of clemency and moderation.

On the 19th of August, which is the date of the letter from Richmond, the royal honeymoon seems yet not entirely to have waned:—

"Their Majesties are the happiest couple in the world, and are more in love with each other than I can say here. He never leaves her, and on the

[1] This was the Marquis of Winchester, not, as Señor Gayangos supposes, Sir Edward Peckham, who was Treasurer of the Mint.

THE COMING OF PHILIP THE PRUDENT. 167

road is always by her side, lifting her into the saddle and helping her to dismount. He dines with her publicly sometimes, and they go to Mass together on feast days."

This letter from Richmond gives the following curious account of the lavish scale on which the royal establishment was maintained :—

"All the rejoicings here consist only of eating and drinking, as they understand nothing else. The Queen spends 300,000 ducats (a year?) in food, and all the thirteen councillors and the Court favourites live in the palace, besides the lord steward, the lord chamberlain, the chancellor, and our people, with their servants. The ladies also have private rooms in the palace, with all their servants, and the Queen's guard of 200 men are also lodged there. Each of the lords has a separate cook in the Queen's kitchens, and as there are eighteen different kitchens such is the hurly burly that they are a perfect hell. Although the palaces are so large that the smallest of the four we have seen is infinitely larger, and certainly better, than the Alcazar of Madrid, they are still hardly large enough to hold the people who live in them. The ordinary (daily?) consumption of the palace is 100 sheep (which are very large and fat), twelve large oxen, eighteen calves, besides game, poultry, venison, wild boar, and a great number of rabbits. Of beer there is no end, and they drink as much as would fill the river at Valladolid."

The writer is very indignant at the scant courtesy paid to his great kinsfolk the Albas, and at the fact that they have had to put up with lodgings that are considered below their dignity even in the villages.

"It is not enough," he says, "to deprive them of their office, but they must needs give them bad quarters as well. . . . These English are the most ungrateful people in the world, and hate the Spaniards worse than the devil, as they readily show, for they rob us in the town itself, and not a soul dares to venture two miles on the road without being robbed. There is no justice for us. We are ordered by the King to avoid dispute and put up with everything whilst we are here, enduring all their attacks in silence. They therefore despise us and treat us badly. We have complained to Bibriesca and the ambassador, but they say it is for his Majesty's sake that we must bear everything patiently."

It was no wonder that under such circumstances these proud hidalgos begged to be allowed to join the Emperor in Flanders for the war. Medina-Celi was the first to revolt at his treatment, and no sooner had he obtained leave to go than eighty other gentlemen followed him with their suites, and so by the middle of August the only Spanish nobles in attendance on Philip were Alba, Feria, Olivares, Pedro de Cordoba, Diego de Cordoba, and three gentlemen, amongst whom was Pedro Enriquez, the supposed author of the letters. The insults upon the Spaniards personally were bad enough; but what was more galling even was the disappointment they felt at the political effect of the match. Instead of a submissive people, ready to bow the neck at once to the new king and his followers, they found a country where even the native sovereign's power was strictly circumscribed, and where the foreigner's only hope of domination was by force of arms; and this they saw in the present case was impossible. Enriquez, if he be the author, says: "The marriage will indeed have been a failure if the Queen have no children. They told us in Castile that if his Highness became king of England we should be masters of France; but quite the contrary has turned out to be the fact, for the French are stronger than ever and are doing as they like in Flanders. . . . Kings here have as little power as if they were vassals, and the people who really govern are the councillors; they are not only lords of the land, but lords of the kings as well. They are all peers, some of them raised up by the Church revenues they have taken and others by their patrimonial estates, and they are feared much more than the sovereign. They publicly say they will not let the King go until they and the Queen think fit, as this country is quite big enough for any one king."

Great preparations were made for the entrance of the Queen and her consort into London. The signs of vengeance had been cleared away, and the city was as bright and gay as paint and gilding could make it. The "galluses," from which dangled the fifty dead bodies of the London trainbandsmen who had deserted to Wyatt at Rochester Bridge, were cleared away from the doors of the houses in which their families lived, and the grinning skulls of the higher offenders were taken from the gates and from London Bridge; but London, for all its seeming welcome and for all its real loyalty to the Queen herself, was more deeply resentful of the Spanish intrusion than any city in the realm, and the few Spaniards who still remained with Philip repaid with interest the detestation of the Londoners towards them. "We enter London (narrative No. 4) on Saturday next, but, considering their treatment of the Spaniards already there, we ought to stay away. Not only will they give them no lodgings,[1] but they affront them on every opportunity, as if they were barbarians, maltreating them and robbing them in the taverns to their hearts' content. The friars brought by his Majesty had better not have come, for these English are so godless and treat them so vilely that they dare not appear in the streets."

Only a few days before this letter was written from Richmond (August 19th) two Spanish noblemen of the highest rank, Don Pedro and Don Antonio de Cordoba, ventured to walk in the streets of London in their habits as knights of Santiago, with the great crimson cross embroidered on their breasts, as they are worn in Spain to this day, and this attracting the derisive attention of the irrepressible London street boy of the period, the two gentlemen were soon surrounded by a hooting crowd, who wanted to know what they meant by wearing so outlandish an ornament, and tried to strip the offending coats from their backs. The affair nearly ended in bloodshed, and the Spaniards had to fly for their lives. The very few Spanish ladies who came with Philip were as resentful as their spouses, and we are told that "Donna Hieronima de Navarra and Donna Francisca de Cordoba have decided not to wait upon the Queen, as there is no one to speak to them at Court, these English ladies being so badly behaved; and the Duchess of Alba will not go to Court again, as she had been so discourteously treated."

[1] The Spaniards had to be quartered in the halls of the City guilds.

With all this grumbling, however, the country itself extorted the admiration of the visitors; the books of chivalry, we are told, have only stated half the truth. The palaces, rich and splendid with the unhallowed spoils of the monasteries; the flowery vales, gushing fountains, enchanted woods, and lovely houses far exceed even the descriptions in Amadis; but there are "few Orianas and many Mavilias amongst the ladies," and the romancers have said nothing about the strange, uncouth beings who inhabit the enchanting land. "Who ever saw elsewhere a woman on horseback alone, and even riding their steeds well, and as much at home on their backs as if they were experienced horsemen?" And after confessing the beauty of the country itself, the narrator concludes that the disadvantages of it outweigh the advantages, and wishes to God that he had never seen the place or the sea that led to it. And things got worse as time went on. The Londoners themselves were in an exaggerated panic, that explains their hard treatment of their guests. The author of the "Chronicle of Queen Mary," who lived in the Tower of London, and faithfully set down from day to day the news he heard, reflects the terror inspired by the presence of Philip's suite in the capital. We have seen that at the utmost the number of Spaniards of all ranks who landed from the fleet did not exceed 500, of whom four-fifths had left for Flanders and Spain before the King entered London, and yet the diarist, writing about this time, says, "At this tyme ther was so many Spanyerdes in London that a man shoulde haue mett in the stretes for one Inglisheman above iiij Spanyerdes to the great discomfort of the

Inglishe nation. . . . The halles taken up for Spanyerdes.' And, again, as showing how complete was the panic, fomented, no doubt, by Noailles and the Protestants, there is an entry in the "Chronicle of Queen Mary" of September 8th, as follows: "A talke of XII. thowsand Spanyerdes coming more into this realm, they said the fetch the crowne." It is not surprising, with such a feeling as this current in the city, that the courtier's next letter, written from London on October 2nd, should be more despondent than ever. They were all ill and home-sick; some had almost died, and the country did not agree with them.

"God save us and give us health, and bring us safely home again. The country is a good one, but the people are surely the worst in the world. I verily believe if it were not for the constant prayers and processions for us in Spain we should all have been murdered long ago. There are slashings and quarrels every day between Englishmen and Spaniards, and only just now there was a fight in the palace itself, where several were killed on both sides. Three Englishmen and a Spaniard were hanged for brawling last week. Every day there is some trouble . . . God help us, for these barbarous, heretical people make no account of soul and conscience; disobey God, disregard the saints, and think nothing of the Pope, who they say is only a man like themselves, and can have no direct dominion over them. The only Pope they recognise is their sovereign."

The futility of the marriage, from a national point of view, rankled in the breasts of the disappointed courtiers as much as did their personal discomfort. They felt that the trouble they had undergone, and the humble pie they had eaten, had added nothing to the power of their country or their sovereign, and their prevailing idea was how soonest and best to wash their hands of an ungrateful and profitless business in which all their sacrifices had been in vain.

"We Spaniards," says the narrator, "move about amongst all these Englishmen like so many fools, for they are such barbarians that they cannot understand us, nor we them. They will not crown the King nor recognise him as their sovereign, and say that he only came to help govern the kingdom and beget children, and can go back to Spain as soon as the Queen has a son. Pray God it may be soon, for he (Philip) will be glad enough, I am sure, and our joy will be boundless to be away from a land peopled by such barbarous folk. The King has forgiven the Queen 2,250,000 ducats she owed him, and has distributed 30,000 ducats a year in pensions to these lords of the Council, to keep them in a good humour. All this money is taken out of Spain. A pretty penny this voyage and marriage have cost us, and yet these people are of no use to us after all."

Bitter disappointment is the note struck all through. The English lords who had been so heavily bribed were ready enough to take all they could get; but they were as patriotic as they were greedy, and did not sell their country's interests for their pensions. Renard for once had made a mistake. He was ready to assent to any conditions the English liked to propose on paper, trusting to the personal influence of Philip on his queen after the marriage was effected. But he forgot that the Queen herself was a mere puppet in the hands of her nobles, as the narrator I have quoted soon discovered, and, whatever ascendency the young bridegroom might obtain over his half-Spanish bride, her councillors, from the stern Gardiner downwards, were Englishmen before everything, to whom the over-weening power of the Emperor had been held up as a terror since their childhood. And so the whole splendid plot failed, and the magnificent nuptials had hardly been forgotten before Philip, recognising that his sacrifices had been in vain, and that he could never rule in England, made the best of an unfortunate speculation, and with all gravity, courtesy, and dignity left Mary to die of a broken heart, alone, disappointed, and forsaken.

*THE EVOLUTION OF THE SPANISH ARMADA.*

## THE EVOLUTION OF THE SPANISH ARMADA.

PERHAPS no character in history has been more misjudged and misrepresented than Philip II For three centuries it has pleased English writers particularly, to portray him as a murderous ogre, grimly and silently plotting the enslavement of England for thirty years before the great catastrophe which reduced his vast empire to the rank of a harmless second-rate power. As a matter of fact he was a laborious, narrow-minded, morbidly conscientious man, patient, distrustful, and timid; a sincere lover of peace and a hater of all sorts of innovations. He was born to a position for which he was unfitted, and was forced by circumstances stronger than himself to embark upon gigantic warlike enterprises which he disliked and deplored.

For ages it had been considered vital in the interests both of England and Spain that a close alliance should exist between the two countries, in order to counterbalance the immemorial connection between Scotland and France; and that the Flemish dominions of the house of Burgundy should under no circumstances be allowed to fall under the sway of the French. It is easy to understand that with France paramount over the North Sea ports and in Scotland, England would never have been safe for a moment; whilst the principal continental seat of English foreign trade would have been at the mercy of England's secular foe. At the same time all central Europe would have been cut off from its Atlantic seaboard, whilst the principal maritime powers, Spain and Portugal, would have been excluded from all ports north of Biscay, except on the sufferance of their jealous rival. This was the tradition to which Philip had been born; inheriting as he did the dominions both of Spain and the house of Burgundy, and almost at any cost he was forced, as his forefathers had been, to cling to the connection between his country and England. Henry VIII. had known full well that he might strain the cord very tightly without breaking it when he flew into the face of all Christendom, and contemptuously cast aside for an ignoble passion the aunt of the Emperor, a daughter of the proudest royal house in Europe. Charles V. dared not, and did not, break with England in consequence; for Henry had taken care to draw close to Scotland and France, and the very hint of such a combination was sufficient to render the Emperor all amiability.

For a time it looked as if the alliance had been rendered proof against all attack by the marriage of Philip and Mary, and it is highly probable that it would have been so if Renard's plan to marry Elizabeth to the Duke of Savoy had been carried out; but here again circumstances were too strong for persons. The marriage would have been useless unless Elizabeth were first legitimised, and Mary

## THE SPANISH ARMADA.

*could* not legitimise her without bastardising herself, which she obstinately refused to do, notwithstanding all the entreaties of Philip and his friends. But Philip ostentatiously favoured his young sister-in-law, in the hope that when she came to the throne he might have some claim upon her gratitude, and induce her to maintain the friendship which was so necessary for his interests. It was no question of Catholic or Protestant yet. He would have supported her—as indeed he did—however firm a Protestant she might be; for the next Catholic heir to the crown, Mary Stuart, was practically a Frenchwoman, married to the heir of the French throne, and with her as Queen of England and France, Spain and the house of Burgundy would have been ruined.

Elizabeth knew as well as any one how vital it was for Philip to be friendly with England; and during a long course of years she traded unscrupulously upon her knowledge that she might assail, insult, plunder, and make more or less veiled war upon him, and yet that he dared not openly break with her whilst France was greedily eyeing his Flemish harbours. From the first moment that Elizabeth's reform policy became evident it was seen by Spanish statesmen that either the government of England must be changed, so as to bring it back to the old cordial alliance, or else Spain must seek new combinations of powers, in order to redress the balance. For the first alternative to be successful promptness was necessary, and the government of the Queen changed whilst the country was yet unsettled and divided. Feria wrote from London to Philip only a day or two after Mary's death that the country must be dealt with sword in hand rather than by cajolery, unless it were to be allowed to slip through their hands; and thenceforward for years all of Philip's agents, one after the other, pressed upon their master the necessity of using force, either by aiding the Catholics to revolt or by a direct attack on England. Angry, almost contemptuous, references to the King's hesitancy and timidity are constantly occurring in the letters of the various Spanish ambassadors in England, but beyond occasional money aid to the English Catholics nothing could be obtained from the King.

Of all things slow-minded, unwarlike Philip desired peace, almost at any price, and he saw, as his advisers did not, the dangers that surrounded him. Marriage designs, cajolery, and other peaceful methods having failed to bind Elizabeth to him, he attempted to form a new combination. He married the French king's daughter as his third wife; and doubtless even thus early had evolved in his mind the idea of a league of the Catholic powers as a counterbalance to Elizabeth's friendship with Denmark, Sweden, and the German Protestant princes. He knew that overt assistance from him to the English Catholics to depose the Queen and stifle Protestantism would increase the enmity of the allied Protestants of the Continent, and perhaps let loose the storm of which the mutterings were already audible in Flanders. So, in answer to Feria's advice and Bishop Quadra's arguments in favour of force, he insisted upon a policy of soft words, pacification, and palliation; and again and again told his ambassadors, "You *must* keep principally in view by all ways and means to avoid a rupture . . . the importance of which is so great that I cannot be satisfied without repeating it so many times."

But if he thus deprecated open warfare he was at all times, after Mary Stuart's French husband was dead, ready enough to subsidise plots to assassinate or depose Elizabeth ; and large sums were sent to England for that purpose. In vain his agents continued to tell him how useless it was to expect that the English Catholics would pull the chestnuts out of the fire for him, unless they were assured of his armed support. But this assurance he would not give. A marriage of his son Carlos with the widowed Mary Stuart, simultaneously with a Catholic rising in England, was an expedient after his own heart, but even here his timidity was so great that he would run no risk of firing a shot in favour of a project in which he would have been the principal gainer. He writes (June 15, 1563) to Bishop Quadra : "With regard to the adherents that the Scots will have in England, and the increase of their number if necessary, you will not interfere in any way further than you have done, but let them do it all themselves, and gain what friends and sympathy they can for their opinions amongst the Catholics and those upon whom they depend. *I say this because if anything should be discovered they should be the persons to be blamed and no one in connection with us.*" He was told plainly that the negotiations could not be carried on in this way, which pledged everybody but himself, but it was all useless : his instructions were firm and undeviating : under no circumstances was he to be drawn into war with England.

In 1564 the English Protestants were almost

openly sympathising with the growing discontent in the Netherlands, and flocks of refugees from Holland were daily crossing to England. Spanish ships were being pillaged on every sea by English privateers, and a war of tariffs and commercial prohibitions was being carried on between England and Spanish Flanders; and Philip's advisers told him that an open war with England would not injure him so much as his present inactivity was doing. But withal when he sent a smooth-tongued ambassador, Diego de Guzman, to mollify the English, his secret instructions were that he was to tell Elizabeth that " his orders were to endeavour to please her in all things, *as in effect we wish you to do, using every possible effort to that end; and striving to preserve her friendship towards us and our mutual alliance.*"

In August, 1568, Philip sent a new ambassador to England, Gerau de Spes. Relations at the time were extremely strained between the two countries, owing to the expulsion of the English ambassador from Spain for some offence against the Catholic religion; and Alba's cruelty in the Netherlands had aroused a bitter feeling in England against Spain, which was increased by the plots which were known to be in progress between the Guises and Alba in favour of Mary Stuart. And yet Philip's orders to his new ambassador were, " that he was to serve and gratify Elizabeth on every possible occasion, *as in fact I wish you to do, trying to keep her on good terms, and assuring her from me that I will always return her friendship as a good neighbour and brother.*"

When Elizabeth a few months afterwards seized Philip's treasure-ships, which had been driven to take refuge in English ports to escape from the privateers, he pursued the same peaceful policy. Fiery de Spes was all for war and retaliation, but beyond seizing English shipping in Spanish and Flemish harbours, Philip would not go. He was driven for money and sorely beset on all sides, his commerce well-nigh swept from the seas, his credit diminished, and his rebellious subjects in Flanders blockading his own coasts against him. Mary Stuart was urging him to action, his own ministers were assuring him ceaselessly that the only way to check English aggression was to "set the fire to Elizabeth's own doors by raising troubles in England or Ireland if he was not prepared to go to war." But in the face of all provocation, in the face of Alba's assurance that his prestige was being ruined by his tame submission, he could only say after long delay (December 16, 1569) that if Elizabeth's hardness of heart continued he should really have to consider what could be done. "We here think that the best course will be to encourage with money and secret favour the Catholics of the North, and to help those in Ireland to take up arms against the heretics and deliver the crown to the Queen of Scotland, to whom it belongs by succession." And the only outcome of it all was the futile aid to the plots of Norfolk and Ridolfi.

It was the same again twelve years later when Drake's appalling atrocities on the South American coasts had aroused the fury of all Spain; and England was enriched by the plunder of sacred shrines and peaceful merchantmen. English troops were in arms against him in Flanders, and public money had been flowing over to the aid of the rebels with the thinnest possible disguise, but still

Philip clung obstinately to the English alliance, hoping against hope that at last Elizabeth would become friendly with him. The most he would do, as before, was to help the Irish Catholics in their revolt, in order to hamper the English queen and prevent her from injuring him further. Certainly in all these years he had never entertained for a moment the idea of the subjugation of England; he only sought either by removing Elizabeth or by diverting her attention to troubles at home to draw her country back again to the old alliance and friendship.

Up to this period (1580) the principal reason, beyond Philip's natural love of peace, which had caused him to follow his long-suffering policy was the fear of finding himself opposed both to England and France. Catharine de Medici was as facile as Elizabeth herself, and could generally, when it suited her, patch up a reconciliation between Huguenots and Catholics and unite them, for a short time at least, under a national banner. But in January, 1580, an event happened which for the first time seemed to hold out hopes that he might be able to revenge himself upon Elizabeth without the fear of France before his eyes. Archbishop Beaton, Mary Stuart's ambassador in Paris, secretly told Philip's ambassador there that he *and the Duke of Guise* had prevailed upon the Queen of Scots to place herself, her son, and her realm entirely in the hands and under the protection of the King of Spain, and would send James VI. to Spain to be brought up and married there to Philip's pleasure. This meant the detachment of the Guises from the French interest, and Vargas, the Spanish ambassador, at once saw its importance. He sent off a special

courier to Philip, urging him now to action:
"Such is the state of things there," he says, "that
if even so much as a cat moved the whole edifice
would crumble down in three days. If your
Majesty had England and Scotland attached to you,
directly or indirectly, you might consider the States
of Flanders conquered, and . . you could lay down
the law for the whole world."

Guise's adhesion to Spain made all the difference,
and Philip welcomed the idea of deporting James
Stuart to Spain as a preliminary measure. Mary
herself was in high hopes, and Beaton said she
was determined to leave her prison only as Queen
of England. Her adherents, he asserted, were
so numerous in the country, that if they rose
the matter would be easy without assistance,
"but with the aid of your Majesty it would soon
be over." The plan was shelved for a time in
consequence of the death of Vargas; and James'
deportation became unnecessary on the fall of
Protestant Morton, and the accession to power of
D'Aubigny, Earl of Lennox, who had already sent
Fernihurst to Spain to assure Philip of his devotion;
but in April of the following year Mary Stuart
opened negotiations with Tassis, the new Spanish
ambassador in Paris. "Affairs," she assured him,
through Beaton, "were never better disposed in
Scotland, than now to return to their ancient condition, so that English affairs could be dealt with
subsequently.' The King, her son, she said, was
quite determined to return to the Catholic religion,
and inclined to an open rupture with the Queen of
England.

Philip, however, wished to be quite sure that

James was really to be a Catholic before helping him to the succession of the English crown. Father Persons and five or six Jesuits were busy in Scotland with Spanish money plotting for the restoration of the Catholic religion, and the young King himself told them, "that though for certain reasons it was advisable for him to appear publicly in favour of the French, he in his heart would rather be Spanish." Even thus early James' duplicity was the subject of wonder to those who surrounded him; and in January, 1582, Mary wrote rather doubtfully about his religion to Mendoza, the Spanish ambassador in England. "The poor child," she said, "was so surrounded by heretics that she had only been able to obtain the assurance that he would listen to the priests she sent him." But she assures the Spaniard that she will bind herself and her son exclusively to Philip in future, and begs that the Scottish courtiers should be bribed in his interest. The Catholic revival in Scotland was being vigorously worked by the Jesuits and the nobles, and it soon became evident to them also that James was too slippery to be depended upon. So they sent Father Holt to London in February with some important proposals. The rank and file of the Jesuits had no idea that their Catholic propaganda in Scotland had been contrived and paid for by Spain with a political object, and Holt was astounded when the person to whom he was directed in London took him to Mendoza. His message was that the Scottish nobles had decided, as a last resource, if James continued obstinate, to depose him, and either convey him abroad or hold him a prisoner until

## THE SPANISH ARMADA. 187

his mother arrived in Scotland. They besought the guidance of the King of Spain in the matter, and begged that 2,000 foreign troops might be sent to them to carry out their plans. This message was repeated in a softened form to Mary Stuart in her English prison, and Mendoza urged his master to send the troops requested, "with the support of whom the Scots might encounter Elizabeth, and the whole of the English north country would be disturbed, the Catholics there being in a majority; and the opportunity would be taken for the Catholics in the other parts of the country to rise, when they knew they had on their side the forces of a more powerful prince than the King of Scotland."

Philip was on the Portuguese frontier at the time, and affairs in Madrid were being managed by the aged Cardinal de Granvelle, who sent to the King notes and recommendations on all letters received.

He warmly seconded Mendoza's recommendations that the troops requested by the Scots nobles should be sent, and says: "The affair is so important both for the sake of religion, and to bridle England, that no other can equal it; *because by keeping the Queen of England busy we shall be ensured against her helping Alençon or daring to obstruct us in any other way.*" Somewhat later Granvelle repeats the same note. Speaking of the fear of the Scots nobles that the landing of a large foreign force might threaten their liberties, he says: "This is not what his Majesty wants, nor do I approve of it, but that we should loyally help the King of Scots and his mother to maintain their rights; and by promoting armed disturbance keep the Queen of England and the French busy, at a comparatively small cost to ourselves, and so enable us to settle our own affairs better. If it had no other result than this it would suffice, but very much more when we consider that it may lead to the re-establishment of the Catholic religion in those parts. It is very advantageous that the matter should be taken in hand by the Duke of Guise, as it will ensure us from French obstruction. *Since we cannot hope to hold the island for ourselves, Guise will not try to hand it over to the King of France to the detriment of his near kinswoman."* He also speaks of the probability of Elizabeth's coming to terms with Spain on being secured to the throne during her life, and the re-establishment of the old alliance between the two countries.

Thus far, then, the aims of Spain were legitimate and honest under the circumstances; and Philip had no avowed intention, or thought, of the conquest of England for himself. We shall see how he was gradually forced by circumstances and the jealousy between the English and Scottish Catholics to adopt a different attitude.

So long as Mary and Mendoza kept the direction of the conspiracy in their own hands all was done wisely and prudently, but as soon as Lennox and the Jesuits had a hand in it a complete muddle was the result. Tassis, the Spanish Ambassador in France, and Guise had been quite outside the new proposition of the Scots nobles, but in March, 1582, Lennox wrote a foolish letter to Tassis, which he sent by Creighton to Paris, laying bare the plan and giving his adhesion to it, but making all manner of inflated and exaggerated demands.

Creighton had promised him, he said, 15,000

foreign troops, of which he was to have command, and he asked in addition for a vast sum of money and a personal guarantee against loss of fortune in any event. Creighton also went to Guise and brought him into the business, and Jesuit emissaries were to go to Rome and Madrid to crave aid from the Pope and Philip. Mary and Mendoza were furious at the ineptitude of Lennox and the priests, and Mary particularly that her name should be used by them as being the head of the conspiracy. Creighton had no authority whatever to promise 15,000 men, and the idea that Lennox was to have command was absurd from a Spanish point of view. Philip was alarmed too at the large number of persons who were now concerned in the affair, and directed that no further steps should be taken. The inclusion of Guise in the project soon produced its result. He wanted naturally to take a large and prominent part, and travelled to Paris to meet Tassis secretly at Beaton's house. He was full of far-reaching, ill-digested plans; but his main desire evidently was to prevent Spanish troops from being sent to Scotland, for fear, he said, of the jealousy of the French. His idea was that a large mixed force should be sent from Italy under the papal flag, whilst he made a descent with Frenchmen on the coast of Sussex. But all these fine plans were soon frozen under the cold criticism of Philip and de Granvelle. Philip, it is true, did not yet think of conquering England for himself, but Mary and James must owe the English crown to him alone, and be bound to restore the close alliance between England and Spain, or the change would be of no use to him: and this could hardly be hoped for if there were too many French and Italian troops concerned in the business, or if Guise had the main direction of the enterprise.

Sir Francis Englefield was in Madrid as Philip's adviser on English affairs, and both he and the numerous English Catholic refugees in France, Flanders, and Spain soon made it clear that their national distrust and enmity of the French was as keen as ever, whilst they looked sourly upon any project which should make the Frenchified Scots paramount over England. This feeling they were careful to urge upon the Spaniards upon every occasion, and it is not surprising that Philip at last came to believe their assurances that all England would welcome a Catholic restoration if it came from their old friends the Spaniards, and not from their old enemies the French.

From that time a change was apparent in Philip's policy. When he heard of the Raid of Ruthven and the flight of Lennox he saw that English Protestant intrigue had conquered, and that the Scottish-Catholic enterprise was at an end for a time. Guise was to be flattered and conciliated, but it is clear that henceforward Philip wished to confine his (Guise's) attention to France. He was told how dangerous it would be for him to leave France with his enemies, the Huguenots, in possession, and was emphatically assured of Spanish support in his own ambitious plans at home.

Guise was flattered, but he could hardly be expected to look upon Scottish affairs from Philip's point of view. So he got one of his adherents, young de Maineville, sent to Scotland to revive the idea of the landing of foreign troops there.

Beaton, who was thoroughly French, was just as anxious to keep the matter afoot in Paris, but Philip had lost faith in the enterprise, and only kept up an appearance of negotiation in order to maintain his hold upon the Guises and prevent them from undertaking anything except under his patronage. De Maineville soon got on intimate terms with James, but the Protestant lords were holding him at the time, and Guise was informed by his agent that the time was not now propitious for a Catholic descent upon Scotland.

Guise thereupon came to the Spaniards in May, 1583, with a fresh plan. He had decided, he said, to begin with the English Catholics. Elizabeth was first to be murdered and the country raised, whilst he landed on the coast, but Philip and the Pope must provide 100,000 crowns to pay for it. His plans, as usual, however, were vague and incomplete, and the English Catholics, as well as Philip, looked coldly upon them. Father Allen and the English exiles were in deadly earnest, "and thought all this talk and intricacy were mere buckler-play." Mendoza in Paris reports to Philip that "they suspected a tendency on the part of the Scots to claim a controlling influence in the new empire, and as the Scots are naturally inclined to the French, they would rather the affair were carried through with but few Spaniards, whilst the English hate this idea, as their country is the principal one . . . and they think it should not lose its predominance."

The English Catholics had a plan of their own which they urged upon Philip. The English North Country was to be raised simultaneously with the landing of a Spanish force in Yorkshire, accompanied by the Earl of Westmoreland, Lord Dacre, and other nobles, with Allen as Nuncio and Bishop of Durham, and some of the extreme Catholic party, even in Scotland, distrusting the French, favoured some such plan as this under purely Spanish auspices.

Guise appears finally to have adopted a combination of this plan and his own. The Spanish forces were to land at Fouldrey, Dalton-in-Furness, Lancashire, whilst the English North Country was to be raised, and the Catholic Scots on the border were to co-operate with the Spaniards. Guise at the same time was to land in the south of England with about 5,000 men. James VI., who had thrown himself into Falkland and had assumed the reins of government, was in complete accord with Guise about it, but the latter, as usual, was for pushing matters on far too rapidly to please Philip. He (Guise) took upon himself to send a priest named Melino to the Pope to ask him to furnish some funds for the expedition and to explain the whole of the particulars, and this deeply offended the King of Spain, who had no idea of having matters arranged over his head by such a bungler as Guise. The latter also sent Charles Paget in disguise to England in August, 1583, to inquire as to the amount of support he might expect when he landed on the south coast, and when Philip in due course saw the instructions taken by Paget, it became clear to him that he must somehow eliminate Guise from the project. On the margin of the instructions Philip scribbled sarcastic remarks as to the futility of Guise's projecting a landing and sending full particulars of his plans to the Pope *before* he had ascertained what support he could depend upon when he *did* land. What opened Philip's eyes more than anything else was that the English " were to be assured on the faith and honour of Guise that the enterprise is being undertaken with no other object or intention than to re-establish the Catholic religion in England and to place the Queen of Scotland peacefully on the throne of England, which rightly belongs to her. When this is effected the foreigners will immediately retire from the country, and if any one attempts to frustrate this intention *Guise promises that he and his forces will join the people of the country to compel the foreigners to withdraw.*"

Well might Philip underline this and scatter notes of exclamation around it, for it marked the parting of the ways, and showed that Guise was more anxious for his family aggrandisement and personal ambition in placing his kin upon the English throne than to serve the interests of Spain by securing a close union between the two countries to the exclusion of France, which was Philip's main object.

Guise was therefore told that he must not be precipitate, and the matter was kept in suspense; but from that moment Philip decided to undertake the matter alone. Allen and the English Catholics had never ceased to urge upon him that his troops should be landed first in England, and not in Scotland; and this now obviously suited Philip best, as he was growing more and more doubtful about James' religious sincerity. Another fact must have also influenced him greatly in the same direction. His great admiral, Santa Cruz, had just brilliantly routed the French mercenary fleet in the service of the Portuguese pretender at the Azores, and in the flush of victory had written to Philip begging to be allowed to direct his conquering fleet against England. "Do not miss the opportunity, sire," he wrote, "and believe me I have the will to make you king of that country and others besides." The grand old sailor made light of the difficulties, and besought the King to let him go and conquer England in the name of God and Spain. But Philip was not ready for that yet, and the idea was only now being forced by events into his slow mind that perhaps he might be obliged, after all, to claim England for his own, since the English Catholics were for ever saying they wanted no French or Scotsmen; and not a single English pretender was otherwise than Protestant. So Santa Cruz was told that the King would consider the matter, and in the meanwhile provide for eventualities by ordering large supplies of biscuits, and by gradually sending men to Flanders. At the same time he wrote to his ambassador in Paris, telling him in confidence that he intended in due time to invade England from Flanders, but no one was to learn this until the preparations had advanced too far to be concealed; "and even then they (the French) must be told in such terms as may not make them suspect an intention of excluding the French from the enterprise."

But what is of more importance still, Philip gave directions in the same letter to Tassis in November, 1583, that his own claim to the English crown as a descendant of Edward III. should be cautiously broached. If England was to remain in close alliance with Spain, it is difficult to see what other course Philip could have taken. James as a successor to his mother was now out of the question, so far as Spanish interests were concerned, for he was playing false all round. No sooner did the Scots Catholics gain the upper hand than he intrigued with Elizabeth and the Protestants for their overthrow, and immediately the English and Protestant faction became paramount he wrote beseeching letters for aid to Guise and the Pope. All this, of course, Philip knew, for he knew everything, and although he intended to put Mary Stuart on the throne, from this time he was determined that her son should not succeed her.

The discovery of the Throgmorton plot and Guise's wild plans in connection therewith threw the whole project into the background for a time, and confirmed stealthy Philip in the idea that in future he must manage matters himself. When Tassis, his ambassador in Paris, was withdrawn from his post, in the spring of 1584, he wrote an important memorandum to his master setting forth at length the arguments on both sides for and against a landing in England or Scotland, by which it is clear that the English and Scottish Catholic factions in France were now bitterly at issue on the subject. As the English plan had gained ground, James had once more considered it advisable to feign a desire to become a Catholic; and Guise had again urged the adoption of the plan of a landing in Scotland, with the invasion of England over the Scots border, James himself being the figurehead. Tassis says that such is the jealousy of the Scots in England that if an army crossed the Border the

English Catholics themselves might resist it. "The English," he says, "would not like to be dominated by Scotsmen, and if the crown of Scotland is to be joined to theirs, they still wish to be cocks-of-the-walk, as their kingdom is the larger and more important one. On the other hand the Scots may be unduly inflated with the opposite idea, so that imperfections may exist on both sides." As Mary Stuart had drawn closer to Spain she had grown distrustful of Beaton and Tassis, whom she considered too much wedded to French ideas; but withal Tassis in this document very emphatically leans to the English view, which he knew was that now held by his master. The full plan for a great armada was evidently slowly germinating in Philip's mind, but the vast expense had first to be provided for. When Guise's envoy, Melino, had gone on his meddling mission to the Pope his Holiness had offered to subsidise the expedition to a moderate amount, and in answer to the second appeal from James VI. himself he had said that he would stand by his previous promise. But this did not suit Philip, and he let the Pope know promptly that he was willing to undertake the great task for the glory of God and the advance of the Church, but that the Pope must subscribe very largely indeed, "and must find ways and means through his holy zeal to do much more than has yet been imagined." He was also warned that Guise ought not to be allowed to leave France, where he might serve the Catholic cause so much more effectively than elsewhere. And so Guise and the Scotsmen are pushed further and further into the background, Philip's aim being evidently to raise civil commotion in France, which was always easy enough to do, and so to paralyse Henry III. and the Huguenots from helping Elizabeth, whilst Guise would be powerless to promote the interest in England of his kinsman James.

When it became apparent that the Pope was to have a large share in the business the intrigue was transferred from Paris to Rome. Sixtus himself was wise, frugal, and moderate, and had no great desire to serve Philip's political aims, but only to signalise his own pontificate by the restoration of England to the Church; but he was surrounded by cardinals who represented the different interests. Medici, D'Este, Gonzaga, Rusticucci, Santorio, and others represented the French view, which was in favour of an arrangement with Elizabeth and James, and desired to exclude Spanish influence from England. Sanzio watched Guise's interests, whilst the Secretary of State Caraffa, Sirleto, Como, Allen, and the Spanish ambassador, Olivares, craftily forwarded Philip's wishes, the Pope himself being carefully kept in the dark as to the ultimate object in view. The cause of religion was invoked all through as being Philip's only motive; inconvenient points were left indefinite, with the certainty that Caraffa would interpret them favourably to Spanish designs; and by the most extraordinary cajolery the Pope was induced to promise a million gold crowns to the enterprise. He was not brought to this without much haggling and misgiving on his part, and was very cautiously treated with regard to Philip's intention to claim the English crown. "His Holiness," writes Olivares, "is quite convinced that your Majesty is not thinking of the crown of England for yourself, and told Cardinal D'Este so. I did not say anything to the contrary. He is very far from thinking your Majesty has any such views, and when the matter is broached to him he will be much surprised. However deeply he is pledged to abide by your Majesty's opinion, I quite expect he will raise some difficulty." Philip's constant orders were that the Pope should be plied with arguments as to the inadvisibility of the heretic James being allowed to succeed, and the need for choosing some good Catholic to succeed Mary. The person that Philip had decided to make sovereign of England was his favourite daughter, Isabel Clara Eugenia, but this was not to be mentioned to the Pope. "But if at any time the Pope moved by his zeal should talk about any other successor, you will remind him, before he gets wedded to his new idea, that he is pledged to agree to my choice in the matter."

In the meanwhile Allen, Persons, and the other English Catholics, were ceaseless in their steady propagation of the idea of Philip's own right to the crown, in consequence of the heresy of James, and the same view was forced upon Mary Stuart by Mendoza and her English confidants in Paris, all of whom were pensioners of Spain. At length Mary was convinced, and wrote to Mendoza at the end of June, 1586, saying she had disinherited her son in favour of Philip.

The full plan of the Armada had now assumed definite form. The King was in possession of Santa Cruz's marvellously complete estimate of cost and requirements of all sorts—a perfect monument of technical knowledge and forethought; the

Pope was pledged to find about a third of the necessary funds, and to leave Philip a free hand with regard to the English succession and the time for the carrying out of the enterprise; whilst Philip's position with regard to his claim to the English crown was regularised by Mary's will in his favour.

Guise, Beaton, and the Scots had thus been routed all along the line, but it was not to be supposed that they would accept their defeat without a struggle. Their next move was within an ace of being successful, and nearly changed the whole plan of the Armada. In July, 1586, Guise wrote to Mendoza that a plan he had long been concocting had at last been brought to a head, and Beaton was commissioned to tell Mendoza what the scheme was. A Scottish gentleman named Robert Bruce had been sent to France with three blank sheets, signed respectively by Lords Huntly, Morton, and Claude Hamilton, which Guise was to fill up over the signatures with letters to Philip, appealing to him to aid the Scots Catholics. They asked for 6,000 foreign troops for one year and 150,000 crowns to equip their own men, and in return promised to restore Catholicism, release James and his mother, compel the former to become a Catholic, and, most tempting of all, to deliver to Philip one or two good ports near the English Border to be used against the Queen of England. Bruce went to Madrid to lay the Scots' appeal before the King, but when he arrived the failure of the Babington plot and the collapse of the Catholic party in England was known to Philip, and he had lost hope of effecting the "enterprise" except with overwhelming forces of his own. He did not wish, moreover, for Guise's interference, and was coolly sympathetic and no more. And yet, in the face of Santa Cruz's advice that he should secure some ports of refuge for the Armada in the North Sea, the offer of the Scots lords to give him two good Scotch harbours was one not to be lightly refused, so whilst he sent Bruce back with vague promises, he instructed Parma and Mendoza to report fully on the scheme. Parma was cold and irresponsive. He would give no decided opinion until he knew what Philip's intentions were. He was apparently jealous that he was not taken fully into his uncle's confidence, and perhaps angry that his son's claims to the English crown, which were better than those of Philip and his daughter, were being ignored. But Mendoza, an old soldier, the last pupil of Alba, as he called himself, was indignant at Parma's doubts, and wrote to Philip an extremely able paper strongly advising the invasion of England through Scotland, instead of risking everything in a vast fleet, to which one disaster would cripple Spain for ever. In prophetic words he foretold the possibility of the very catastrophe which subsequently happened, and prayed Philip, ere it was too late, to close with the Scots lords' offer. But Philip and Parma were slow and wanted all sorts of assurances; so Bruce was kept in France and Flanders for many months, whilst his principals lost hope and heart. At last, when they were on the point of going over to the Protestant side, on a promise of toleration for their religion, Bruce was tardily sent back with 10,000 crowns to freight a number of small boats at Leith to send over to Dunkirk for

Parma's troops, and the 150,000 crowns demanded by the lords were promised when they rose.

During all this time the juggle in Rome was going on. Gradually Sixtus was familiarised with the idea that Philip could not go to war for the sake of putting heretic James on the throne; then Allen took care that he saw the genealogical tree showing Philip's claim, and at last, in the summer of 1587, it was cautiously hinted to him that, though Philip would not add England to his dominions, he might perhaps appoint his daughter to the throne. Sanzio, Mendovi and the French cardinals were straining every nerve to persuade the Pope that the King of Scots might be converted, and the Capuchin monk Bishop of Dunblane, amongst others, went to Scotland for the purpose of forwarding this view.

The result of Bruce's appeal at Madrid was concealed from Guise, but of course he learnt it indirectly, and was greatly indignant at his exclusion from a project of which he was the originator. It was really no secret, however, for in July, 1587, Father Creighton, sent by Guise, arrived in Rome full of it; he, like other Scotsmen, being in favour of James' conversion and his acceptance by Spain as King of England. But Allen, Persons, and the rest of them soon silenced Creighton, with threats, cajolery, and money.

When Catharine de Medici got wind of the business she seems to have thought it a good opportunity for getting rid of Guise and checkmating Philip at the same time, and urged him (Guise) to go himself to aid his kinsman James to the crown, in which case she would largely subsidise him; and Guise himself was so incensed at the way

Philip had treated him that he threatened to divulge the whole of Bruce's plot to James, and very probably did so. Elizabeth, too, sent young Cary to warn James of what was going on, so that when Bruce arrived in Scotland the King was fully prepared for him; and although he appeared to acquiesce in the hint from Bruce that the Spaniards would aid him to avenge his mother, he was now surrounded by ministers favourable to the Protestant interest, who saw that James had more to hope for from Elizabeth than from Philip, and the matter was deferred indefinitely. It was late in autumn when Bruce arrived in Scotland, too late in the season to freight ships, and he suggested that in the following summer ships for the transport of Parma's 6,000 men to Leith should be freighted in Flanders. This was impossible—in fact, the long delay whilst Philip and Parma were hesitating had ruined the project, which was now public and consequently impracticable, though Bruce and the Scottish lords continued to clamour for Spanish men and money until the Armada appeared. And so again Philip's want of promptness lost this chance, which might have saved the Armada.

By this time, late in the year 1587, the final plan of the Armada had been settled. Parma had received his full instructions from Philip some months before; all Spain and Catholic Christendom were ringing with preparations for the fray, and the great fleet —or what Drake had left intact of it on his summer trip to Cadiz—was mustering at Lisbon under gallant old Santa Cruz, who was already dying brokenhearted at the neglect of his wise precautions, at the confusion, waste, and ineptitude which foreboded the crowning disaster.

# THE SPANISH ARMADA.

With the subsequent mishaps and catastrophe this study is not concerned. My object has been to show how circumstances drove Philip to adopt the course he did, both with regard to the invasion itself and his claim to the English crown; and to demonstrate that the ostensible prime object of the Armada, the conversion of England to Catholicism, although undoubtedly desired by Philip, was mainly used as a means to his real end—namely, a close political alliance with England, without which Spain was inevitably doomed to the impotence which eventually fell upon her.

*A FIGHT AGAINST FINERY.*

## *A FIGHT AGAINST FINERY.*

(A HISTORY OF THE SUMPTUARY LAWS IN SPAIN.)

IT is a curious reflection that whilst all the serious acts and surroundings of civilised life have been rendered amenable to the law, whilst the very instincts inherent in the nature of mankind have been dominated and regulated by authority, utter failure has attended the persistent efforts of rulers to cope with the trivial follies of fashion, or to limit the vanity and extravagance of personal adornment. For long ages men, and particularly women, have insisted upon making themselves absurd and uncomfortable, at great cost and in an infinite variety of ways, in obedience to dictates or impulses springing from nobody knows where, and have only consented to forego each succeeding caprice when the taste for it has worn itself out and has given place to another, perhaps still more preposterous than its predecessor.

It has been from no fault of the rulers that they have

been beaten in their fight with fashion, for they have tried their hardest for centuries. Our Plantagenet and Tudor sovereigns made many attempts to regulate the dress and adornment of their subjects, but the motive which mainly prompted them was the desire to differentiate the classes and prevent the humbler citizens from emulating, in appearance at least, their social superiors. In a state of society which depended upon the subjection of the majority by the privileged classes, this motive was perfectly reasonable; as was also the alternative one of protecting a particular national industry, which, in Tudor times especially, often furnished a reason for the imposition of sumptuary enactments; but both of these motives, from their very nature, were necessarily more or less ephemeral and artificial, because, on the one hand, the continual social development, the growing wealth of the traders and the emancipation of the labourers made the classes interdependent; and, on the other, the extended seaboard of England and the maritime enterprise of the inhabitants made the protection of a particular industry by prohibiting foreign competition impossible for any great length of time. The attempted interference, therefore, of English sovereigns with the dress of their lieges was intermittent and spasmodic, and was, at a comparatively early period, admitted to be useless.

Such, however, from various reasons was not the case in Spain. There the fight against finery was kept up persistently for nearly six centuries, and hardly a decade passed during that time without one or more petty and ridiculous attempts being made to interfere with the dress, food, personal habits, and surroundings of the people. The ostensible motives were usually different from those which operated in England. The separation of the classes has never been so complete in Spain as elsewhere in Europe, owing to the fact that from a very early period in the history of the country all Christians were banded together and dependent upon one another for protection against the common enemy, the infidel. Manual industry, moreover, was never a strong point with Spanish Christians, and the main reason for the various attempts to exclude foreign goods was the dread that Spanish gold would be sent out to pay for them. Nothing is more striking, indeed, than the absolutely murderous effect upon Spanish industry exerted by most of the paternal attempts at interference with trade, but political economy was even more of a dead letter amongst that nation of warriors than with our own ancestors. The earliest object of the great mass of sumptuary laws in Spain was to restrict the dreaded taste for luxury and splendour which was felt to be a characteristic of the hated Moor, who had been conquered bit by bit by people who were content to live roughly, feed frugally, and dress plainly. But with victory came wealth, with peace came intermixture, and the subtle, refined, Oriental blood, with its love of pomp and brilliancy, gradually permeated the rough Gothic-Iberians, until its manifestations alarmed rulers whose power still largely depended upon the self-sacrificing frugality and hardy endurance of their subjects. Thus it was that the attempt was made to keep people frugal and homely whilst they were growing rich, and the tendency continued during all the centuries that the struggle against Spanish luxury went on, although during the last three centuries of the period the original motive had disappeared, and the usual excuse for the interference of the King with the dress of his subjects was the desire to prevent them from spending so much money upon themselves, in order that they might spend more upon him.

But, whatever the motives may have been, the fight against extravagance was carried on as persistently as fruitlessly until quite recent times, and there exists a mass of information with regard to the dress and manners of the people in the Spanish sumptuary enactments unequalled elsewhere. The decrees usually took the form of a representation from the Cortes to the sovereign, setting forth in a preamble the particular abuses to be remedied, and then proposing a remedy which the sovereign usually confirmed by what was called his "pragmatic sanction," and the decree was then proclaimed and had the force of law. A large number of these decrees or "pragmatics" of the highest interest will be found in the British Museum manuscripts (MSS. Add. 9933 and 9934), and many more are set forth in Sempere's "Historia de las leyes suntuarias" (Madrid, 1788), whilst the familiar and festive traditions of old Madrid teem with quaint stories of ingenious evasions and jovial defiance of the laws under the very noses of the sable-clad Acaldes and Alguaciles, whose grave and solemn duty it was to clip lovelocks and measure frills and furbelows.

The first vicious extravagance which seizes upon a hardy, simple people who find themselves safe after a period of struggle is naturally that of gluttony; and the earliest sumptuary decrees of the Castilian kings were directed against this particular excess.

In point of date the first decree extant in Spain of a sumptuary character was that issued by Don Jaime (El Conquistador) of Aragon in 1234. He was extremely devout and ascetic himself, and was shocked at the growing extravagance of his subjects, who having in his remote mountain kingdom finally expelled the Moors, turned their attention to tourneys, shows, and mimic warfare, at which great sums were spent both in feasting and adornment. The Jews too, who at the time nearly monopolised Spanish trade, encouraged the growing taste for the fine stuffs and precious ornaments, from the sale of which they derived so large a profit. So in 1234 Don Jaime decreed from his capital of Zaragoza that no subject of his should sit down to a meal of more than one dish of stewed, and one of roast meat, unless it were dried and salted. As much game as they pleased might be eaten, on condition that it had been hunted by the eater, but otherwise only one dish of game might be served. No jongleur or minstrel might eat with ladies and gentlemen, and no striped or bordered stuffs were to be worn. Gold and silver, as well as tinsel, were prohibited, and ermine and other furs were only to be used as a trimming to hoods and hanging sleeves. Jaime since his childhood had been trying to crush the rising power of his feudal nobles, and had already embarked on that long career of conquest by which he subdued the Moorish kingdoms of Majorca and Valencia, so that, although he himself was now safe in his mountain realm from invasion, his decree was as much prompted by his dread of the softening effect of luxury upon his subjects as by his own rough, simple tastes.

His kinsman of Castile was in worse case, for his dominions were more open to the Moor. Saint Ferdinand conquered the splendid Moorish city of Seville in 1248, where he died four years later, leaving his son, Alonso the Wise, to succeed him as King of Castile. Oriental luxury surrounded the frugal Castilians on all hands. The wealth of plundered cities, the spoils of Moslem palaces were to be had for the grasping, so that it was natural that extravagance in attire and eating should soon threaten to soften the Christian conquerors dwelling in the midst of the gentler, vanquished Moor. Alonso the Wise, in 1256, therefore issued in Seville his first great sumptuary enactment. By it no saddles were allowed to be covered or trimmed with plush. No gold or silver tinsel was to adorn them, excepting as a border of three inches wide, the saddle itself being of uncovered leather. Gold and silver might be used on caps, girdles, quilted doublets, saddle-cloths or table-covers, but not for draping shields or cuirasses. No jingling bells were to be used as trimmings, except on the saddle-cloths at the cane-throwing tourneys, but even then no device was to be embroidered on the cloths. Bosses upon the shields were not to be allowed, but the latter might be adorned with a painted or gilded-copper device. No milled cloth was to be worn, nor were the garments to be cut and pinked in fanciful shapes, or trimmed with ribbons or silk cords; the penalty for infringing any of these regulations being the loss of one or both thumbs by the offender, which of

## A FIGHT AGAINST FINERY.

course meant his disgrace and ruin in the career of arms. Women were allowed a little more latitude, but not much. They might wear ermine and otter fur to any extent, but they were forbidden to adorn their girdles with beads or seed-pearls, or to border their kirtles or wimples with gold or silver thread, or to wear them of any other colour than white.

With regard to eating, Alonso the Wise held similar notions to those of his neighbour Don Jaime, and ordered that his lieges should not have upon their tables more than two dishes of meat and one of bought game, and on fast days not more than two kinds of fish. As if recognising the difficulty of enforcing this, the King solemnly undertook to comply with his own regulations. Great extravagance had arisen in wedding feasts, which were said (as in Oriental countries they do to-day) to often ruin the contracting families, and Alonso made strict rules to limit the excess in this direction. No presents of breeches were to be given, and the entire cost of a wedding outfit was not to exceed 60 maravedis, whilst not more than five men and as many women might be invited to the wedding banquet by each of the contracting parties. The money spent upon marriage rejoicings, indeed, had become so great that Alonso made this reform a great point in his decree, and provided against evasion by strictly limiting the time during which the feast might continue and wedding presents be given. Moors were said to be dressing like Christians, and this was rigidly forbidden. They were to wear no red or green clothes, and no white or gold shoes, and their hair was to be parted plainly in the middle of the head, with no topknot, whilst they were enjoined to wear their full beard, which made the distinction between them and the shaven-chinned Christians the more marked. The penalties imposed for disobeying this decree of 1256 were savage in the extreme, varying from loss of a thumb and a fine for the first offence, to death for the third; but savage as they were, they can hardly have been effectual, except perhaps in Seville, for only two years later, in 1258, Alonso came out with a perfect code of conduct for his subjects, far too minute to even summarise here, but of which some specimens may be given, as they served as a model for subsequent decrees for many years afterwards. Alonso had apparently got tired of his self-denying ordinance and says the King may eat and dress as he pleases, but agrees to limit his daily table expenditure to 150 maravedis a day, which in spending power would represent about £40 at the present time at least. But he orders his "ricoshomes," ruling men, to eat more sparingly and to spend less money. None of the members of the royal household, squires, scribes, falconers, or porters, except the head of each department, were allowed to wear white fur or trimmings, or to use gilt or plated saddles or spurs. They were forbidden to indulge in breeches of scarlet cloth, gilt shoes, and hats of gold or silver tissue. Priests, it appears, had been reducing the size of their tonsures and ruffling in fine colours, so as to be undistinguishable from laymen, and they are sternly ordered to have their tonsures the full size of their heads, gird themselves with a rope, and eschew red, green, and pink garments. The old regulations about eating were repeated with the addition of one plate of meat for supper, and the prohibition of fish on meat days. No man, however rich, was to buy more than four suits of clothes in a year, and no ermine, silk, gold or silver tissue, no slashes, trimmings, or pinked cloth might be worn by men. Two fur mantles in a year, and one rain-cape in two years was the limit of extravagance allowed to a man in this direction; and the King alone was to wear a red rain-cape. Lawn and silk for outer garments were confined to royalty, but the "ricoshomes" might employ them as linings. No crystal or silver buttons were to be allowed, nor was shaving or other signs of mourning permitted, except to vassals who had lost their overlord and to widows. Jews and Moors are cruelly treated in this decree, and their offences and those of the poorer classes are to be punished by torture or death, whilst those of the "ricoshomes" are left to the King's discretion. Ermine, vair, and otter furs would appear to have been amongst the principal articles of luxury, as the wearing of them is very strictly regulated, and white furs seem to come next in estimation after them.

For ninety years these laws of Alonso the Wise were repeated and reimposed with slight variations, but apparently ineffectually; since in 1348 the Cortes of Alcalá made a presentment to Alonso XI. of Castile bewailing the luxury and extravagance of the age, and proposing a new code of sumptuary rules, which in due course the King confirmed. These rules are very interesting because they demonstrate the great strides which had been made in luxury, refinement, and civilisation since the issue of the decrees of Alonso the Wise nearly a century before. No gold ornaments, no ermine or grebe-neck trimmings, no seed-pearl embroidery, gold or silver buttons or wire, and no enamels were to be worn except by nobles. No gold tissue or silk was allowed except for linings, and no man below the rank of a knight might wear vair fur or gilt shoes. Even the princes of the blood were strictly limited in their dress, and were ordered to use tapestry cloth or silk, but without gold or trimming of any sort. The Spartan wedding regulations of Alonso the Wise had now become obsolete with the advance of wealth, but the new rules, although wider, were to be enforced with equal or greater severity. No gentleman was to give his bride within four months after marriage more than three suits of clothes, one of which might be of gold tissue, and one embroidered with seed-pearls to the value of 4,000 maravedis, an enormous sum when we consider that ninety years before 150 maravedis were the limit of the monarch's daily expenditure, and that at this date, 1348, the value of a sheep was only eight maravedis. The bride's trousseau is regulated down to the smallest details, and the penalty for exceeding them is the loss of one-quarter of his land by the too-generous gentleman who does so. The decree sets forth that some women are wearing trains, "which are both costly and useless," but in future they are to be confined to those ladies who are travelling in a litter—a privilege limited to nobles. All other women are to wear pelisses without trains, just reaching the ground, "or at least not to drag more than two inches upon it." Ladies who broke this rule were to be fined 500 maravedis. Great stress is again laid upon the limitation of extravagance in wedding feasts, and burials, but the cost still allowed shows to what an excess luxury had been carried. The bride's wedding clothes might cost 4,000 maravedis and the groom's outfit 2,000; and thirty-two people were now allowed at the wedding feast. Much more latitude was permitted in the use of seed-pearls, gold, and silver, to people above the rank of knights, but the principal point to be noted in these decrees of Alonso XI. is the incidence of the penalty. In the decrees of Alonso the Wise, as has been shown, the most savage penalties were imposed upon the poorer classes, whilst the punishment of the nobles was left to the King's discretion. But much more even justice is dealt out by Alonso XI. The nobles who break the law are to lose one-quarter of their land, the knights one-third, the citizens 500 maravedis, whilst the poorer classes for slight offences against the sumptuary rules are condemned to lose the offending garment and its cost in money.

But whatever the penalty might be, extravagance, checked in one direction, broke out in another, and Peter the Cruel, the son of Alfonso XI., only a few years after the date of the decree just mentioned, issued a complete sumptuary code in which the punishments were positively ferocious. Fines, scourging, mutilation, and banishment for first and second offences, and death for the third, were imposed for the smallest infraction. Peter was particularly hard on priests, who were said to be swaggering about with women, tricked out in gay finery, and they were ordered in future to be sober and frugal, wearing no ornaments of any kind, and only sad-coloured garb. Workmen, too, were to labour from sunrise to sunset for a fixed wage on pain of punishment as severe as those imposed by our own labour laws. The King, moreover, fixed stringently the cost which was to be incurred by cities and towns in entertaining him when he visited them. The dietary scale appears a pretty generous one from the point of view of to-day, consisting as it does of 45 sheep at 8 maravedis each, 22 dozen of dry fish at 12 maravedis a dozen, 90 maravedis worth of fresh fish, with pork, grain, wine, &c.; the total value of the feast being limited to 1,850 maravedis. Villages and nobles were not to spend more than 800 maravedis on a similar occasion.

In 1384 Peter the Cruel's nephew, John I. of Castile, was well beaten by the Portuguese at the battle of Aljubarrota, and marked his sorrow by issuing a decree prohibiting the use in any form of dress of silk, gold, silver, seed-pearls, precious stones, or ornaments of any kind, and everybody was ordered to don a simple mourning garb. When, four years after this, John of Gaunt's daughter Catharine came to marry the heir to the crown of Castile, she brought something else with her besides the wide, pointed coif which Spanish widows wore for the next three hundred years. Part of her dower consisted of great herds of merino sheep, which crossed and thrived so well in Spain that the coarse duffel, which had been the only native cloth, gave place in a few years to beautiful fine woollen textures which could vie with those of England and Flanders.

Intercourse between nations, the growth of wealth, the spread of learning, and the advance of civilisation were moving with giant strides. The soft arts of peace were practised with greater success than ever, now that the Moslem and the Christian were fast merging into one people in Seville and Toledo, and the refinement of the one was strengthened by the energy of the other. Beautiful stuffs, stiff with gold and gems, gauzy silk, soft cloths, and fine linens, had no longer to be brought from the Moors or the kingdoms across the sea. Seville, Toledo, and Cordova could produce everything that the most luxurious extravagance could desire, and the sumptuary laws for a time were forgotten.

In 1452 the Cortes of Palenzuela presented a petition to John II. asking that the stringent sumptuary code of Alonso XI. should be re-enforced. The King, in reply, admitted that the law was a dead letter, and that the extravagance in dress was greater than ever. He says that gold tissue and silks are now ordinary wear, and that gold trimmings and marten-fur linings are used even by people of low estate. "Actually working women," he says, "now wear clothes that are only fit for fine ladies; and people of all ranks sell everything they possess in order to adorn their persons." Still the remedy proposed to him of a revival of the stern code of a hundred years before he saw was an impossible one, and the matter was held in suspense. He died soon afterwards, and his feeble successor, Henry IV., was equally powerless to stem the rising tide of industry and wealth with their natural consequences.

In 1469, during the interregnum which followed the deposition of Henry, the Master of Santiago issued a proclamation deploring the growing extravagance of the age, and enjoining more moderation. Amongst other similar things it says,

"Such is the pomp and vanity now general, even amongst labourers and poor people in their dress and that of their wives, that in appearance they seek to vie with persons of rank, whereby they not only squander their own estates but bring great poverty and want to all classes." But it was useless: and luxury went unchecked until Ferdinand and Isabel the Catholic were firmly seated on the twin throne of a united Spain and the last Moslem stronghold had fallen. Then, in 1495, a "pragmatic" was issued which superseded all previous obsolete sumptuary codes and established a new one, which formed the model for similar decrees for the next two centuries. Probably a more economically unwise decree under the circumstances was never penned. All other previous pragmatics had forbidden the wearing of extravagant apparel, and this did the same, especially severely as regarded the precious metals; but it did more than this. It absolutely forbade the introduction and sale of every sort of gold and silver tissue, and rendered criminal the exercise in Spain of the industry of embroidering or weaving gold, silver, and every other metal. The Christianised populations of the south of Spain were greatly excelling already in this industry. Their gold embroideries on velvet were in great demand for church vestments and royal trappings all over Europe. The taste for chivalrous splendour was not confined to Spain, and the beautiful half-Oriental tissues of Andalusia were eagerly sought for in every Court; gold was just beginning to find its way direct to Spain from the new-found Indies, and if the industry had remained untrammelled there was no reason why the country should not have provided the world with textile splendours to its own great advantage. The ingenious, industrious people—for they were industrious until the strangling of their handicrafts made them idle—did their best to avert ruin. In 1498, only three years afterwards, the Cortes made a presentment to the Queen saying that things were worse than ever. It was true that gold brocade was no longer made and the wicked waste of the precious metal was thus avoided, but all sorts of strange devices and novelties were being introduced in the manufacture of silks, whereby the people were tempted to squander their money on useless finery. The Spanish silk factories were then the finest in Europe, and great quantities of raw silk were raised in the south-east of the Peninsula : and yet a "pragmatic" was issued the next year, 1499, stringently forbidding the manufacture, sale, or use of silk, except for lining. It was a staggering blow to a flourishing industry, and in order to prevent total ruin a decree was given that no raw silk from abroad was to be introduced into the country, and only Spanish-grown silk used. But this was not enough, and some of the silk-making provinces, reduced to desperation, petitioned for the relaxation of the law. Their prayer was granted, as if in irony, to the extent of allowing them to *wear* silk against the law. But they did not want to wear silk, but to make it for other people to wear, and their industry languished, never entirely to recover.

By the time Isabel the Catholic had died the Spanish silk industry was nearly at an end, and the skittish young Bearnaise princess, Germaine de Foix, who succeeded her as old Fernando's wife, came too late to do it much good. It is true she snapped her slender fingers and threw up her pretty chin at the straitlaced sumptuary laws, and surrounded herself with silks and velvets, gold brocade and gems, wherever she went; but unfortunately they mostly came from the looms and workshops of Southern France, and gave no work to Spanish hands. Money, of course, had to be sent out of Spain to pay for the finery, and in 1515 the Cortes of Burgos complained of this to Jane the Mad, Isabel's nominal successor, who thereupon issued a decree entirely forbidding brocades and gold or silver embroidery and trimmings to be worn at all, and strictly limiting the wearing of silk in any form to people of rank.

But Jane's power was the merest shadow; Spain was in the throes of a great struggle for its democratic institutions, which it lost, and no notice was taken of poor Crazy Jane's decree. If she understood it she probably had as little sympathy with it as her young stepmother, for she had lived for years with her handsome husband Philip as head of the most pompous and splendid Court in Europe, in busy Flanders, surrounded by all the traditional magnificence of the house of Burgundy, and her young son, the coming Emperor Chares V., Fleming as he was by birth and instinct, was even less likely than she to revert willingly to the simple, democratic, and patriarchal traditions of the Spanish Court.

He came to his new country with a whole host of Burgundian, Flemish, and German nobles, whose taste for finery had never been checked; and whatever decrees Charles might issue for the dress of his people, he and his Court were the first to disregard the letter and spirit of his precepts. It is not to be wondered at, therefore, that they were not obeyed for long together by any one else. The initiative, moreover, did not come from the King or his courtiers, but from the Cortes of Castile, who were naturally swayed entirely by Spanish ideas, of which Charles had at this time, boy as he was, but little knowledge or sympathy. This was so clearly recognised that when he was about to leave Corunna in 1520 to assume the imperial crown, the Cortes held there petitioned him at least to order that the sumptuary laws with regard to silks, brocades, gold embroideries, and gold and silver lace, should be strictly enforced during his absence from Spain, since they saw that, with such a Court as his, they would not be enforced in his presence. But the example of the Court had struck too deeply, and the fury for splendour had now really taken hold of the Spaniards, who in their ages of struggle had been so simple and homely.

In the pragmatic of 1537 it is said that during the Emperor's absence the use of brocades, silks, and precious embroideries had increased more than ever, and they are absolutely prohibited, and the rigid law of 1498 again repeated. The preamble of the decree of 1537 says that this law against gold embroidery was generally evaded by making the gold lace and devices separately and then stitching them on to the cloth, which cost much more even than embroidery would have done; and the making of such adornments was consequently prohibited altogether. Only nine years afterwards, in 1548, the Cortes of Valladolid made a presentment to the Emperor saying that things were worse than ever, and the cost of clothes had been increased instead of decreased by the ingenuity of tailors, who had taken to the plan of cutting out the most elaborate patterns of coloured cloth with fine scissors and sewing them on to the cloth garments, almost covering the latter with delicate lace-like snippet work of applied cloth. In face of this abuse the Cortes prayed the Emperor to forbid the use of any and every sort of trimming, lace, or adornment on the garments, both of men and women, which might give an excuse for the wicked tailors to charge extravagant prices. Charles V. thought this too sweeping, but in 1552 he issued a "pragmatic" prohibiting the applied snippet work, and also the use or manufacture of gold and silver lace and ornaments, the wearing and making of velvets, silks, and satins being also rigidly limited. Spain, flooded with the precious metals from the Indies, richer perhaps in actual bullion than ever a country was before or since, with home-grown silk in abundance, and the most deft and tasteful weavers in the civilised world, was therefore obliged to import its manufactured gold and fine stuffs from abroad, whilst its own humbler citizens languished amidst the wealth they were not allowed to earn. No decrees could prevent rich people from squandering their money on dress, least of all when the Emperor and his Court were in a constant blaze of magnificence.

Philip II., who in his later years usually wore black velvet trimmed with jet or bugles, with the simple chain of the Golden Fleece about his neck, was in his youth as splendid as his father; and the preparations for his voyage to England to marry Mary

Tudor in 1554 included the making of more solid magnificence in the way of dress than probably was ever made for one event in modern history. His son's valet [1] was of a literary turn of mind, and has left us a precise description of the dresses and trappings made for Philip and his army of courtiers—the flower of Spain—in which the language of extravagance is exhausted. Horse furniture, bed-hangings, canopies, quilts, and upholstery, as well as dress, were all of satin or velvet covered with gold embroidery and seed-pearls. There were twenty great nobles, Spaniards, Flemings, and Italians, each with scores of followers, all dressed in silks and satins with gold chains. Philip's German bodyguard, even, of 100 troopers, wore facings of silk on the gaudy red and yellow uniform of Aragon, and the common sailors of the fleet had crimson silk caps with white plumes. Some few amongst Philip's numerous suits may be mentioned as an example of the dresses then in vogue, although many of his nobles appear to have fully rivalled him in splendour. For some years, as has been shown, gold-embroidered dresses had been strictly prohibited; and Muñoz, in his description of the sartorial wonders prepared for the wedding, mentions the revival of gold embroidery as a novelty. Prince Philip had one suit consisting of surcoat, doublet, trunk-hose, and jacket of crimson velvet covered with little lozenges formed of twisted gold chains, the interstices being filled with a running sprig of silver braid, the leaves formed of silver filigree. The surcoat was lined with silver cloth of satin, embroidered in the same way. Another surcoat was of grey satin covered with alternate stripes

[1] Andrés Muñoz' MSS., National Library, Madrid.

of applied gold chains and silver bugles. It was lined with stamped cloth of silver, and the doublet, trunks, and jacket were of white satin ornamented in the same way. Another "pretty suit," we are told, consisted of a French surcoat of black velvet embroidered all over with gold and silver bugles, the trunks and jacket being of crimson velvet, and the doublet of crimson satin with the same embroidery One of his dresses consisted entirely of white silk velvet covered with a costly embroidery of gold filigree; and another had a surcoat of black velvet with a border of gold bugles and heavy twisted silver cords, the garment itself being almost hidden under a closely embroidered running sprig in gold, the leaves being filled in with silver filigree, and in the spaces between the sprigs were slashes of white satin. With this gorgeous coat went a suit of white velvet and gold. Precious stones were worn at the neck and wrists, and gold chains and gems were looped around the hat. Heavy gold chains rested on the shoulders, and arms and housings flashed with riches inestimable, the spoils of the two Indies.

This will give some faint idea of the fashions of a time when the rulers were fruitlessly trying to repress extravagance in dress amongst their subjects. Most of this finery was prepared in the city of Valladolid, whence Philip left on his journey, and it is not entirely surprising that in the following year 1555, the Cortes of Castile, sitting in that place, boldly presented a petition asking that the sumptuary laws should be done away with altogether. They say that they are entirely a dead letter, and are consequently a scandal, as well as being useless and vexatious. Their petition was not granted, for Philip and his father still thought that all the growing wealth of the country should come to them, instead of being used for decking the undistinguished persons of private citizens.

There had been no finer flax than that of Galicia, and no better linens than those made from it, but the trade had been crippled by the sumptuary restrictions, and the business had already fallen into the hands of Flemings and Frenchmen, who got paid for their stuffs with Spanish gold. The wool industry was still more cruelly treated. Thanks to the merino stock, the manufactory of fine cloths, serges, and friezes had been very prosperous, and Spain could, and did, export these textiles largely; but in 1552 the export of such goods was strictly prohibited, and even wool in the fleece might not be sent out of the country except on condition that for every twelve sacks exported two pieces of foreign cloth and one bale of foreign linen should be introduced to prevent the export of gold.

The silk growers of Valencia and elsewhere had been ruined, but the looms remained, and the weavers attempted to obtain raw silk from Italy and France. The introduction of raw silk was thereupon forbidden, and most of the weavers went the way of the growers, to idleness and ruin, or across the seas to the Indies. The Cortes of 1555 saw the evil that was being done and, as usual, made a presentment on the subject. They pointed out the paralysis of Spanish industry and the large sums of coin sent out of the country to pay for French and Flemish linens, and ascribed the evil to its secondary and not its primary reason. They say flax-growing is neglected and decayed, and suggest that public lands, where suitable, should be cultivated, and every landowner forced to plant a certain proportion of flax on his estate. It was useless and absurd, of course, as the sumptuary laws limiting the making or wearing of lawns and fine linens had killed the industry, and the coarse linens were still spun and woven at home; so nothing came of it.

But the acme of absurdity and political perverseness was reached in the Cortes of 1552, which presented a petition begging that the export of manufactured goods of all sorts to the new Spanish empire in America should be strictly prohibited. They say that the people there are getting their money so easily and becoming so rapidly rich, that they buy such great quantities of Spanish goods as to raise the prices in the Peninsula, "*whereby we who work here cannot live.*"

The Cortes of 1560 reported that the nation was fast being ruined by extravagance in dress, and begged that a "pragmatic" should be issued forbidding every sort of ornament or tissue in which metal entered, and strictly limiting the trimming of garments to a plain piping round the edge. This pragmatic was duly granted, but during the next few years a considerable change was seen. Philip had married the beautiful young French Princess Elizabeth of Valois, who had been brought up with Mary Stuart in that light-hearted court that Brantome described so well. She had no patience with the rigid puritanism and peddling interference of stern authority with beauty's armoury, and French fashions for ladies became general. A "pragmatic" was published in 1563, ostensibly re-enforcing that of 1537 (which, as has been shown, prohibited the use of gold lace or embroidery in any form), but really relaxing the regulations greatly, for the benefit of the ladies. They might in future wear sleeves of point lace in gold or silver, gold or silver gauze, or silk shot with gold, and their jackets might be made of similar stuffs, whilst they might deck their coifs, wimples, stomachers, and underlinen with as much gold as they pleased. Gold, silver, or crystal buttons could now be worn, but not on the skirt, and only on the head, bosom, bodice, and sleeves; whilst the hat might be trimmed with gold gimp. Some concessions were made to their spouses as well, for they were permitted to clothe their nether limbs in silk hose, and their trunks might be slashed and trimmed with silk, and, generally speaking, the wearing of silk was greatly extended.

Contemporary writers are full of the great extravagance in dress which followed this period. Moncada says that it was not uncommon for a man's dress to cost 300 ducats a suit, whilst the abuse of precious stones, both by men and women, was carried to a ridiculous excess. Contemporary portraits show that things were bad enough in this respect in England at the time, but they were much worse in Spain.

Only one year after the proclamation of the pragmatic just mentioned, namely, in December, 1564, another elaborate decree was issued, on the pretext that the previous one had left several points in doubt, and the authorities had consequently been lax in enforcing it. The decree of 1563 had said that one year's grace was to be given for garments already made, and this concession had served as a loophole for the evading the regulations altogether. The authorities are therefore ordered strictly to enforce the decree; but the opportunity is taken of elucidating doubtful points and still further modifying the severity of the orders. It is now explained that the prohibition of gold, silver, and silk stitching, gimp, or trimming of any sort on the garments, referred only to applied trimmings, and was not meant to include the weaving of gold or silk threads or stripes in the textures, or even the sewing of stripes of silk or leather on to the garment, which stripes might be bordered by a piping and held by two rows of ornamental backstitch on each side, provided that no other sort of adornment is used. Silk gimp even may be applied on garments for indoor wear, whilst silk frogs may be sewn on to overcoats and travelling cloaks. Fringes were also allowed on horse furniture and harness now, and swordbelts and baldricks might be worn as rich as the taste and extravagance of the owners cared to make them. Some doubt is said to exist as to the legality of stuffing the trunk-hose with baize to extend them, and whether the slashes might be lined with baize for the same purpose, and these practices are strictly forbidden, "nor may piping be inserted like farthingales, nor may threads, nor wires, nor gummed silk be employed to extend the trunks unduly, as we are informed has fraudulently been done." The previous pragmatic had imposed the same penalties for infraction of the decree by people in their own houses as in public, which appears to have caused much vexation by the invasion of domiciles by inferior officers, on pretext of searching for forbidden garments, and the right of search was now abolished.

An attempt to shame ladies into obeying the law was made for the first time, of many, in these pragmatics of 1563-4 by giving to women of bad character the right to deck themselves in prohibited finery in their own houses. But Madrid was already commencing upon the downward career which made it for more than a century the most dissolute place in Europe, and women of rank even were proud of their effrontery, so that no attempts to induce them to obey the law by appeals to their modesty ever succeeded. The brazen-faced impudence of the Madrileñas, which so shocked foreigners in the seventeenth century, still remains as a cherished tradition of the fast-disappearing race of *majas* and *manolas* of Lavapies and other low neighbourhoods of the capital, and is encouraged in them as a national trait by their social betters.

In 1568 Philip lost both his beautiful young wife and his only son. Defeat and disappointment met him on all sides, and his gloom, deepened by fanaticism, became heavier as the years rolled on. Henceforward he and his Court dressed in black, and the fashions of his people followed him, to the extent of relinquishing almost entirely the use of gold tissues and embroidery on their garments. But poor as was the King's exchequer, and in despite of Drake and the buccaneers, gold still poured into Spain from the Indies, and luxury, if checked in one direction, was certain to break out in another. Coaches had been brought by Charles from Flanders when he came to Spain, and by the end of the sixteenth century a perfect rage for coaches had seized upon the people of the capital—a form of extravagance which for the next century at least was carried to a ridiculous excess, and even now remains the principal foible of the Madrileños. The new taste was supposed to threaten the art of horsemanship and the breed of horses; so for some years pragmatics were issued ordering that no coach or wheeled litter or chariot was to be drawn by less than four horses. To encourage men to ride on horseback, doctors, lawyers, and licentiates of universities were authorised in 1584 to use long housings to their steeds, and whilst mules were still to be housed with plain harness, horses might be decked with velvet saddles, gold and silver fringes, gimp and nails, and made as smart as possible, in order to encourage their use.

In 1593 Camillo Borghese was sent to Madrid by the Pope, and has left behind him for our enlightenment a minute account of the fashions of his day,[1] by which we may see the effects that had been produced by the "pragmatics" we have described. "The dress of this country," he says, "is as follows. The men wear long breeches, with a surcoat and hat, or else a cloak and cap, as it would be a great breach of decorum with them to wear a hat and cloak together. This costume would certainly be very pretty if the breeches were not cut so long as to be disproportionate. Some men have taken to wearing hose in the Seville style, which they call

[1] "L'Espagne au 16$^{me}$ et 17$^{me}$ siècles," par Morel Fatio. Paris, 1878.

## A FIGHT AGAINST FINERY.

galligaskins, and with these it is proper to wear a cloak and hat instead of a cap. The ladies, like the men, usually dress in black, and have a veil round their faces like nuns, their heads being enveloped by their mantillas in such a way that their faces are hardly visible. Indeed if it were not for the pragmatic issued by the King on the subject they would still cover their faces completely, as they used to do a few years ago. When they do not wear these veils over their faces, they have on collars with enormous ruff pleats. They are naturally dark-skinned, but the use of paints is so common that they all look fair, and though small in stature their high pattens make them look tall, so that it may be truly said that all Spanish ladies turn themselves from little and dusky to big and bright. The main street of Madrid would be fine if it were not unutterably filthy and almost impassable on foot, and the better class of ladies are always in carriages or litters, whilst the humbler ones ride on donkey-back or pick their way through the mire. They (the ladies) are naturally impudent, presumptuous, and off-handed, and even in the street go up and talk with men whom they do not know, looking upon it as a kind of heresy to be introduced properly. They admit all sorts of men to their conversation and are not a bit scandalised at the most improper proposals being made to them.

"The gentlemen now rarely ride on horseback but often go in carriages. They are preceded in the streets by a group of pages and a couple of servants they call lacqueys, the pragmatic not allowing them more, although the grandees may be attended by four. The pragmatics only allow saddle cloths to be worn from October to March, but for the rest of the year velvet saddles may be used. The one pastime of these people is to drive up and down the Calle Mayor (High Street) from midday to midnight."

The good churchman was much shocked at the effrontery of the people and their filthy habits, but this branch of the subject is foreign to the present article. Rough magnificence, side by side with boorish rusticity, seems to have been the characteristic of the Spain of Philip II. In the same year that Borghese wrote, a very severe pragmatic had been issued prohibiting the use of silver ornaments on household furniture, which, it says, had reached a pitch of extravagance which could no longer be endured. Decrees were issued in 1586, 1590, and 1594, which are interesting as showing that the inevitable extravagance of dress had now turned into the direction of the starched ruff. "No man," says the last-named pragmatic, "may wear either at his neck or wrists on any sort of ruff or frill, fixed or loose, any trimming, fringe ravelling, or netting, starch, rice, gums, rods, wires, gold or silver threads, or any 'alchemy' or anything else to extend or support them, but only a plain holland or linen ruff with one or two little pleats, on pain of forfeiture of shirt and ruff and a fine of 50 ducats." Great resistance was offered to this, and it was found, somehow or other, whether by "alchemy" or what not, the "lettuce-frill" ruffs still stood stiffly from the neck, and the Council of State gravely considered the matter, with the result that the decree of 1594 insists upon the law being enforced, the ruffs to be as described, and not more than three inches wide from the band to the hem, the colour to be pure white. The penalties for infraction were tremendous—for a first offence, 20,000 maravedis fine, for the second, 40,000, and for the third, 80,000 and a year's banishment.

This was not by any means the only sumptuary law promulgated in this year of 1594; a much relaxed code of dress was issued with regard to gold and fancy silk textures, of which the universal use of unadorned black for so many years had greatly decreased the manufacture in Spain. Women were now allowed to wear fine cloth or silk jackets, and cover the seams thereof with gold or silver braid or scrolls, whilst their dresses and mantles might be trimmed as profusely as they pleased with the same ornaments. Doublets, jackets, and waistcoats were now allowed to be of quilted silk, satin, or taffety; whilst the trunk hose of the men might be slashed, and double-stitched at the edge of the slashings. The said breeches, moreover, might be stiffened by a single thickness of baize and all the fine stuffs used for gentlemen's garments could now, for the first time for many years, be stamped with patterns. New and more severe measures were adopted at the same time to keep up the breed of horses, which animals were thought to be almost in danger of extinction, as horsemanship was less than ever indulged in, and mules were preferred for drawing the coaches.

In the same year, 1594, a curious pragmatic was proclaimed dealing with the extravagant abuse of honorific titles. It commences in the King's name by saying that, although it is unnecessary to make rules for himself or his family, he will begin at the top for regularity's sake. The King must be addressed in writing simply as "Sir" at the head of the letter, which must end with "God guard the Catholic person of your Majesty," at the bottom. The heir to the crown was to be addressed in the same way, but with "Highness" substituted for "Majesty," the Princes of the blood being given the style of Highness, but "his Highness" alone standing for the heir to the crown. The rest of the Princes were to be addressed on the outside of a letter, "To his Highness the Infante Don So-and-so." The titles "Excellency" and "Illustrious Sir," which had become very general forms of courtesy, were forbidden, and "Most Reverend Sir" was only to be applied to Cardinals and the Primate of Spain, the Archbishop of Toledo. The highest grandees, bishops, and members of the Council of State were in future to be addressed by the inferior title of "Señoria," or Lordship, whilst, out of courtesy and at the option of the person speaking or writing, the same title could be given alone to Marquises, Counts, Presidents of Councils, and Grand Commanders. All letters of every kind were ordered to begin at the top with a cross, and then to state the business without any address or name, ending with "God guard your lordship'—or other title—and the date, place, and signature of the writer. Absolutely no further compliment was to be permitted, no matter what the relationship or rank of the parties. As a further attempt to enforce simplicity, the same pragmatic provides that in future, on pain of a fine of 10,000 maravedis, no coronet may surmount any coat of arms, except such as are borne by Dukes, Marquises, and Counts.

The proclamation of this pragmatic caused a dreadful fluttering of the dovecotes of the Calle Mayor. "Liars' parade" (the raised terrace before the church of St. Philip), the favourite lounge of the gilded youth, rose in revolt, the cadets of the Cordobas, the Mendozas, the Maquedas, the Leivas, the Manriques, and the rest of them, who had been called " Excellencies " and " Lordships " from their cradles, turned like the worm at last. Dress without gold they might, but they, the sons of Dukes, to be addressed with no more ceremony than dustmen—perish the thought! that they would not stand. So they and the rest of the rufflers, led captains, kept poets, bullies, and blacklegs, swept down the Calle Mayor carrying the grave Alcalde and all before them. Shops were shut, water was boiled to throw out upon the base " Corchetes," who dared to call such gallants plain " Mister," and the gloomy recluse in the Alcazar at the end of the street himself heard the row. When he was told the cause of it, he only remarked, so the chronicles say : " Bah! what does it matter to me what they are called? Let them be Lordships, or what they will, so long as they serve me well." And the pragmatic thus died on the day it was born, for no attempt was ever made to enforce it, and " Señorias " in the Calle Mayor remained as plentiful as blackberries in an English hedgerow.

The isolation of Philip II. in his gloomy old age, together with the relaxation of the enactments already mentioned against the use of gold and silver tissues, had allowed luxury in dress practically to go unchecked during the last years of the sixteenth century, and when the King died, in 1598, he left Spain, and particularly the capital, in a perfect frenzy of prodigality. The most brazen dissoluteness accompanied the blindest religious fanaticism; the exchequer was bankrupt, the fields untilled, the aforetime busy workshops of the south silent and abandoned, the people starving or flocking across the seas in search of the easily won gold that was ruining them; and when the coveted gold came to the few who survived the pursuit, it was lavished in insensate waste on the adornment of their outer persons—for they always fed frugally in that lean land—and most of the wealth left the country as fast as it entered it, the idleness it engendered being its net result to the country that won it.

For the next hundred years the same process went on. The monarch of Spain and the Indies was reduced to beg his subjects in the name of charity to provide food for himself and his family, whilst the mines of Peru and Mexico were sending millions. The splendour of the polished Court of Philip IV. was only rivalled by that of his nephew, the Grand Monarque, but it was soaked to the core in sloth and squalor, whilst the humbler people found the purchasing power of gold grow less and less as the metal poured in and the workers, dazzled by wealth so lightly won, ceased to produce commodities for consumption. Philip III. was a narrow bigot without his father's industry or intellect, but he was well-meaning and sorely beset, and was unequal to the propping up of the great empire into which his father's narrow and halting policy had introduced the dry rot. The regulation of dress, however, and the repression of profane extravagance was just the task which appealed to his tastes and sympathies, and he set about it as soon as he mounted the throne.

His pragmatic of 1600 was a new departure in many things and was the pattern of all similar enactments for the next hundred years. It is very minute, but a few of its provisions are worth preserving, as they throw much light on the tastes of the time. The King in his preamble sets forth that he is informed that the sumptuary pragmatics are quite disregarded, and seeing that the great excess and extravagance in dress constitutes a national scandal which must be moderated, he has conferred with his wisest councillors and has decided to issue a new pragmatic which shall supersede all previous ones.

To begin with, the following sweeping order is given: No one of whatever rank, except the King and his children, shall wear any sort of brocade or cloth of gold or silver, or stuff shot with gold or silver, or silk in which metal is woven. No cord, gimp, ornamental stitching or quilting, either of silk or metal, is to be permitted, excepting on religious vestments and uniforms, and no precious stones or pearls are to be worn on housings or accoutrements in any shape. There is an absolute prohibition of the employment of lute-string, twist, ruchings, flat braid, cording, chainlets, crewels, cross-stitching, through-stitching, tangle trimming, puffs, and any sort of bead or steel trimmings; and the following dress is alone prescribed: The cape or other over-garment may be of any sort of silk with stripes, on each edge of which may be an ornamental stitching. Surcoats and ropillas (a sort of half-tight over-jacket with double sleeves, the outer ones hanging loose from the shoulder) may be also of silk and trimmed in the same way, and, if desired, a piping of another sort of silk, but not the same, may be put between the stripes. The inside of the capes may have similar stripes of silk, satin, or taffety, but not velvet. Shoulder capes may be made of velvet, and the hoods of riding-cloaks or rain-capes may be lined with the same. Silk gimp and frogs may be sewn on to duffel cloaks, &c. The trunks may be worn of any kind of silk, and each slashing may be edged with a velvet or silk piping and an "eyelash" border. If the slashing is a wide one this edging may be worn on both sides of it, but if otherwise only on one side. The slashings may be lined with taffety. Silk gimp or braid of any sort may be worn on the trunks excepting lutestrings or crewels. Galligaskins may also be made of silk, but with no trimming but a row of gimp on each side and at the opening. Dressing-gowns for women and men may be of any material or fashion, so long as gold or silver is not used. Doublets, ropillas, or trunks made of satin may be ornamented by silk stitching of any colour, but on no account may the stuff be pinked, ravelled, or fringed. The rules generally apply to women as well as men, but the former are allowed to wear jackets of light cloth of gold or silver, which may be trimmed with a braid of the same over the seams, and the whole jacket may be covered with "whirligigs" or scrolls of gold or silver, so long as there is no working in the stuff

## A FIGHT AGAINST FINERY. 241

itself. The frills and flounces of these garments may also be ornamented in the same fashion. Hats, belts, baldricks, &c., were all treated in the same way; gold or silver gimp, braid, and lace were allowed to be sewn on, but not embroidered or woven in, the texture.

A rather curious point in this decree of 1600 is the distinction in it of different classes of citizens. Thus women of known evil life were allowed to wear what they liked inside the houses, but were to conform to the law in the streets; pages might dress in silk jackets, coats, trunks, and caps, but their capes were to be of cloth or frieze; no lackeys were to have silken clothes or velvet scabbards, but they were allowed to wear taffety caps. The punishments for the breaking the orders seem severe but unequal. Offending wearers were to lose the peccant garment and pay a sum equal to its value for pious uses, but tradesmen who made or sold the goods were to be condemned to four years' exile and a fine of twenty maravedis for a first offence, double the punishment for a second, and the pillory and ten years' exile from Spain for a third. All this sounds very severe, but there were plenty of ways out of it. For instance, garments already made might be worn for four years by men and six by women, although they were not in accordance with the law. This pragmatic was proclaimed with the usual ceremony by one of the Alcaldes de Casa y Corte with the sound of drum and trumpet in the High Street of Madrid on the 8th of June, 1600. The month must have been a busy one for the dignified officials in question; for during the first fortnight of it decrees regulating almost every conceivable subject were issued. The rigid and unpopular decree about courtesy titles was superseded, and nearly everybody of position might now be called Señoria. No gold or silver in any form was to be used in furniture or household decoration, "as the King is shocked at the waste of the estates of his subjects in such superfluities, and considers it high time that the money were employed in useful and necessary things." Velvet or silk might be employed in upholstery, but no gold or silver except a gold fringe on the edges. The same rule applied to the lining of carriages and litters, but no silk was to be used on the outside of vehicles.

The regulation of jewellery was just as minute and severe, and to judge from that which was in future to be allowed, the excess in this respect must have been very great, since after pages of prohibitions with regard to the fashions of jewellery, and the limitation of enamels and precious stones, men were still allowed to wear as many rings as they liked, chains and girdles of gold pieces, sets of cameos mounted in gold, and strings of pearls in their caps. The use of silver plate is also much limited, but still side-saddles might be made of silver, if plain, and the harness and horse-cloths covered with the same metal. Here, again, the same loophole for evasion was given; for all things already made were exempt if registered within six months.

Attempts were made at the same time, as on many subsequent occasions, to suppress the ostentatious promenading up and down the Calle Mayor, which grew more scandalous as the years went on, until it reached its apogee in the reign of Philip IV., and for which the taste has never yet quite died out. No women of loose life were to promenade in coaches, nor might coaches be hired for the purpose on pain of confiscation. No person but a grandee might have more than two torches carried before him under penalty of one hundred ducats fine, and if any person hired a lackey by the day, or for less than a month, he was to be put in the pillory and exiled for four years. The reasons for these regulations will be well understood by those who have studied the characteristic picaresque novels of the period, and have smiled at the amusing subterfuges adopted by impecunious scamps to pass themselves off as noble hidalgos, the better to prey upon their fellow-creatures.

Amongst other things Philip III. in his youthful zeal tried to deal with the vexed subject of ruffs. He made no attempt to stand against starch any longer—indeed, to judge from his portraits, no one ever wore such stiff or extensive ruffs as he did himself, but he sternly draws the line at trimming. There must be no lace edges or ravellings; they must be pure white, with two little pleats only, and not more than $4\frac{1}{2}$ inches wide, half as wide again as had been allowed by his father. For the next few years pragmatics positively rained in Madrid, altering, restricting, relaxing this or the other detail of the various decrees; but all to no purpose apparently, for in 1611 Philip came out with another long proclamation, saying that the extravagant abuse of dress being worse than ever, he has consulted discreet experts and has decided to alter the rules. The use of gold and silver thread and foil, and of coloured silks, is more restricted than ever, the only exceptions being for church vestments and the dresses of officers actually engaged in war. In other respects, however, the trimmings allowed appear to be exceedingly elaborate, and in the pragmatic of 1611 about a dozen different specimen trimmings of trunks alone are described with all the finnicking minuteness of a modern Court dressmaker's bill; the sum total of it all being that the employment of silk, velvet, and other fine stuffs, stamped and plain, was now almost unrestricted, whilst bullion was more severely forbidden than before, except for ladies' jackets and a few of their trimmings.

Another desperate attempt was made in the same year to restrict the unprofitable idling in the streets with carriages and an order was issued that no new coaches were to be made without a license from the President of the Council, and no man was to ride in a coach without leave, "as the King is informed that gentlemen are forgetting how to ride." Women also are to refrain from covering up their heads and faces, in order that they may be seen and recognised, and they may only be accompanied by their husbands, fathers, sons, or grandfathers. The girls of a family may ride in a coach without the mistress of it, and the owners of coaches may be accompanied by a friend, but with this exception no coach is to go out without its owner, and may not be lent, exchanged, or sold without special license.

Ruffs had now apparently become general with all classes, as a pragmatic was issued in 1611, saying that, notwithstanding the former prohibition of the use of long-lawn and muslin for ruffs, frills, and collars, poor people would insist upon wearing them, and they consequently might now be made of those cheaper materials as well as of fine linen.

In March, 1621, Philip III. died, leaving luxury and extravagance in his capital more rampant than ever, and Philip IV., a mere boy, at once set to work to grapple the evil with as much confidence as if he were the first to attempt it. If economy had ever been needed it was so now, for the public treasury was empty, the people ruined with oppressive taxation, ecclesiastical extortion and official peculation, and the country was rapidly becoming depopulated. A curious pamphlet is still in existence which contains a series of exhortations addressed to the King in the year of his accession by a noble member of the Cortes of Castile, setting forth the various evils from which the country was suffering, and proposing remedies for them.[1] There is much plain speaking and boldness on many matters therein, and, amongst others, on the eternal question of sumptuary extravagance. The representation on this subject has so direct a bearing upon what has already been said as to the inoperativeness of the pragmatics, that some of it is worth transcribing.

"Your subjects spend and waste great sums in their abuse of costly garb with so many varieties of trimmings that the making costs more than the garments themselves, and as soon as they are made there is a change of fashion and the money has to be spent over again. When they marry, the

[1] "Discursos y apuntamientos de Don Mateo de Lison y Biedma." Secretly printed in 1622.

vast wealth they squander on dress alone ruins them, and they are in debt for the rest of their lives ; and although this expenditure may be voluntary, it has become, so to speak, obligatory, and such is the excess that the wife of an artisan nowadays needs as much finery as a lady, even though she and her husband have to get the money for it by dishonest means, to the offence of God. Many weddings, indeed, are prevented by the excessive cost and the vassals are therefore unable to serve your Majesty as they ought. They are unable to pay their debts, the costs incurred in the recovery of which still further reduce their fortunes. . . . As for collars also, the disorder in their use is very great, for a single one of linen, with its making and ravelling, will cost over 200 reals, and six reals every time it is goffered, which at the end of the year doubles the cost of them and much money is thus wasted. Besides this, many strong young men are employed in goffering them, who might be better employed in work necessary for the commonwealth or in tilling the soil. The servants, too, have to be paid higher wages in respect of the money they have to spend in collars, which consumes most of what they earn, and a great quantity of wheat is wasted in starch, which is wanted for food. In addition to this, the fine linens to make these collars are brought from abroad, and money has to be sent out of the country to pay for them. With respect to coaches, great evil is caused and offence given to God, seeing the disquiet they bring to the women who own them, as they never stay at home but leave their children and servants to run riot with the bad example of the mistress being always abroad. The praiseworthy and necessary art of horsemanship too is dying out, and those who ought to be mounted crowd, six or eight of them together in a carriage, talking to wenches rather than learning how to ride. It must be evident how different gentlemen must grow up who have all their lives been rolling about in coaches instead of riding, besides which the breed of horses is deteriorating and money is being squandered by the keeping of coaches often by people of moderate means who can ill afford it but who are over-persuaded by their wives, who say that because So-and-so, who is no better off than they, have a coach they must have one as well, and so the bad example spreads."

Don Mateo proposed some very drastic remedies, and, whether in consequence of this or not, the King and his favourite, the masterful Count-Duke of Olivares, put their heads together during the first few weeks of the reign, and came out with tremendous series of pragmatics repeating the most stringent provisions of the decree of 1611 with regard to the use of gold or silver, either in dress, furniture, saddlery, or upholstery. No trimmings were to be allowed of any sort, and no silk capes, cloaks, or overalls were to be worn, cloth, frieze, and duffel being substituted in those garments. Above all Don Mateo's suggestion about the ruffs was adopted. No person was permitted, on pain of the pillory and exile, to pleat or goffer linen in any shape. Starch was placed in the *index expurgatoris* again, and ruffs were to be for ever suppressed in favour of the large, square, flat Walloon collar, which fell over the shoulders and breast like a bib.

The expenses of the palace were cut down to

a minimum, and Philip himself, the most prodigal and lavish of men in after years, went on short commons. Amongst other efforts at economy made by him one originated a fashion which became deeply rooted in the Spanish character, and which the Italian minister of another Philip—the Frenchman—a hundred years afterwards, said had a large share in making Spaniards the leisurely and dignified people they were. The wide, falling Walloon collar, with little or no stiffening,—as will be seen in portraits of the time—was apt to wrinkle round the neck and very soon became dirty; so an ingenious tailor in the Calle Mayor submitted to the young King and his brother Carlos a new device, consisting of a high square collar of cardboard covered with light-coloured silk inside and with the same stuff as the doublet outside. By means of heated rollers and shellac the cardboard was permanently moulded into a graceful curve which bent outwards at the height of the chin.[1] Philip was pleased with the novelty and ordered some of the new "golillas," as they were called, for himself and his brother. The tailor, in high glee, went to his shop to make them, but alas! heated rollers turned with handles and smoking pots of shellac were suspicious things in those days, and the spies of the Council promptly haled the tailor and his uncanny instruments before the President, who sagely decided that there was some devilish witchcraft behind it all; and if not—well, the accursed

[1] As first invented, the golilla opened in front, as shown in the portrait of Quevedo, facing page 256, but later, when the hair was worn long, it was made square in front and was fastened behind, as shown in the portrait of Charles the Bewitched.

things he was making were lined with light blue silk in violation of the pragmatic, so he must be punished anyhow. A bonfire was made of the poor man's stock before his door and he was put under lock and key; but when Olivares heard of it he was furious. He and the Duke of Infantado sent for the President and rated him soundly as a meddling old fool for burning the King's new collars. The President declared his ignorance that they were for the King, but pointed out how outrageous they were in shape, and how they sinned against the pragmatic; but he was soon silenced by the Count-Duke, who told him they were the best and most economical things ever invented, as they did away with the need for constant washing of collars, and would last ten years without further expense or trouble.

The golilla "caught on" with high and low. It is true that heads had to be carried stiffly and turned slowly, but Spanish heads were intended so to be used and no complaint was made. No more pragmatics against ruffs, moreover, were ever needed again, and the costly, cumbrous fashion went out for good. This was in 1623, the same year as Charles Stuart went on his hairbrained trip to Madrid, and during his stay all the pragmatics were suspended, in order that he might see how splendid the Madrileños could be if left to themselves. They did their best to sustain their reputation and the poverty-stricken country was again plunged into the maddest vortex of prodigality that even dissolute Madrid had ever seen, and flaunting Buckingham himself was outshone in brilliancy and lavishness by the nobles of Philip's Court. The strict law of Charles V. limiting the wearing of jewellery and precious stones had been re-imposed, but the list of gems displayed, given, and received as presents during Charles' visit, and the sumptuous dresses worn, has been left on record, down to the smallest detail, by one of the King's attendants ;[1] and shows an inconceivable lavishness which naturally would, and did, make it difficult to revert in Madrid to the severe orders of the pragmatics again.

The tendency of the time, however, was against barbaric spendour, and gradually the taste for gold and silver tissues and embroideries in civil costume was modifying itself, but new extravagancies sprang up as old ones languished. Philip's sister Anna had married Louis XIII. of France in 1615 with great pomp, and all the Spanish Court had assembled on the historic ford of the Bidasoa which marked the French frontier. They brought back some new fashions with them, caught from the Parisians. Since Charles V., for good reasons, was obliged to have his curls cropped at Barcelona, Spaniards of all classes had worn the hair short, and parted as it is in England at present. The French wore it longer and the Spaniards now followed their lead. But not all at once. They first adopted the mode of having two ugly locks like long, limp Newgate-knockers, called "guedejas," hanging before the ears, the back of the head being cropped and the top surmounted by a twist or curl called a "copete." In the early portraits of Philip IV. this style of headdress may be seen.

[1] Manuscript of Don Diego de Soto y Aguilar in the Royal Academy of History in Madrid, transcript in the author's possession.

Another fashion brought from France was much more objectionable, but took a stronger hold in Spain than elsewhere. Round hoop-skirts or farthingales had been common in most parts of Europe for over fifty years before, but the new refinement, called a "guarda-infante," was a very large farthingale flattened back and front so as to stick out inordinately at the sides, particularly at the hips. The jaunty Madrileñas added to it a new feature, which made it worse than ever, namely, a metal section or facing to the bottom hoop which resounded against a similar plate on the heels of their clogs, or clanked upon the ground, so that a musical clickety-click accompanied them wherever they went; even as it did that aged equestrienne of Banbury famed in English nursery lore. As the bold wenches minced along they prided themselves upon the eccentric or rhythmical effects they produced. They would be neither shamed, coerced, nor persuaded to abandon the foolish caprice until they tired of it themselves, but Don Philip did his best by pragmatics to suppress it. In 1639 the famous fulmination against female extravagance in dress was issued, part of which ran as follows:

"His Majesty orders that no woman, whatever her quality, shall wear a guarda-infante; which is a costly, superfluous, painful, ugly, disproportionate, lascivious, indecent article of dress, giving rise to sin on the part of the wearers and on that of men for their sakes. The only exception to this rule shall be public prostitutes.

"No skirts shall consist of more than eight yards of silk or a proportionate quantity of other stuff, nor shall they measure more than four yards round; the same rule shall apply to polonaises, over-skirts, hen-coop skirts and petticoats.

"No woman wearing shoes shall have a bottom hoop, farthingale, or anything else in the skirt for the purpose of making a noise, and bottom hoops or farthingales shall not be worn except with pattens at least five inches high.

"No woman shall wear low-cut bodices except women of known evil life. Any person guilty of infraction of this pragmatic shall lose the offending article of dress and pay a fine of 20,000 maravedis for the first offence, and for the second double that amount, with exile from the Court."

The unfortunate dressmakers who made the garments were to be much more severely punished than the fair wearers, and four years' penal servitude was their sentence for a second offence.

The offended Madrileñas did not put up tamely with such tyranny, and, led by three frisky damsels, the daughters of a famous judge, they came out the day after the pragmatic was proclaimed, swaggering and jingling up and down the Prado in the widest guarda-infantes, the most outrageous farthingales, and the noisiest of hoops; and dared the scandalised alguaciles to touch them, since they could hardly arrest all the rank and beauty of the Court; and the fair ones practically had their own way, for Philip only issued a grave and sorrowful remonstrance against the indelicacy and expense of their constantly changing caprices, and begging them to conform to their duty. But they pleased themselves as usual, although it is said that their three fair ringleaders did no go quite scot-free, as their father the judge, scandalised that his own daughters should be the first to break the law, condemned them to dress in nun's garb of the coarsest frieze. Nothing daunted, the recalcitrant "Gilimonas,"[1] as they were called, managed, with nods and winks and frisking skirts, to look more deliciously provocative than ever in their penitential garb, and their pastors and masters were glad enough to get them back again into their clicking farthingales to avoid the scandal.

Nor were the gallants of the other sex more submissive about their lovelocks. An order was proclaimed at the same time, saying, "His Majesty orders that no man shall wear a topknot, or lovelock before the ears, or any curls upon his head —and barbers who dress the hair in this fashion shall be fined 200 maravedis and be imprisoned for 10 days." Men who wore the offending curls were to be excluded from Court and all public offices. "Liars' Parade" was as much upset about this as about titles, and made a desperate attempt to resist. It was in the very heyday of poetry in Spain— Calderon, Lope de Vega, Quevedo, and a host of others were for ever firing off poetical squibs and satires at the foibles of the age, the "Liars' Parade" being the central exchange for the "good things" of poets, big and little, from the monarch downwards. A cloud of barbed poetical arrows from scores of poetical bows were consequently shot at the royal decree against topknots and guedejas; and ridicule and satire were poured out unsparingly upon those who were responsible for it. But to be shut out from the presence of king and ministers, to have the public service closed against them, was

[1] Their father's name was Gil Imon de la Mota.

too hard to be borne by the noble swaggerers and kept poets of the Calle Mayor, so they gave way and took to the long, lank, straight hair all round, which Philip himself wore for the rest of his life, though others, particularly away from the Court, still clung to the guedejas and short backhair.

When Philip IV. had been gathered to his fathers in the jasper vault of the Escorial, and his sickly son had married a French princess, Spain began to conform its fashions to those which ruled in the Court of the Roi-soleil, but somehow the three-cornered plumed hat, so general in France and England, never became popular in Spain. The large flap-brimmed hat with feathers still lingered when the Queen Regent Mariana, during her rivalry with her bold step-son, Don Juan José of Austria, raised a regiment of Swiss and German mercenaries. These soldiers wore a very broad-brimmed hat, flat all round, and slightly turned up at the edge, much like the wideawakes of to-day. This hat caught the fancy of the Spaniards, who dubbed it "Chambergo," a Spanish variant of "Schomberg," after whom the regiment was called, and this hat has to this day never lost its hold upon the Spanish populace, although they had to raise a revolution to keep it, as will be related presently.

A very absurd craze at the end of the seventeenth century, which official remonstrance was powerless to put down, was the universal wearing of great horn-rimmed spectacles, such as may be seen in the portrait of Quevedo, facing page 256; men and women of fashion insisted upon wearing these ugly appendages, whether they needed them or not, and literary fashion though it was in a litterary age, much sport was given to the poetasters in attacking it.

By the time Charles the Bewitched had grown up, French fashion ruled in Madrid, with the sole exceptions of the golilla (somewhat changed in shape to suit the long backhair) and the round-brimmed hat, which resisted all attempts to displace them; but the old vice of extravagance still continued in spite of changed fashions, and in 1674 a pragmatic was issued deploring again the costly excess in dress, the abuse of adornment of equipages, and the idle luxury of the time. The severe decrees of Philip IV. are re-enacted, and a code of permissible dress laid down, in which velvets, silks, satins, taffeties, of all colours, stamped and plain, are allowed, but foreign textures are to be equal in weight and fineness to Spanish goods.

The pragmatics now, however, had altered their tone. They were exhortatory rather than comminatory during the last years of the House of Austria. A change came with the advent of the first Bourbon Philip V. The Spaniards were sensitive, and resented the inferiority implied by the adoption by the Court and society of the French fashions, high heels, wide-skirted coats, full-bottomed wigs, and the rest; so the mass of the people clung to their cropped backhair, their broad-brimmed hats, long cloaks, and above all their stately stiffened "golillas." Philip was too wise to run atilt against the golilla at first, and indeed adopted it himself, as may be seen in his portrait as a youth in the Louvre. But he wrote an anonymous pamphlet against it, and lost no opportunity of pointing out its unfitness for working people and soldiers. Alberoni, with his caustic

Italian wit, was for ever sneering at it, so that when Philip abandoned it and took to a collar and white lace cravat public opinion was prepared for the change and the golilla fell, after a reign of a hundred years.

When Philip was firm upon his throne after his long struggle, he issued a pragmatic, in 1723, once more trying to stem the tide of extravagance, precisely as if it had never been tried and failed before. No gold or silver either in texture or trimming was to be worn. No gold, glass, pearl, or steel buttons were to be allowed. No precious stones, real or false, might be used in trimming or fastenings, there were to be no foreign ornaments, and sham gems and jewellery were strictly prohibited. No silk might be worn but such as was of Spanish manufacture. Servants were to be clothed in plain cloth and woollen stockings, and no person but a grandee was allowed to keep more than two lackeys; and no silk was to be used on harness or the outside of coaches. No person might drive more than four horses in the capital, and no lawyer, notary, or tradesman was permitted to keep a coach. Doctors and priests alone might ride a pacing mule, all other men were bidden to mount horses only. Artisans and workmen were to dress exclusively in baize, serge, or frieze; their cuffs alone might be of silk. The pains and penalties in this great pragmatic were many and severe, but the decree aimed at doing too much. So many fine and delicate doubtful points arose with regard to its provisions, that for years after fresh proclamations were constantly being made to elucidate this pragmatic of 1723; and through the many loopholes offenders escaped, and the act became a dead letter.

VELASQUEZ, Pinxt.

FRANCISCO DE QUEVEDO VILLEGAS
*from the collection of his Grace the Duke of Wellington.*

Indeed, sumptuary laws were already growing out of date, even in Spain; the courtiers copied the latest fashions from Paris, and the common people, more out of patriotism and mute resentment than anything else, made their cloaks longer and longer and their hats wider and wider. The long ends of the cloaks had to be put out of the way somehow, so they were thrown across the face to the opposite shoulder, and, what with the broad-brim over the brow and the cloak over the mouth, none of the face was seen but the eyes.

Spain during the greater part of the eighteenth century had the ill-fortune to be governed by foreign ministers, mostly Italians, and one after the other they tried to cut stubborn Spain to the same pattern as the rest of the world. The more they tried the more sulky and determined became the people, and it resolved itself into a national article of faith to resist all change; things Spanish being better than things elsewhere. When Philip's younger son, Charles III., came from Naples to rule them he brought with him his Neapolitan ministers. Grimaldi said that the Spaniards all looked like conspirators slinking about in the darkness with their covered faces. An attempt was made to light the streets with oil-lamps, but the people resented such a foolish foreign fad, and smashed the lamps as fast as they were put up. The offenders could not be identified with their covered faces and slouch hats, so the King was persuaded by the Marquis of Squillaci (Esquilache, as the Spaniards called him) to issue a new pragmatic. Its tone was more one of sorrow than of anger. The King was shocked for foreigners to see such a boorish fashion in his capital, and had determined that in future no long cloaks or round-brimmed hats were to be worn. Either a short cape or a skirted coat was allowed, and men might wear either their own hair or a wig, but they must cover it with a three-cornered hat and not a Chambergo, and the face must not be hidden in any way.

This order was proclaimed on the 4th of March, 1766, and police were posted in the principal places with shears to curtail cloaks and lop hat-brims. It happened that a man pursued by alguaciles for wearing the forbidden garments took refuge in the precincts of the church of the Trinity, where he was followed by the officers and beaten, in defiance of sanctuary. An infuriated crowd collected and overpowered the authorities, who were dismayed at the feeling evinced, and withdrew their men. For the next few days men all over Madrid ostentatiously flaunted their cloaks and broad-brims before the barracks and police posts, and there is no doubt that the feeling was taken advantage by politicians for their own ends to goad the people to fury against the Italian ministers. Matters came to a head on the 23rd of March, when a soldier attempted to seize a man with his face covered. A crowd, ready for mischief, collected immediately, and the authorities were overpowered. The mob swept up the Calle de Leon across the Calle de Alcalá to Squillaci's house (the famous "house with the seven chimneys") which they wrecked, although the minister had fled. With broad-brimmed hats on the top of poles they scoured the streets, making all men they met uncock their hats. Overpowering all resistance, they assembled before the palace. The guards used force in vain, and that night the capital was in the hands of the mob. The gaols were opened, houses wrecked, foreigners assailed and killed, the King's Walloon Guard especially being singled out for vengeance. Squillaci and Grimaldi had fled, and the Spanish ministers, either out of timidity or sympathy, practically sided with the rioters. The rising spread rapidly to the provinces, old grievances were raked up again, and a dangerous revolution was in progress, when the King surrendered unconditionally. People were to wear what they pleased, food and oil were to be reduced in price, and the Italian ministers were smuggled away, never to return.

That practically ended the fight for sumptuary control. Finery was triumphant in the long struggle, and the strong arm of authority was obliged to confess itself powerless to dictate on the question of personal adornment. Half-hearted attempts were made after this to interfere in sumptuary matters by Spanish sovereigns, but the effects of their decrees were hardly felt outside their own households. In 1780, for instance, a pragmatic as severe in form as ever was issued, minutely regulating the wearing of mourning and prohibiting mourning coaches, but little notice was taken of it after the first few weeks; and later still a curious mild little decree was issued by Charles IV. limiting the number of dishes which, according to custom, many officials were entitled to receive daily from the royal kitchens. It is a long drop from Alfonso the Wise to the silly dodderer who handed over his kingdom to Napoleon because his son had offended him; but the same feeling, almost the same phraseology, pervades the first pragmatic we have quoted and the last. Both deplore the lavishness and luxury of the people, and exhort them to correct the excess and superfluity which characterises their tables; and in both of them the King promises that he himself will rigidly conform to his own decree and reform the extravagance of his private repasts.

Custom, taste, and perhaps necessity, have done what five hundred years of "pragmatics" failed to do. The Spaniards are the most sober and frugal-feeding nation in Europe, and certainly do not exceed in the matter of gaudy or ostentatious raiment. The only traits left to them perhaps by the extravagant old fashions we have described, are their consuming love for driving about the streets in a fine carriage, however much they may stint in all else; and the grave stiff-necked dignity which a century of the golilla left behind it.

*A PALACE IN THE STRAND.*

## A PALACE IN THE STRAND.[1]

PROBABLY not one person out of a thousand of those who hurry along the busiest part of the Strand notices even the existence of a closed iron gate by the side of a public-house opposite the Vaudeville Theatre. If you peer through the grating you will only see a dark, narrow court, now blocked up by the building operations connected with the Hotel Cecil, and you will have no difficulty in coming to the conclusion that this avenue, which has been gradually going down in the world for the last two centuries, is destined before very long to be blotted out altogether. For this was an important thoroughfare once, called Ivy Lane, one of the three public roadways by which access was obtained from the Strand to the river and the boats, the other two being Milford Lane and Strand Lane, the entrance to which latter still exists, a mere passage between two shops opposite Catherine Street. Down the centre of Ivy Lane ran a brook, over which the roadway of the Strand was carried by a bridge called Ivy Bridge. This lane, which separates the liberty of the Duchy of Lancaster from the city of

[1] *The Fortnightly Review*, September, 1893.

Westminster, ran sloping down to the river between the garden walls of two of the great Strand palaces which, erected, as they all were at first, by bishops, were subsequently grabbed by kings and courtiers for their own use. To the east stood, on the Savoy demesne, the house of the Bishop of Carlisle, which was granted to the Elizabethan Earl of Bedford, and subsequently came into the possession, by exchange, of Robert Cecil, afterwards the first Earl of Salisbury, second son of the great Burleigh, whose own house stood nearly opposite, on the site of Exeter Hall; and on the west, covering all the space now occupied by the Adelphi as far as Coutts' bank, there rose the ancient mansion which for centuries was the town palace of the prince-bishops of Durham, known to history as Durham Place.

In the lawless times, when these mansions were first founded, it would have been dangerous for any but ecclesiastics to have resided outside of the protection afforded by the City boundaries, and so it came about that all the way from the Temple to Whitehall, along the banks of the silent highway, which then was the principal thoroughfare of London, there ran a string of bishops' palaces and religious foundations. Their outhouses and stable gates opened on to the rough country road we still call the Strand—a road which even in the time of Mary, we are told, was filthy and unseemly, and remained so, indeed, until the great nobles made these palaces their homes. Many books have been written about the Aldelphi and its site, and Durham Place, which was by far the most important of the Strand palaces until the Protector built Somerset House, has come in for its own full share of notice, but the writers

## A PALACE IN THE STRAND.

upon the subject have copied each other with slavish fidelity, errors and all. The same set of facts and assumptions has invariably done duty in all descriptions of Durham Place. I wish in the present article to break new ground, and relate some hitherto unnoticed episodes in its history.

Stow has not much to tell of Durham Place, except of the great festival of 1540, when the future rivals, Dudley and Seymour, with Poynings, Carew, Kingston, and Richard Cromwell, challenged all Europe to a tourney, and held open house with regal lavishness for a week at Durham Place, lent to them for the purpose by the King, who rewarded each of them, moreover, with an income for ever of a hundred marks a year and a house out of the plunder of the Hospital of St. John of Jerusalem. The State Papers now and again give us a ray of side-light on the history of Durham Place. We know how Somerset granted it to Elizabeth for her life after he had beheaded his brother, who there had coined the doubloons with which he thought to bribe his way to the throne. We know on Somerset's fall how jealous Northumberland gave to the Princess the great unfinished palace of the dead Protector, and took for his own town house Durham Place, in which, although it was nominally hers, she had never lived. We know something, but not much, of the fastuous splendour of Dudley's life during the three years he lived here, of Jane Grey's ill-starred wedding in the house, of the plotting of her father-in-law, verily a lath painted like a sword, and the weaker time-servers around him, to perpetuate their rule and confirm them in their ill-gotten gains, of the pitiably crumbling down of the house of cards when the supreme moment came; and how Northumberland went forth from the Tower to the scaffold, never to see Durham Place again, hoping in his craven soul, till the axe fell, that his abject recantation would purchase his worthless life.

The Egerton Papers (Camden Society) tell us somewhat in detail of the arbitrary expulsion of Raleigh from Durham Place, where, by the grace of his mistress, he had lived happily and splendidly for nearly twenty years. These facts and some others in the subsequent history of the house are recited by every writer who has touched upon the subject, and I have no desire to repeat at length incidents which are already well known. One error into which most writers have fallen has been to jump at the conclusion that whenever recorded history is silent on the subject of Durham Place, the house reverted to the possession of the See of Durham. Such does not appear to me to have been the case. It is usually asserted that Henry VIII. first took possession of the house by forcing the Bishop, Cuthbert Tunstal, to exchange his palace for some other property. This is founded on Stow's statement that Cold Harbour, in Thames Street, was granted to the Bishop because of "his house near Charing Cross being taken into the King's hands, Cuthbert Tunstal was lodged in this Cold Harbour." It is certain, however, that Katherine of Aragon lived here during her widowhood, before Henry VIII. came to the throne, as many of her letters to her father in Spain are in existence dated from this house, ranging over several years prior to her marriage with Henry in 1509. On the very year of Mary's death Cuthbert Tunstal wrote a letter [1] to Cardinal Pole thanking him for obtaining for him the *reversion* of the house ; [1] and it is usually assumed from this that he actually entered into possession of it. But he did not; and it is the story of Durham Place during this time, namely, the last years of Mary and the first few years of Elizabeth, that I wish to tell.

The historians of the house generally make short work of the matter by saying, "When Elizabeth came to the throne Tunstal was again driven from this house, and about 1583 Elizabeth granted it to its greatest tenant, the glorious Raleigh." [2] In all probability Tunstal only lived in the house a short time if at all. He was appointed to the See in 1530, and in 1540, as we know by Stow's description of the already-mentioned festival, Durham Place was a royal house, and so it remained until 1603, when Lord Salisbury used Toby Matthew, Bishop of Durham, as his catspaw to claim it, in order that he might filch the best part of it—the Strand frontage —for himself, which he did to his own great profit. In any case, it is certain that Tunstal never got the house back again from Mary or Cardinal Pole, whatever promises may have been made to him.

Of the few Spanish nobles of high rank who stayed with Philip II. during the whole of his residence in England after his marriage with Queen Mary, one was Gomez Suarez de Figueroa, Count de Feria, a prime favourite and close friend of Philip. This nobleman had fallen deeply in love with Miss Jane Dormer, one of Mary's maids of

[1] Calender of State Papers, 1547-1580, p. 105.
[2] "The Adelphi and its Site," by H. B. Wheatley, F.S.A.

honour, and married her, and although the secret of the union had been well kept, circumstances made it necessary to openly avow it before the King and his suite left London for Flanders in September, 1555. Feria was again in London with the King in March, 1557, for a few months, but in January, 1558, he came back in another capacity. The war was going badly for Philip and England. The French had taken Calais, and Guines was on the point of falling; if the contest was to be carried on at all more money and more men must be squeezed out of unwilling England, or otherwise peace must be made, with England for a scapegoat. Philip could not come himself, so he sent his haughty, overbearing favourite Feria as his ambassador to bully and bribe the English courtiers and coerce the sorely beset Queen. He came with a large train of servants and with great magnificence; his English wife, a country knight's daughter only as she was, as proud as himself; and he was granted the use of Durham Place, furnished from the Queen's own house, as other great ambassadors had been granted it before him. Egmont had been lodged there with his splendid train in January, 1554, when he had come to offer Philip's hand to Mary. Chatillon, the French ambassador, too, had been given the use of the house during his short embassy in 1550, so that there was nothing extraordinary in the granting of the house to Feria. Only that former ambassadors had stayed for a few weeks, whereas Feria and his successor remained in possession for five years and a half, and made of Durham Place a trysting-place for treason during the most of that time.

## A PALACE IN THE STRAND. 269

Whilst Elizabeth was striving against terrible odds with all her subtle statecraft to lay the foundation of a united nation on the broken elements of civil and religious discord, her task was hourly rendered more difficult by the plots hatched in her own house at Durham Place. All the disaffected and discontented found a welcome there; emissaries from Shan O'Neil flitted backwards and forwards at night by the river gate. Stukeley whispered here his willingness to desert with the Queen's ships to the King of Spain, and here Hawkins himself humbly begged to be bought. Lady Sidney, Robert Dudley's sister, Dudley himself, Arundel, Lumley, Montague, and Winchester found in the secret rooms at Durham Place open but discreet ears to listen to their plans for preventing the establishment of Protestantism in England, and for bringing the country again under the sway of the Pope. Madcap Arthur Pole appealed first to Durham Place when he wanted aid for his silly plot in favour of Mary Stuart, and long-headed Lethington came at dead of night by the silent river on a similar but far more serious errand. The publication of the correspondence of the Spanish ambassadors in England during the reign of Elizabeth (Rolls Series) adds many interesting pages to the history of Durham Place, and renders the memories of the house more important than ever to the students of the Reformation period in England.

Feria arrived in London and took up his residence at Durham Place on the 26th of January, 1558, having, as he says, lingered on the way in order not to bring the unwelcome news of the surrender of Guines by the English, which news had crossed the Channel with him. In addition to Durham Place, where he and his household were lodged, he had the same privileges as to an apartment in the Queen's palace as those which appertained to an English Privy Councillor—privileges which he tried hard to have confirmed to him by the new Queen when Mary died, in order, as he says, that he might keep his foot in the place and spy out what was going on. But Elizabeth and Cecil knew full well what his object was, and were quite shocked at the idea of the representative of a possible suitor for her hand sleeping under the same roof as the maiden Queen, so Feria had to depend upon his paid agents in the palace, and even in the Council itself, to bring him news to Durham Place of what was going on.

With the evidence now before us we can form an approximate idea of the appearance of Durham Place at the time. The Strand was a rough, unpaved road, with a fringe of shops and taverns on the northern side, whilst on the south side were the back walls and outer courts of the riverine mansions. The principal land gateway of Durham Place stood exactly opposite the spot now occupied by the Adelphi Theatre. The English custodian or porter, who was in the pay of the Queen, had his dwelling just inside the gate, where he could spy those who went in and out on the land side. On each side of the gate in the outer courtyard were stables and outhouses, and in and around the gateway in the street were benches where idlers and hangers-on sat and lounged through the day gossiping, in various tongues, and boasting of the prowess of their respective countrymen. On the other side of the street, nearly opposite, was a tavern called the "Chequers,"[1] which drove a roaring trade with the men-at-arms, Court-danglers, and serving-men who were constantly passing to and from Whitehall and St. James'. Opposite the gateway, across the large outer courtyard, was the door of the great hall, generally standing open for the neighbours to pass through[2] it to the inner or smaller courtyard, in which stood a water conduit fed by a "spring of fairwater in Covent Garden."[3] Beyond this inner courtyard stood the house itself at the bottom of the slope on the bank of the river at the spot now occupied by the arches that support Adelphi Terrace. It was a castellated structure, with its water-gate placed in the middle of the curtain between two turrets, and leading not, as usually was the case, through a garden, but straight from the steps into the house itself by an enclosed pent-house doorway. The domestic offices, and probably the chapel, were on the ground floor, but the principal dwelling-rooms were all upstairs and in the turrets. Aubrey, in his letters (vol. iii. 573), thus speaks of Raleigh's occupancy of one of these turrets: "Durham House was a noble palace. After he came to his greatness, he lived there or in some apartment of it. I well remember his study, which was on a little turret that looked into and over the

[1] It was afterwards called the "Queen's Head," and here Old Parr lodged when he came to London.
[2] In the next century, when the Strand front was built over, the parishioners wanted this hall for a church for St. Martin's parish, the hall, they said, being only used as a passage.
[3] A century later the water of this spring was found to be foul, and, as its source had been forgotten, an examination was made. The spring was rediscovered under a cellar of a house in Covent Garden.

Thames, and had a prospect which is as pleasant as any in the world."

The water-gate of the house was not the only approach to the river, as there was a space with trees on each side of the house, with a dwarf wall fronting the water, and a descent on one side by which the neighbours were allowed to get water from the stream for washing and similar purposes. It will thus be seen that the only really private part was the house itself between the inner courtyard and the river; the great hall and both courtyards being practically open to the public under the supervision of the custodian at the outer gate, who was responsible only to the Queen, and was a constant source of friction with the foreign occupants of the house.

Feria stayed at Durham Place until August, 1558, taking an active part in the distracted Councils of the Queen; and then, having found that Mary's hopes of an heir were again fallacious, and having bullied and frightened the Queen and Council into raising all the money they could beg or borrow for Philip's service, he went back to Flanders, leaving his English wife in London, with a Flemish and a Spanish ambassador of lower rank than himself to represent his master. But when Mary was known to be dying, he posted back again to be on the spot when the great change took place, and Durham Place was avoided like a plague-spot thenceforward for many days by the courtiers and time-servers who wished to stand well with the new Queen.

The proud Spaniard repaid distrust by bitter resentment, and soon found that his arrogance made him unfit instrument for cajolery. So he sent for a softer spoken diplomatist to act as his "tender," and the wily, silken Bishop of Aquila became his guest at Durham Place. Feria could not for long brook the need of paying supple court to the people over whom he had ridden roughshod, and an excuse was soon found by which he might be withdrawn without an open confession of his unfitness, and in May, 1559, he left Durham Place for good, leaving his English Countess and the Bishop of Aquila in possession.

At Dover he met Baron Ravenstein, who was coming from the Emperor to offer the hand of the Archduke Charles to Elizabeth, and as such a match would only have subserved Spanish interests if it had been effected by the aid of Spanish diplomacy, Feria asked the German to become his guest at Durham Place, which he did, and was made much of by the Countess and the Bishop. But he wore out his welcome very soon, particularly with the latter, a portion of whose apartments he occupied, and the Bishop sneers at him for his constant attendance at Mass. "He is quite a good fellow," he says, "but surely this must be the first negotiation he ever conducted in his life." The Countess soon came to high words with the new Queen, and in a month or so left Durham Place in a dudgeon to join her husband in Flanders, thenceforward to see England no more. With her went, in addition to her escort, Don Juan de Ayala, her grandmother, Lady Dormer, and that Mistress Susan Clarencis who was Queen Mary's most devoted attendant. From that time, namely, July, 1559, the Bishop was temporary master of Durham Place by favour of the Queen, against whom he never ceased to intrigue as far as he dared.

We have already glanced at the structure of the house itself; it may be now interesting to give some account of the household of the Bishop, which may probably be considered a typical one. First there was a chaplain at three crowns a month and his board, a chief secretary at twelve crowns a month, a chamberlain, two or three gentlemen-in-waiting, a groom-of-the-chambers, and six pages—all without any fixed wage, but who lived on promises, perquisites, and what they could pick up, eating, however, at the Bishop's expense, and mostly clothed by him. Then there were two couriers at three shillings a month, which they rarely got; a cook, a buyer, a butler, and a pantryman, at a crown a month each; two cantineers, two "lacqueys," two Irish grooms, and two washerwomen at nominal wages of from three to five shillings a month when they could get them, which was very uncertain. Small as the wages seem to us, the expense of the establishment was very great, as these people and a host of friends and hangers-on were fed roughly but abundantly at the Bishop's cost, the humbler sort eating in the great hall and the gentlemen of the household in the upper chambers.

The Bishop had hardly been in possession of the house for a year when Challoner, the English Ambassador in Spain, warned Cecil that the "crafty old fox" was getting to know too much about what went on at Court, and that some decent excuse should be sought for turning him out from so advantageous a coign of vantage as Durham Place, with its water-gate and its close proximity to the palace, whence spies and courtiers might come and go secretly, as we now know they did, at all hours for the information of the King of Spain's Ambassador. We may be sure that the hint was not lost on Cecil, but the Bishop was cunning, and to turn him out without good ostensible cause would have been too risky at a time when Philip's future action was still uncertain. So the Queen's porter in charge of the house was told to take careful note of those who went in and out by the Strand gate, and particularly those who attended Mass in the Ambassador's chapel. But still the weak point in the position was the water-gate, the key of which always remained in the possession of the Bishop or his major-domo. Various stratagems were resorted to by the English porter to obtain possession of it, but in vain, and more decided measures had at last to be taken. The Bishop's confidential secretary, an Italian named Borghese, was bribed by Cecil to tell all he knew of his master's practices, and great promises of high position and a rich marriage in England were held out to him as a further reward for his treachery. This made him arrogant and boastful, and led to a slashing match with the Bishop's Italian gentleman-in-waiting, whom Borghese nearly killed. He boasted that he had friends at Court, snapped his fingers at the officers of the law and at the Bishop's cajolery and threats, made a clean breast of it to Cecil, and things began to look bad for his late master. Dr. Wotton, a member of the Privy Council, went to Durham Place, and gravely formulated a series of complaints founded on the secretary's information. Most of these complaints were trivial, being to the effect that the Bishop had said and written various depreciatory things against the Queen: but one accusation was serious, namely, than Shan O'Neil had taken the Sacrament at Durham Place, which was true, although the ecclesiastical diplomatist solemnly denied it.

The Bishop was nearly beside himself with rage and chagrin, and begged plaintively to be relieved from his irksome post among heretics such as these. But all in vain. It did not suit the Queen and Cecil for the moment to perpetrate the last indignity of turning him out of the house, but after this they kept a closer watch upon him than ever and bode their time. They had not to wait long. There were four French hostages in London, held in pledge for the due fulfilment of the Treaty of Château Cambresis, and very troublesome guests they were.

The most turbulent of them was a certain Nantouillet, Provost of Paris, a fanatical Catholic and partisan of the Guises. He had for some reason or another conceived a grudge against a mercenary captain called Masino, who was in the pay of the Vidame de Chartres, a Huguenot nobleman. So, in the manner of the times, he sought to have him killed, and, seeking for an instrument, he came across a young lad of bad character called Andrea, who was a servant of a lute player at Court, Alfonso the Bolognese. To this lad the Provost gave a dagger and a coat of mail, and promised a reward of a hundred crowns if he killed Masino. Andrea left his musical master and hung about the Strand door of Durham Place for several days at the beginning of January, 1563. At meal times he went into the great hall as others did and ate his fill, and then lounged outside on the benches again.

At last, in the dusk of the afternoon of the 3rd of January, 1563, Captain Masino came swaggering up the Strand on his way to Whitehall, and Andrea fired at him point blank, at a foot distance, with a harquebuss. But the captain's swagger saved his life, for the bullet passed between his left arm and his body, making a hole through his swinging cape and burning his doublet, and then glanced off into a shop on the other side of the way, "and came near killing an honest Englishman therein." Out came the swashbuckler's long rapier, and off ran the assassin into the outer courtyard of Durham Place, shrieking for mercy, followed by the captain and the English neighbours. The Bishop's household in the great courtyard seized their arms, and slammed the doors in the faces of the pursuers, whilst the terrified assassin fled through the great hall, through the inner courtyard and pell-mell up the stair leading to the Bishop's apartment.

Quite by chance, of course, the Provost of Paris happened to be playing at cards with the Bishop and the French Ambassador, whilst Luis de Paz and other friends looked on. The banging of the crowd at the closed door of the great hall, the terror-stricken cries of the criminal, and the tramping of the servants on the stair, brought out the Bishop and his friends to ask indignantly the cause of the uproar. Andrea on his knees at the door begged for protection and mercy. Captain Masino had beaten him, he said, some days ago, and he had fired a shot at him and missed him, so no harm was done, but still the captain wanted to kill him. Calming the clamour, the Bishop asked whether the shot had been fired inside or outside of Durham

Place. "At the gate!" they said, and the boy had only entered when pursued, to save his life. "Then," said the Bishop to Bernabe Mata, his majordomo, "turn him out by the water-gate." By mere chance again a boat was in waiting, hired by the Provost of Paris, who slipped outside himself to see the assassin safely off, gave him ten crowns, and whilst the crowd still battered and stormed at the door of the great hall, Andrea was carried to Gravesend as fast as strong oars could propel him. But he was captured next day, and under torture told the whole story. The Provost himself was closely imprisoned in Alderman Chester's house, whence he carried on for weeks an interesting correspondence with his friends outside, written with onion juice on the inside lining of the breeches of a servant.

This attempted murder was the opportunity for which Cecil had long been waiting. Strong hints about treachery founded on the secretary's information, galling interference with attendance at Mass, flouts and insults, had been more or less patiently borne by the Bishop at his master's behest, but harbouring a criminal was an infraction of the ordinary law of the land, and if it could be brought home to the Ambassador the Queen would have a good excuse for taking her house away from a tenant who put it to so bad a use. The news was not long travelling from the Strand to Whitehall; Cobham and a posse of the Queen's guard came straight to Durham Place, and in the name of the law demanded the surrender of the criminal. They were told he was not there, but had left by the water-gate, and, this reply being unsatisfactory, they came back again directly with the Queen's command that the keys of the water-gate, as well as those of the Strand entrance, should be given up to the English custodian, in order that he might render an account of all those who went in and out. The Bishop writes to Philip:—

"This custodian is a very great heretic, who for three years past has been in this house with no other duty than to spy out those who come to see me, for the purpose of accusing me. I have put up with it for all this time, although at great inconvenience to myself, so as to avoid having disputes with them on a matter of this description. When the Marshal made this demand, however, I answered him that for twenty years the Ambassadors here had been allowed to reside in the royal houses, nearly all those sent by your Majesty and the Emperor having done so, and they had invariably been accustomed to hold the keys of the houses wherein they lived. I said that it was not right that an innovation should be made in my case after my four years' residence here, especially on so slight a pretext as this matter, in which I was not at all to blame, and considering that this is the first case of the sort that has happened since I have been here, it cannot be said that my house is an habitual refuge for criminals. I would, however, go and give the Queen an account of the matter, which I endeavoured to do."

But the Queen would not see him either that day or the next. She was too busy she said; and on the following day, which was Twelfth Day, just as people were coming to Mass, some locksmiths came in a boat to the water-gate and put a new lock on, notwithstanding the protest of the Bishop's household, and the keys of all the gates were now held by the Queen's officers. The Bishop was in a towering rage, and said, that as the Queen imprisoned him in his own house, and made a goal of it, he demanded the keys back, or else that she should find him another residence where he might be free. A long account of the solemn conference between the Bishop and the Council is given in the Calendar of State Papers (Foreign), the 7th of January, 1563, and the Bishop's version is now published in the Spanish State Papers of Elizabeth, vol. i. According to both accounts, the Bishop got decidedly the worst of it. Cecil was the spokesman, and, instead of taking up a defensive position about the keys, he turned the tables by piling up all the complaints which his spies had accumulated for the last two years, and the poor Bishop found himself the accused rather than the injured party. The escape of the criminal by the water-gate was made the most of—such a thing in law-abiding England had never been heard of before—but after all this was a bagatelle to the other charges.

The neighbours had complained over and over again, Cecil said, of the quarrels and fights of the Bishop's dependants, and had asked for his removal from the house. There had been a squabble, one of many, between the English porter and the Bishop's scullions about the water, which, after serving the conduit in the inner courtyard, ran down to the basement kitchen of the house itself. The Bishop's servants kept their tap running in the kitchen out of malice, in order to deprive the upper conduit of water, and when the English porter complained, they shut the door of the great hall, so that neither he nor the neighbours could get to the conduit at all. Then the porter said he would cut the pipe and stop their supply, and at this threat they went to his house with weapons in their hands and said they would kill him if he did so; and he was the Queen's servant! But, worst of all, Cecil accused the Bishop of plotting with Shan O'Neil and Arthur Pole, and said that since the house had been in the Bishop's occupation it had become sadly dilapidated and damaged as regarded the lead, glass doors, and so on, and that the Queen had decided to put it into proper repair and find another fitting residence for him. The Bishop retorted by denying all the charges, and saying that as the house was low-lying and damp and he was old and ailing, he would be glad to leave it. But soft spoken as he was to the Council, he was burning with rage, and wrote to Granvelle in a very different tone.

It was some months yet, however, before he moved from Durham Place, and during that time the Queen's Marshal again descended upon the house one morning of a Catholic feast-day, and haled all those who were attending Mass to the Marshalsea. The guard had, it appears, concealed themselves betimes in the porter's house, and Cecil had given them orders that if any resistance whatever was offered they were to attack the house in force and capture all the inmates at any cost. But at last the poor old Bishop, heart-broken at having to suffer so much indignity, was got rid of and lodged elsewhere. Deeply in debt and penniless, he went in the summer of 1563 to Langley, Bucks, where he died in August, some say of poison, some of plague, and some of grief. Then Durham Place, refurbished and repaired, again became a royal guest-house.

On the 16th of July, 1565, the Queen lent Durham Place to Sir Ambrose Cave, one of her Privy Council, for the celebration of his daughter's wedding with the son of Sir Francis Knollys, the Vice-Chamberlain, and the new Spanish Ambassador, Canon Guzman de Silva, was invited to the supper in the evening, at which the Queen had promised to be present. By mutual consent it had been arranged that the French and Spanish Ambassadors should never meet at Court, or where the vexed question of precedence might arise; but the two diplomatists, wily Churchmen both, were for ever on the look out for a chance of scoring off each other. No doubt Ambrose Cave thought he had cleverly evaded the difficulty by asking the French Ambassador to the more important meal, namely, the eleven o'clock dinner, and the Spanish Ambassador to the supper in the evening, at which the Queen was to be present. But when De Foix learnt at the hospitable feast at Durham Place that the Queen was coming later, he announced his intention of staying to supper as well. If Guzman did not like it, he said, he might stay away, and poor Cave, foreseeing an unseemly squabble in the Queen's presence, rushed off in despair to the Spanish Ambassador to beg of him not to come. But this was too much for the Toledan pride of the Canon, and he told Cave that he had not sought an invitation to the feast, but since it had been given and accepted he was not going to stay away for the French Ambassador or any one else. As for precedence, his master was the greatest King on earth, and if the worst came to the worst he would fight out the question. In vain Cave protested that the Queen would not come if there was to be any quarrelling, and he would be ruined at Court. He could not, he said, get rid of the Frenchman, who flatly refused to go, and he could hardly throw him out of the window. Guzman said if there was much ado about it he would throw him out of window himself, and sent off Cave in a huff. Then Guzman hurried to Whitehall in order to catch the Queen before she started for Durham Place. He waited for some time, he says, in the privy garden by which she would have to pass to her barge; and after she had vainly attempted to smooth matters over, and said she herself must refrain from going if there was to be any disturbance, she pretended to fly into a rage at Cave's management of the affair, and sent Cecil and Throgmorton off to Durham Place to get rid of the French Ambassador somehow. What arguments they used Guzman neither knew nor cared, but when he arrived with the Queen the rival Ambassador was gone, and he was the principal guest next to the sovereign. "The Queen stayed through the entertainment, and the Emperor's Ambassador and I supped with her in company with the bride and some of the principal ladies and the gentlemen who came with the Emperor's Ambassador. After supper there was a ball, a tourney, and two masques, and the feast ended at half-past one in the morning."

In September, 1565, Durham Place received a royal guest in the person of Cecilia, Princess of Sweden, Margravine of Baden, who came principally to spy how the land lay with regard to the oft-repeated suit for Elizabeth's hand made by her brother Eric XIV. The English queen, as was her wont, made much of her at first; but she, too, wore out her welcome during the months she stayed, for, as we have seen, the housekeeping of great folk in those days was far from economical, and when the Swedish princess ran short of money and wanted pecuniary help, as she soon did, frugal Elizabeth's friendship began to cool, and it ended in the poor Princess having to pledge even her clothes to satisfy her more pressing creditors before they would let her go; and her husband, a ruling prince, was put into gaol at Rochester by the irate tradesmen who had trusted his wife. But all this was at the end of her visit; the beginning was certainly brilliant and auspicious.

The Princess arrived at Dover in the Queen's ships, and was there received by Lord Cobham and his wife, the Mistress of the Robes, and a knot of courtiers sent by the Queen from Windsor. They rode as usual through Kent to Gravesend, where the Queen's barges awaited them, and the Queen's cousin, Lord Hunsdon, and six pages in royal livery received the Princess, who was thus carried up the river with all pomp and circumstance to the water-gate of Durham Place. Her dress on the occasion attracted attention in London by its strangeness. She was attired, we are told, in a long black velvet robe, with a mantle of cloth of silver and black, and on her fair hair she wore a golden crown. At the top of the water-stairs at Durham Place she was received by the Countess of Sussex, Lady Bacon, and Cecil, and installed in the house with all honour. A day or two afterwards the Queen came from Windsor to visit her. "She received her Majesty at the door, where she embraced her warmly, and both went up to her apartments. After the Queen had passed some time with her in great enjoyment she returned home, and the next night, the 15th, the Princess was delivered of a son." In due time the young Prince of Baden was christened with great pomp, and Durham Place was a scene of festivity on that and many other occasions whilst the Swedish Princess resided there.

We have rather a full account of one of Queen Elizabeth's visits to the Princess at Durham Place, as Guzman, the Spanish Ambassador, happened to be at Whitehall when her Majesty was starting, and, at her invitation, accompanied her thither in her barge. He says he was with her alone for some time in the cabin of the barge, until, probably, her Majesty becoming tired of a *tête-à-tête* with an elderly clergyman, called her new pet Heneage to her, and began to whisper and flirt with him. The Princess awaited the Queen at the water-gate as usual, and led her to the principal apartments upstairs, although neither royal lady would consent to be seated until a stool was brought for Guzman, who relates the incident. The Queen came by water, and returned in a coach by way of the Strand. When she was seated in the carriage with Lady Cobham, her maiden Majesty could not resist the opportunity afforded by the condition of her companion to make rather a risky joke to the Ambassador, who, ecclesiastic though he was, retorted fully in the same vein, and carefully repeated the conversation in a letter to his royal master the next day.

For the next few years Durham Place gave shelter to many courtiers, ambassadors, and honoured guests of the Queen, and was occasionally lent, as we have seen, for parties and merrymakings, its large size and easy access by land and water making it peculiarly appropriate for such uses. But the elder Earl of Essex, Walter Devereux, made a somewhat longer stay in some of its apartments. It was here, probably enough in the turret-rooms which were Raleigh's favourite abiding-place, that Essex planned that expedition to Ireland with which his name was destined for all time to be linked. From here he started in August, 1573, and, with the exception of one flying visit in 1575, never saw Durham Place again.

In 1583 the Queen granted the house to Raleigh. It was in a dilapidated condition, and he spent, as he says, £2,000 in repairing it; certain it is that during twenty years that Raleigh lived there Durham Place reached its apogee of splendour. The Strand had greatly altered for the better since the time when Feria lived at Durham Place. The Bishop of Carlisle's house, on the other side of Ivy Lane, had disappeared, and Robert Cecil had built a splendid house for himself on its site. His father and elder brother, too, across the Strand had another palace, and between them they had paved and made up the roadway for a considerable distance before their properties. But slowly, too, the Strand was becoming a great fashionable thoroughfare, and long-headed Robert Cecil knew well that as shops grew up along its line the street frontage would increase in value. So he cast covetous eyes across his own boundary at Ivy Lane on to the great ramshackle congeries of stables and outhouses which fronted the Strand at Durham Place. As long as his mistress lived he dared not disturb Raleigh, but no sooner had the great Queen passed away than Raleigh was turned out with every circumstance of harshness and insult, and Lord Salisbury got his street frontage, upon which he built Britain's Burse, which was to be a rival to the Royal Exchange.

Thenceforward Durham Place went down in the world. A sort of square, with entrance by what is now called Durham Street, was built on a portion of the garden and great courtyard, but the hall and mansion themselves were left intact, and the latter was still used for the lodging of ambassadors and others, and the Bishops of Durham appear to have had lodgings in what formerly was their own palace. Lord Keeper Coventry lived, or at all events wrote, his letters here, and Lord Keeper Finch died at Durham Place in 1640. Lord Pembroke bought the whole site soon after, intending to build himself a house there, but although the plans were made the project fell through. The Commonwealth soldiers were quartered in the house for nearly two years, and Lord Pembroke had to find himself a house elsewhere, for which the Parliament voted him £200.

The Strand front became more and more valuable, and by and by another exchange was built on the rest of the frontage, whilst the property in the rear continued to get more squalid as the time went on. In the middle of the last century the exchanges were pulled down and a fine row of shops built on the site, whilst projects for dealing with the space still occupied by the old palace were busying many men's minds. At last came the brothers Adam and made a clean sweep of it all, back and front, and built the Adelphi as we see it to-day. The wide expanse of mud which at low tide formerly spread from the walls of the old palace is now replaced by the waving trees of a public garden. Great railway stations, gigantic hotels, towering masses of "flats" and "mansion" rear their high heads all round the site of old Durham Place. The wealth and power have passed from the hands of the few to the hands of the many, and instead of one man living in squalid splendour in the comfortless palace surrounded by hosts of unproductive hinds, hundreds live in comfort, usefulness, and self-respect upon the spot. There is probably more money spent in a week by working people in the garish music-hall that occupies the Strand front than would have sufficed to keep Durham Place in full swing for a year during the time of its greatest grandeur.

*THE EXORCISM OF CHARLES THE BEWITCHED.*

CHARLES II. OF SPAIN, "The Bewitched."
*(From a painting by Claudio Coello.)*

## *THE EXORCISM OF CHARLES THE BEWITCHED.*[1]

THE pallid little milksop in black velvet, with his lank, tow-coloured hair and his great underhung chin, who will simper for ever on the canvas of Carreño, had grown to be a man—a poor feeble anæmic old man of thirty-seven,[2] the last of his race, to whom fastings and feastings, the ceremonies of the Church, and the nostrums of the empirics had been equally powerless in providing a successor for the crumbling empire of his fathers. The

[1] *The Gentleman's Magazine*, November, 1893.
[2] Stanhope, the English minister in Madrid, writes to the Duke of Shrewsbury, September, 1696 : " They cut off his hair in this sickness, which the decay of nature had almost done before, all his crown being bald. He has a ravenous stomach, and swallows all he eats whole, for his nether jaw stands out so much that his two rows of teeth cannot meet, so that a gizzard or a liver of a hen passes down whole, and his weak stomach not being able to digest it he void it in the same manner."

strong spirits upon whom he had leant in his youth and early manhood had passed away. His imperious mother, who reigned so long and unworthily in his name, had died of cancer only a year or two ago. His virile brother, Don Juan José of Austria, in whom the worn-out blood of the imperial race had been quickened by the brighter but baser blood of his actress mother, had been poisoned. His beloved first wife, the beautiful Marie Louise of Orleans, had faded away in the sepulchral gloom of that dreary Court, and his new German wife, Marie Anne of Neuberg, with her imperious violence, frightened him out of what little wit he had left by her advocacy of new ideas. For new ideas to that poor brain were the inventions of the very Devil himself. He had been drilled for years into the knowledge that the claims of his French kinsmen to his inheritance were just; and, though for years past all the diplomatists of Europe had been plotting and planning for one or the other claimant with varying success, all that poor Charles the Bewitched himself wanted was to be left alone in peace whilst he lived, and that one of his French cousins should succeed him when he died. There was not much chance of either wish being fulfilled from the time that England and the Austrian faction juggled Marie Anne of Neuberg into the palace as Charles' second wife. She made short work of all the courtiers and ministers who favoured the French succession—they had one after the other either to come round to her side or go. Most of the best of them—not that any of them were very good—sulked in their own provinces awaiting events, whilst others still plotted in the capital.

In the meantime the Queen and her camarilla were all-powerful. After various weak and futile explosions, the smashing of crockery and breaking of furniture and the like, the poor King, for the sake of peace, let her have her own way, and ostensibly favoured the claims of the Austrian Archduke to his inheritance. But like most semi-idiots he could not relax his grasp on an idea of which he had once become possessed, and though he was surrounded day and night by the Queen's creatures, and was content that they should have their way whilst he was well, he no sooner fell into one of his periodical fits of deadly sickness than, with all the terror and dread of death, and constant fear of poison and witchcraft upon him, he yearned for the presence of those who had been with him in earlier and happier days, before the German Queen and her base blood-suckers had come to disturb his tranquillity.

The story of the strange and obscure Court intrigue which resulted in the gaining by the French faction of the upper hand in the palace during the critical time preceding Charles's death, has often and variously been told, mostly with an ignorant or wilful distortion of events. M. Morel-Fatio has shown how Victor Hugo has deliberately falsified the character of the Queen Marie Anne of Neuberg, in order that he might make use of the local colour furnished by the Countess d'Aulnoy's letters written from Spain fifteen years before the period represented by the dramatist;[1] and many other writers, French and

[1] "L'Histoire dans Ruy Blas" in "Études sur l'Espagne," by A. Morel-Fatio, Paris.

English, who have been attracted by the romantic elements of the witchcraft story, have surrounded it with a cloud of fictitious persons and incidents which makes it difficult now to distinguish between history and romance. Every writer on the subject, so far as I know, moreover, has stopped short at the story of the exorcism itself, whereas it really developed into a great struggle of many years' duration between the Grand Inquisitor on the one hand and the Council of Inquisitors on the other, in which, curiously enough, the latter body championed the cause of legal process as against the arbitrary power assumed by its own chief.

There is in the British Museum [1] a full manuscript account from day to day of the whole transaction from beginning to end, written at the time by one of the clerks or secretaries in the Inquisition, who, although he avows himself a partisan of the French faction and of the King's confessor, Froilan Diaz, around whom all the storm raged, declares that he has set down the unvarnished truth of the whole complicated business, in order that people may know after his death what really happened, and how much they "owe to his Sacred Majesty Philip V. for preserving the privileges of the holy tribunal of the Inquisition, or, what is the same, our holy faith." By the aid of this set of documents, and another set in the Museum (part of which has been published in Spanish),

---

[1] Add. MS. 10241, British Museum. See also "Proceso criminal fulminado contra el Rmo. P.M. Fray Froylan Diaz, de la sagrada religion de predicadores, Confesor del Rey N.S.D. Carlos II. : Madrid, 1787."

the story, which is well worth preserving, may be reconstructed, and the hitherto unrelated particulars of the actual exorcism rescued from oblivion.

The most powerful person at Court next to the Queen was Father Matilla, the King's confessor, whose hand was everywhere, and who said on one occasion that he would much rather make bishops than be one. Then came the other members of the Queen's camarilla, an obscure country lawyer who had been created Count Adanero, and Minister of Finance and the Indies, who provided the crew with money to their hearts' content, and squandered and muddled away the national resources, whilst all Spain was groaning under impossible imposts; Madame Berlips, a German woman who had an extraordinary influence over the Queen, and an insatiable greed; two Italian monks, and a mutilated musician of the Royal Chapel. There were two great nobles also who, after several periods of disgrace and hesitation, had at last thrown themselves on to the Queen's side —the Admiral of Castile and Count Oropesa, the ostensibly responsible ministers; but these practically only carried out the designs of the Queen's camarilla, and were content with the appearance and profits of power without its exercise. The populace, as may be imagined, were in deadly opposition to the Queen and her foreign surroundings, and were strongly in favour of one of the younger French princes whom they might adopt and make a Spaniard of, as they never could hope to do with a German archduke, and thus, as they thought, avoid the threatened partition of their country.[1] This was the position of things in March, 1698, when the King, who had partly recovered from his previous attack eighteen months before, was again taken ill.[2] He was dragged out by the Queen to totter and stagger in religious processions, was made to go through the ceremonial forms of his position, nodding and babbling incoherently to ministers and ambassadors whom he was obliged to receive, and at last, weary and sick to death, haunted by an unquiet conscience and with the appalling fear of hourly poison, he sent word by a trusty messenger to the wise, crafty old minister of his mother, Cardinal Portocarrero, who had been banished from the Court by the Queen, that he wished to see him.

The Cardinal needed no two invitations, but posted off to the palace. He had still plenty of

[1] Stanhope to his son, March 14, 1698: "Our Court is in great disorder: the grandees all dog and cat, Turk and Moor. The King is in a languishing condition, so weak and spent as to his principles of life that there is only hope of preserving him for a few weeks.... The general inclination is altogether French to the succession, their aversion to the Queen having set them against all her countrymen, and if the French King will content himself that one of his younger grandchildren be King of Spain, he will find no opposition either from grandees or common people. The King is not in a condition to give audience, speaking very little and that not much to the purpose. The terms in which they express it to me is that he is *embelecado, atolondrado, and dementado*. He fancies the devils are very busy in tempting him."

[2] "The King is so very weak he can scarcely lift his hand to his head to feed himself, and so extremely melancholy that neither his buffoons, dwarfs, nor puppet shows, all of which show their abilities before him, can in the least divert him from fancying everything that is said or done to be a temptation of the Devil, and never thinking himself safe without his confessor and two friars by his side, whom he makes lie in his chamber every night" (Stanhope to the Earl of Portland, March 14, 1698).

friends of various ranks, notwithstanding the Queen, and amongst them was Count de Benavente, the Gentleman of the Bedchamber. By him he was conducted at night to the King's bed-side, after the Queen had retired, and heard the heart-broken recital of the monarch's troubles. The King told him he was ill and unhappy and in trouble about his soul's health. He was conscious of a struggle going on within him between his knowledge of the right thing to do and his incapacity to do it, and this left him no peace or happiness. The people who surrounded him were distasteful to him, his confessor, Matilla, gave him no real consolation, and he ascribed much of his own illness and misery to the bad management and ceaseless worry he had to endure from those who had the direction of affairs. The King unburdened himself to the Cardinal in his lisping, mumbling fashion, his utterance broken with sobs and tears, but sufficiently plainly for Portocarrero to see that if he and his friends acted boldly, swiftly, and secretly they might again become predominant and dispose of the splendid inheritance of Spain and the Indies. He said some consoling, soothing words to the King, and promised him that steps should be taken to insure him tranquillity, and then he took his leave. The interview took place in the ancient Alcazar, which stood on the site of the present royal palace in Madrid, for poor Carlos had no spirits for the new Buen Retiro Palace, where his father had been so gay and splendid. It was nearly eleven o'clock at night, but as soon as the Cardinal got back to his own house he summoned his friends to a private conference. They were all of them courtiers in disgrace with the Queen, and most of them extremely popular with the mob in Madrid. There was Count Monterey, mild and temporising, with his hesitating speech and his irritating "hems and hahs"; there was the Marquis of Leganes, a hot-headed soldier, rash and pugnacious; Don Francisco Ronquillo, ambitious, intriguing, and bold, who, with his brother, was the idol of the "chulos" of the capital; Don Juan Antonio Urraca, honest, uncouth, and boorish; and, above all, quiet, wise, and prudent Don Sebastian de Cotes, a close friend of the Cardinal's. First, Monterey was invited to give his opinion as to what should be done, but he dwelt mainly upon the danger to them all presented from the King's infirmity of purpose; and how one minister after the other who had for a moment succeeded in persuading him to make a stand, had been disgraced and banished the moment the Queen got access to her husband and twisted him round her finger, as she could. He had no desire to take risks, apparently, and could recommend nothing but that the Cardinal Archbishop should keep his footing in the palace, and gradually work upon the King's mind. Leganes scoffed at such timid counsels; where the disease was so violent as this a strong remedy must be adopted. This should be the immediate banishment, and, if necessary, the imprisonment of the Admiral of Castile, the principal minister. He (Leganes) had plenty of arms at home, and had hundreds of men in Madrid who would serve him, with experienced officers to command them, and could soon make short work of the Admiral and his train of poets and buffoons. Ronquillo went further still. He said that was all very well, but at the same time they must seize the Queen and shut her up at the Huelgas de Burgos. Monterey called him a fool, and said such an act would be the death of the King and would ruin them all before he could alter his will; and the two nobles rushed at each other to fight out the question on the spot before the Archbishop himself. When they were separated the Cardinal no doubt thought it was time to do something practical, and asked his friend Cotes his opinion. Cotes was prosy enough, but practical. He said of course Portocarrero could easily get the King to sign any decree he liked, but the Queen could more easily still get him to revoke it; and, although it would be well to strike at the Queen herself, he did not know who would dare to do it. But after all she could only influence him by mundane means; the confessor, Matilla, whom the King hated and feared, and flouted only yesterday, must be got rid of, and the Queen would lose her principal instrument. This was approved of, but no one could suggest a fitting successor except Ronquillo—who, of course, had a nominee of his own!—who was promptly vetoed. Each of the others doubtless had one too, but thought best to press his claims privately. So it was left to the Archbishop to choose a new successor and gain the King's consent to his appointment. The choice fell upon a certain Froilan Diaz, professor of theology at the University of Alcalá. One of his recommendations was that he was near enough to the capital to be brought thither quickly, before the affair got wind, and no sooner did the Ronquillos learn that Cotes had recommended him to the

Archbishop than they sent a mounted messenger post-haste to Alcalá to inform Father Froilan of his coming greatness, and claim for themselves the credit of his appointment.

A few days afterwards, in the afternoon, the King lay in bed languidly listening to the music which was being played in the outer chamber, with which his own room communicated by an open door. The outer room, as usual, was crowded with courtiers, and in the deep recess of a window stood the confessor, Matilla, chatting with a friend, alert and watchful of all that passed. Suddenly Count de Benavente entered with a stout, fresh-coloured ecclesiastic, quiet and modest of mien and unknown to all. They walked across the presence chamber without announcement, and entered the King's chamber, shutting the door behind them. Matilla's face grew longer and his eyes wider as he saw this, and he knew instinctively that his day was over. Turning to his friend, he said, "Good-bye; this is beginning where it ought to have left off," and with that he left the palace, and went with the conviction of disaster to his monastery of the Rosario. They had all known for some days that something had been brewing. Spies had dogged every footstep of the Archbishop and those who attended the midnight meeting at his house, but they had left out of account the King's own Gentleman of the Bedchamber, Count de Benavente, who had arranged the whole affair. It is true that when the Queen had, as usual, entered the King's bedroom that day, at eleven o'clock, to see him dine, he had told her in a whisper, unable to retain his secret, that he had changed his confessor. She, astounded and disconcerted at the news, pretended to approve of the change—anything, she said, to give tranquillity to her dear Carlos. But when she could leave, she flew with all speed to her room, summoned the Admiral and the camarilla, and told them they were undone. Panic reigned supreme, the general idea being that Matilla himself had betrayed them. In any case they saw that *he* was past praying for, so they threw him overboard, and decided to try to save themselves, and see if, in time, they could not buy over the new confessor.

The only man of them who kept his head was a great ecclesiastic, a brother of the Admiral of Aragon, and of a member of the Council of the Inquisition, one Folch de Cardona, Commissary-General of the Order of San Francisco, who was subsequently to play an important part in the tragicomedy. When Matilla learnt that the Queen and her friends had known of the change an hour or two before it happened he broke down. "Oh, for that hour!" he exclaimed; "in it I would have set it all right." Divested of all his offices, dismissed from his inquisitorship, with a pension of 2,000 ducats, he died within a week of poison or a broken heart, and he disappears from the scene.

In his place stands Froilan Diaz, a simple-minded tool of the courtiers who had appointed him. He did not look very terrible, even to the panic-stricken Queen and her friends, and they decided to make the best of him, and try to confine the changes to the confessorship. Henceforward Froilan Diaz was a man to be courted and flattered. Honours and wealth were lavished on him, and for a year no great change was made in the palace or outside; but under the surface intrigue was busy, both at the King's bedside and in the haunts of the Madrid mob. At the end of a year the latter element made short work of the ministers and the Queen's gang and drove the lot of them out, to be replaced by Arias, the Ronquillos, and the French party; but with this revolt the present study has nothing to do.

The King's extreme decrepitude for a young man had several years before given rise to rumours amongst the vulgar that he was bewitched, and the assertion had been made the subject of grave consideration by the Grand Inquisitor of the time, who reported that he could find no evidence to act upon. At the time of the first serious illness of the King, in 1697, he had of his own action sent to the new Grand Inquisitor a terrible and austere Dominican monk called Rocaberti, and had confessed to him his conviction that his illness was not natural but the result of some maleficent charm, and besought him earnestly to have an exhaustive inquiry made. The Inquisitor told him that he would, if he pleased, have inquiry made, but saw no possible result could come of it, unless the King could point out some person whom he suspected or some plausible evidence to go upon. And so the matter remained until some weeks after Father Froilan had become confessor. As may be supposed, Froilan Diaz's elevation had reminded all his old friends of his existence, and, amongst others, an old fellow-student visited him, with whom he fell into talk about past days and former acquaintances. "And how is Father Argüelles getting on?" said the confessor. "Ah, poor fellow!" was the reply; "he is confessor at a convent at Cangas, terribly ill, but in no-wise cast down, for the Devil himself has assured him in person that God is preserving him for a great work yet that shall resound through the world." The King's confessor pricked up his ears at this, and wanted further particulars. It appeared, according to the friend, that Argüelles had had much trouble with two nuns of his convent, who were possessed, and in the course of his exorcisms had become quite on intimate terms with his Satanic Majesty. Froilan thought this was too important to be neglected, so he consulted the Grand Inquisitor, the Dominican Rocaberti. The grim monk did not, apparently, much like the business, but consented to a letter being written to the Bishop of Oviedo, the superior of Argüelles, asking him to question his subordinate as to the truth of the assertion that the King was suffering from diabolical charms. The Bishop, determined that he would not be made the channel for such nonsense, wrote a sensible answer back, saying that he did not believe in the witchcraft story. All that ailed the King was a weakness of the heart and a too ready acquiescence in the Queen's wishes, so he would have nothing to do with it.

Then Froilan sent direct to Argüelles, who himself was afraid of the business unless he was secured from harm, and refused to put any questions to the Devil unless he had the warrant of the Grand Inquisitor. A letter was therefore written by the latter on June 18, 1698, ordering him to write the names of the King and Queen on a sheet of paper, and, without uttering them, to place the paper on his breast, summon the Devil, and ask him whether the persons whose names were so written were suffering from witchcraft. Froilan sent the letter in a long one of his own to his old friend Argüelles with an elaborate cipher and other devices for secrecy in subsequent communications. No names henceforward were to be written. The vicar, Argüelles, replied, expressing no surprise at so strange a request, but said the Devil had previously told him that he was reserved for great things, but had not given particulars, only that he should receive an order from a superior. Then he tells the result obtained by his first effort. He says he placed the hands of the possessed nun upon the altar, and by the power of his incantations commanded the Devil to answer the question put to him. The Devil was not at all shy, but "swore by God Almighty that it was the truth that the King was bewitched," "et hoc ad destruendam materiam generationis in Rege et eum incapacem ponendum ad regnum administrandum.' He said the charm had been administered by moonlight when the King was fourteen years of age.

So far the Devil. Then the vicar, as an expert, gives some advice of his own. He says the King should be given half a pint of oil to drink, fasting, with the benediction, and the ceremony of exorcism which the Church prescribes.[1] He

[1] How fit the King was to undergo such a regime as this may be judged by Stanhope's letter to his son, dated Madrid, June 15, 1698 : "Our gazettes here tells us every week that his Catholic Majesty is in perfect health, and it is the general answer to all inquiries. It is true that he is abroad every day, but *hæret lateri lethalis arundo ;* his ankles and knees swell again, his eyes bag, the lids red as scarlet, and the rest of his face a greenish yellow. His tongue is *trabada*, as they express it ; that is, he has such a fumbling in his speech, those near him hardly understand him, at which he sometimes grows angry, asks if they all be deaf."

must not eat anything for some time afterwards, and everything he eats and drinks must be blessed. The case is a very bad one, he says, and a miracle will be performed. If the King can bear it he should be given, in addition, the charm prescribed by the Church, but not otherwise.

He gives the not improbable opinion that as the King will vomit dreadfully he must be held in the arms of the "master," by which name it was agreed that the Grand Inquisitor should be referred to in the correspondence. But he says not an hour is to be lost, and the master himself must administer the draught.

But this remedy was too strong, and Froilan and the Inquisitor, or the friend and the master, as they are called henceforward, write to say that, although they are much obliged to the Devil and the vicar, such a draught as that recommended would certainly kill the King, and they beg the exorciser to ask the Devil again for a more practical and a safer remedy. "How much and in what form is the Church charm to be given; at what hour; on what parts of the body?" And so on—queer questions indeed to be addressed by two pillars of the Church to the Devil. But this is not all. They draw up a series of questions that would do honour to a cross-examining barrister. "What is the proof of witchcraft? In what way does it act so as to make the King do things contrary to his own will? How are the organs affected cleansed by the charm? What compact was made with the Devil when the witchery was effected? Was it administered internally, or externally?

Who administered it? Has it been repeated? Is the Queen included in its operation?" And other questions of a similar sort. The vicar is rather shocked at their inquisitiveness, and refuses to put such questions. How can he ask the Devil anything that the Church does not deal with in its exorcising ceremonies?

Another letter is sent asking him to consult the Devil as to whether it will be well to take the King to Toledo, to which the vicar replies somewhat evasively, reproaching his associates. What is the good, he says, of all their professed desire to heal the King whilst they refuse to carry out the directions sent them? A change of place is useless if he takes the malady with him, and until they follow out the instructions already given it is no good for him to consult the Devil again. "Besides," he says, getting into dangerously deep water for a country vicar, "how can you expect the King to be well? Justice is not done, the churches are starved, hospitals are despoiled and closed, and souls are allowed to suffer in purgatory because money is begrudged for Masses, and above all, the King does not administer justice after swearing on the cross that he would do so. The Divine message has already been delivered to you. I have told you all it is fitting for you to know and how to cure the patient, and you do nothing but ask a lot more questions. I tell ye, then, that you will find no excuse for this at the supreme judgment, and the death of the King will be laid at your door, since you could cure him and will not." This was almost too bold to be borne, and the Inquisitor's secretary writes back in grave condemnation. He again insists upon the questions being put to the Devil. "You are presumptuous to dare to suppose that you know better than the friend and the master, and that you can command in this way whilst refusing to obey. You want to get out of it now by attributing the King's illness to other causes. The 'friend and the master' are deeply offended, and if you do not do as you are commanded all will be frustrated, and we distressed to feel that, just as God had begun to open the door of knowledge to us, all is spoilt by your presumption and obstinacy."

After a good deal more of mutual recrimination the vicar gave way, and on September 9, 1698, he wrote that he had sworn the Devil on the holy sacrament, and he had declared that the charm had been administered to the King in a cup of chocolate on April 3, 1673. "I asked," he writes, "what the charm was made of, and he said three parts of a dead man." "What parts?" "Brain to take away his will, intestines to spoil his health, and kidney to ruin his virility." "Can we burn any sign to restore him?" "No, by the God that made you and me." "Was it a man or a woman who administered the charm?" "A woman; and she has already been judged." "Why did she do it?" "In order to reign." "When?" "In the day of Don Juan of Austria, whom she killed with a similar charm, only stronger."

This of course was directed against the late Queen-mother—a dangerous line to take, considering that the Cardinal Archbishop Portocarrero, whose creature Froilan was, had been her friend and minister. Lucifer continued, that the remedies were those that the Church prescribed. First, drinking of blessed oil fasting; secondly, anointing the whole body with the oil; next, strong purges and absolute isolation of the King even from the sight of the Queen. Then the Devil got sulky, said he was tired and knew no more, and refused to say another word. The adoption of such a course as that prescribed, with a man who was dying already of exhaustion would have been murder; and of course the associates again hesitated, writing to the vicar directing him to inquire of the Devil if any witchery has been practised since the first, and why the King cannot do right when he wishes to, instead of being, as he complains, impelled to act wrongly against his will. It seems impossible that this can be the result of the original charm, particularly as the person who gave it is dead. Has anything been given since? "Yes," says the Devil, "in 1694, only four years ago, on September 24th, a similar charm was given in food and left no outward sign," and this the Devil swears by God and the Holy Trinity. Then Lucifer, tired of answering questions, apparently gives a bit of advice. He says they are thwarting Providence by their delay, and if they do not hurry up the King will be past help.

But again the friend and the master want more information, and on October 22nd write to say that it is of the highest importance that they should know the name and residence of the witch; who ordered her to act, and why. This the Devil absolutely refuses to answer; but as his past proceedings proved him to be a demon somewhat infirm of purpose, they do not seem to have been at all discouraged, but a week or so afterwards return to the charge with a perfect catechism, which they order the vicar to put to his diabolical interlocutor. "Who was the witch? What was her name, condition, and residence? Who ordered the charm, and why? Who got the corpse and prepared the conjuration? Who handed the chocolate to the King? Had the witch any children?" And so on at great length. The answer came from the vicar on October 7th, in which the Devil seems to have made quite a clean breast of it. The Queen-mother, he said, had ordered the first charm; the first witch was a woman named Casilda, married, with two sons, who lived away from her. The go-between was Valenzuela (the Queen-mother's favourite), and the witch had no accomplice but the Devil. She sought the corpse and prepared the charm, and handed it to Valenzuela. The second charm, in 1694, was administered by one who wishes for the *fleur-de-lis* in Spain; one who is a great adulator of the King, but hates him bitterly. The Devil could not mention names, he said, but they knew the person well. This witch was a famous one named Maria, living in the Calle Mayor; but he could not give the number of the house or her surname.

The Grand Inquisitor's secretary wrote in answer to this, thanking him, but regretting that his information was so limited. The street mentioned as the residence of the first witch, namely, the Calle de Herreros, did not exist in Madrid, and the friend and the master beg the vicar to ask his friend the Devil for more information as to the houses and husbands of both witches, "as to seek a Maria in the High Street of Madrid was like looking for a needle in a haystack." They want also the name of the person who ordered the second charm, and the secretary ends his letter with an astounding invocation of the Devil's aid. He is conjured in the names of God, of His holy Mother, and of St. Simeon of Jerusalem, the King's patron saint, to intercede with God, " who, the lessons tell us, is a relative," to aid in the King's recovery. No reply appears to have been received to this letter, but it was soon followed by another, saying that the friend and the master have administered the charm recommended by the Devil, and the King is better; but they urgently beg for further aid from the same quarter, and more charms if possible. This letter was written on November 5, 1698, and produced two replies from the vicar, who said that he had been conjuring all the afternoon fruitlessly, and at last the Devil burst out in a rage, " Go away! don't bother me." In fact, it is quite clear at this point that the vicar, having got himself into a perfect net of confusion and contradiction, was getting very frightened indeed; and his next letter said the Devil was sulky, and would only reply to all his conjurations that he, the Devil, had been telling him a lot of lies and would say no more. All would be known by and by, but not yet. The vicar added to this a remark to the effect that all the King's doctors were false and disloyal, and should be dismissed; the doctor to be appointed in their place was to be chosen more for his attachment to the old Church than for his medical science, and, in the meanwhile, the King's abode and garments were to be changed and the exorcisms continued.

The vicar was thereupon again gravely rebuked

for daring to say that the King's physicians are disloyal, but they, the friend and the master, will refrain from employing them. A further letter of November 26th urges the vicar not to stand any more of the Devil's nonsense. Tell him he *must* give the names and addresses, as the friend and the master are put to great trouble seeking them, and he is exhorted to be diligent in completing the good work he has begun, as the King is much better for the exorcisms administered to him. The doctors were, of course, nominees of the new dominant French party, and the friend and master did not like their loyalty to be called into question; but the vicar was firm, so they were changed, and the poor King was taken on his journey to Toledo and Alcalá. He certainly had got much better, and Stanhope ascribes his improvement to the plasters of his new Aragonese doctor, or "rather," he says, "what I believe has done more is that he has of late drunk two or three glasses of pure wine at every meal, whereas he has never taken anything before in all his life but water boiled with a little cinnamon."

As soon as the King was well enough, the intrigue that had been brewing since the new confessor had got a footing was completed, and the third claimant to the succession, the young Prince of Bavaria, was solemnly adopted as heir to the crown. This, of course, offended most of the great Powers of Europe, but it had the effect of reconciling with each other the Spanish courtiers who had espoused either the French or the Austrian cause, and for a few months, until the new heir died, the Court quarrels were patched up. Still the inquiries of the Devil went on, and the vicar stumbled and blundered deeper into the mire. He tried to correct his mistake about the street where the first witch lived by saying that the street called Herreros was now the Cerrajeros, and the surname of the witch was Perez, the commonest name in Spain. The secretary wrote to say that the friend and the master could not make head or tail of it all, and begged the Devil to be more explicit—first he said the witch was alive, and then dead. The King was much better.

By this time, the beginning of the year 1699, the vicar evidently thought that, as he had so far come out of the affair with flying colours, he ought to be brought to the capital and placed on the main road of promotion, instead of being kept in a remote village: and he wrote that the Devil had declared that the whole truth could only be divulged in the church of the Virgin of Atocha in Madrid, and that as he, vicar, had begun it, so he must conduct the affair to the end. A week or two later he wrote, again pressing to be allowed to carry on the rest of the conjuration at the Atocha, in order, as he says, to reanimate the devotion to the image, which he thought was cooling. He gives the name of the second witch as Maria Diez, another extremely common name, and then falls ill, sulks, and refuses to invoke the Devil again except at the Atocha. Still his correspondents continue to press him for fresh signs and information, without result except to produce fresh demands that he should be brought to Madrid. The confederates, however, deemed this too dangerous, and the correspondence with Argüelles closes in the month of May, 1699.

About this time the Queen's suspicions were aroused by a hint dropped by the King, and she at once set spies around those who had access to the monarch's room, particularly Froilan Diaz. She soon learnt something of what was going on, and, as the chronicler says, "roared from very rage." She called her friends together, and in a tearing passion told them what she had discovered, demanding immediate vengeance on the King's confessor. Some of her friends, particularly Folch de Cardona, were cooler-headed than she was, and pointed out that as the Grand Inquisitor was mixed up in the business, it would be imprudent to take any steps until it was seen how far the holy tribunal itself was implicated, and that in any case the Queen's vengeance should be wreaked on Froilan by the action of the Inquisition if possible, so that she might avoid the unpopularity of appearing in the matter herself.

The next day Folch de Cardona sounded his inquisitor brother, and found that the Council of the Holy Office knew nothing of what was going on, and when the Inquisitor was informed and asked whether the tribunal would consider Froilan guilty if the facts were proved, he cautiously answered his brother that he would not venture of himself to decide, but personally he considered so much hobnobbing with the Devil both delicate and dangerous. In June the Grand Inquisitor Rocaberti died suddenly, probably of poison, and left Froilan to face the matter alone; and a few days afterwards a report was sent from Germany, having been transmitted to the Emperor by the Bishop of Vienna, containing a declaration, said to have been made by the Devil to an exorciser in the church of St. Sophia, to the effect that Charles II. was bewitched by a certain woman called Isabel living in the Calle de Silva, in Madrid, and that if search were made the instruments of her incantations would be found beneath the threshold of her house. The Queen thought to prove that this was another of Froilan's tricks, and had the whole matter discussed by the Inquisition, who, however, could find nothing to connect him with it, but proceeded to excavate the spot indicated in the Calle de Silva, and there found sundry dolls and figures dressed in uniforms, which dolls were borne in solemn procession and burnt with all the ceremonies of the Church at the end of July. All this was of course conveyed to the King by Froilan, and it, together with the positive assurance that he was bewitched given to him by a German exorciser named Mauro Tenda, who had been secretly summoned to Spain, threw the poor creature into such an agony of terror that his state became more and more pitiable.

In September a mad woman in a state of frenzy presented herself at the palace and demanded audience. She was refused admittance, and thereupon began to scream and struggle in a way that attracted the attention of the King, who told his attendants to admit her. She burst in foaming and shrieking with a crucifix in her hand, cursing and blaspheming at the poor trembling King, and she had to be borne out again on the shoulders of the guards, the King nearly dying of fright on the spot. The maniac was followed, and it was found that she lived with two other demoniacs, one of whom was under the impression that they were keeping the King subject in their room. This nonsense was also conveyed to the monarch, who was now thoroughly persuaded that he was under the influence of sorcery, and he ordered that all three of the women should be exorcised by the German monk. This was done, Froilan standing by and dictating the questions that were to be asked of the Devil by the exorciser. Unfortunately for the confessor, the questions he asked were rather leading ones, in which his desire to injure the Queen was evident. "Who was it," he asked, "that had caused the King's malady?" The answer given was that it was a beautiful woman. "Was it the Queen?" was next demanded, to which the reply was somewhat confusing, as it was merely the name of an unknown man, "Don Juan Palia." "Is he a relative of the Queen? What countryman is he?" received no reply; but when the Devil was asked in what form the charm had been administered he said, "In snuff." "Any of it left?" "Yes, in the desk." "What queen was it that caused the malady?" was again asked. "The dead one," said the Devil. "Is there any other charm?" "Yes." "Who gave it?" "Maria de la Presentacion." "Who ordered it?" "Don Antonio de la Paz." "When was it given?" No answer. "Of what was it made?" "Of a dog's bone." "Why did you send the woman to frighten the King?" No answer. Other questions and answers were given of the same sort, the latter mentioning at random the names of unknown people, and in some cases libelling the Queen and the ministers—all of it obviously the babble of a mad woman. Secret though the exorcism was, the Queen had a full report of it, and was of course furious with rage at the open attempt to cast upon her the blame of the witchcraft.

The first step towards her revenge was to get a new Grand Inquisitor in her interest, and she pressed the King to appoint her friend Folch de Cardona. He refused, no doubt prompted by his confessor Froilan, and, notwithstanding the Queen's passionate protests, appointed a second son of one of the noblest houses in Spain, Cardinal Cordoba, to whom the King unburdened himself completely, and Froilan told the whole story of the exorcism from beginning to end. From these confabulations a most extraordinary resolution was arrived at. Probably the Queen herself was too high game to fly at, so the new Grand Inquisitor and his friends decided that the Devil and the Admiral of Castile, the late Prime Minister, were at the bottom of all the King's trouble, and they ordered the Admiral with his papers to be secretly seized and imprisoned by the Inquisition of Granada, whilst all his household were incarcerated in another prison. They had no doubt, they said, that he would confess all, even if his papers did not incriminate him. No action, however, could be taken until the new Grand Inquisitor's appointment was ratified by the Pope; but on the very day the bull of ratification arrived the Cardinal Grand Inquisitor died of poison, and the Queen once again urged her nominee for the place, but without success as before. She then cast about for an ambitious man who was unobjectionable to her opponents, but who might nevertheless be bought over by her. She found him in the person of Mendoza, Bishop of Segovia, to whom she promised her support and a cardinal's hat if he would serve her. He was appointed Grand Inquisitor, and the Queen had now the whiphand of her enemy, the confessor. First the German monk was netted, and under torture by the Inquisition made a clean breast of his exorcism in the Calle del Olmo, when Froilan was present. Then a monk of the Atocha, who had been sent by the Provincial to investigate the strange doings of Friar Argüelles at Cangas, produced the letters from the "friend and the master," and told the story of the conjurations. This was quite enough evidence to ruin Froilan, and he was apprehended. He refused to answer any questions, as all he had done had been by the King's own orders, and as the confessor of his Majesty his mouth was closed. He was at once dismissed from his offices, and the Grand Inquisitor appealed to the King to allow all privileges to be waived, and his confessor punished. Poor Charles the Bewitched was dying in good earnest now, and could only mumble out that they might do justice. But Froilan had powerful friends both at Court and in the Council of the Inquisition, and before the blow fell he retired, ostensibly to his monastery, but thence fled to the coast, and so to Rome. But he was not safe even there, for the Grand Inquisitor had him seized for heresy by the Papal officers and brought back to Spain. Then came the long struggle between the Inquisition and its head. First, Froilan's case was submitted to the theological committee of the Holy Office, who unanimously absolved him. On June 23, 1700, he was fully acquitted by the General Council of the

Inquisition, the Grand Inquisitor alone voting for his secret imprisonment without further trial.

At the next meeting of the full Council, to the intense surprise of the members, a decree for the secret imprisonment of Froilan was placed before them for signature. They unanimously refused to sign it, and came to high words—almost blows—with their chief, who threatened them all with dire consequences for their obstinacy, and, to show that he was in earnest, there and then sent five of them down to their dungeons on his own responsibility. This was too high-handed even for the meekest of the Inquisitors, and the Council broke up in confusion. The Council of Castile, the supreme advisers of the Crown, appealed at once to the King against the imprisonment of the Inquisitors; but the King was helpless now, for the Queen and a new confessor were at his bedside, bound to stand by the Grand Inquisitor through thick and thin. They got the dying King to sign a decree appointing new Inquisitors enough to swamp the votes of those left, but lo and behold! they turned against their own creator at the very first meeting, and refused to endorse the Grand Inquisitor's action, either as to the imprisonment of Froilan or that of the Inquisitors. The strong man who led the revolt was Lorenzo Folch de Cardona, the brother of the Queen's old friend, now Bishop of Valencia, and it was decided that he must be silenced somehow. They offered him a bishopric, which he refused. They threatened him with prison and banishment, and he told them that they dared not touch him; and he was right, for all Madrid was looking on. Then the Inquisitor-General sent the case to be judged by a provincial council of the Inquisition at Murcia, which was subservient to him, but the General Council at Madrid told them they would be acting illegally if they decided against the verdict already given by the Committee of Theologians and the General Council, and even they did not dare to find Froilan guilty. In the meanwhile, guilty or not guilty, the poor man was kept a close prisoner in a dark cell of a monastery of the Dominican Order, to which he belonged.

In November, 1700, the King died, and the Grand Inquisitor was one of the regents, making himself remarkable for his splendour and ostentation during the short period of uncertainty after the King's death. But the arrival of the French King, Philip V., put an end to the Queen's hopes, and the Grand Inquisitor was sent off in disgrace to his diocese. As soon as his back was turned the General Council of the Inquisition, with Folch de Cardona in the chair, demanded of Prior of the Atocha by what right he still kept Froilan in prison. His answer was that he did so on the warrant of the Grand Inquisitor. An appeal was made to the King, but the fortune of war kept Philip for ever on the move, and for years no decision was given. In the meanwhile the Pope espoused the cause of the Inquisitor-General, and protested against his deprivation. The King appointed a new Inquisitor-General, and the Pope vetoed the appointment. Then the Pope sent special power to the old Grand Inquisitor to sentence Froilan to whatever punishment he liked without more ado, and the Council of the Inquisition and Folch de Cardona protested to the King against the attempt of the Pope to override the law of Spain; and at last Philip V. put his foot down once for all—dismissed the Inquisitor-General, reappointed the old Council, and authorised them to release Froilan in the King's name. They found him, after five years' close confinement, nearly blind in the dungeons of the monastery of the Atocha, and brought him out in triumph to be appointed Bishop of Avila. In vain the Pope protested and the dismissed Grand Inquisitor fumed. Philip the Magnanimous was a very different monarch from Charles the Bewitched. The black bigotry of the House of Austria was gone, and thenceforward, though the Holy Office existed in the land for a century longer, the arbitrary power of the Inquisition to override the law of the land was gone with it.

*A SPRIG OF THE HOUSE OF AUSTRIA.*

**PHILIP IV. OF SPAIN.**
*(After the painting by Velasquez.)*

## A SPRIG OF THE HOUSE OF AUSTRIA.[1]

No dead and gone human visage looms so clearly through the mist of ages as that strange lymphatic face of Philip IV., which the genius of Velazquez delighted to portray from youth to age. The smooth-faced stripling in hunting dress, with his fair pink and white complexion, his lank yellow hair, and his great mumbling Austrian mouth, shows more plainly on canvas than he could have done whilst alive how weak of will and how potent of passion he was, how easily he would be led by the overbearing Count-Duke of Olivares to sacrifice all else for splendid shows and sensuous indulgence; how his vanity would be flattered by poets, painters, and players, whilst the world-wide empire of his fathers was crumbling to nothingness

[1] *The Gentleman's Magazine*, September, 1892.

beneath his sway, and his vassals were being robbed of their last maravedi to pay for the frenzy of waste and prodigality with which Charles Stuart was entertained or a royal wedding celebrated. Thenceforward, through his fastuous prime, stately and splendid in his black satin and gold, to the time when, old and disappointed, with forty years of disastrous domination, the rheumy eyes drawn and haggard, but the head still erect, haughty and unapproachable in its reserve, the great painter tells the King's story better than any pen could write it. There is something not unlovable in the shy, weak, poetic face, and one can pity the lad with such a countenance who found himself the greatest king on earth at the age of sixteen, surrounded by fawning flatterers and greedy bloodsuckers who plunged him into a vortex of dissipation before his father's body was cold in the marble sarcophagus at the Escurial. The old man's face, too, cold and repellent as it is, shocking as are the ravages that time and self-indulgence have stamped upon it, has yet in it an almost plaintive despair that explains those terrible broken-hearted letters in which the King, icy and undemonstrative as he was, poured out his agony and sorrow undisguised for years to the only person in the wide world he trusted, the nun Maria de Agreda.

His long reign, which saw the ruin of the Spanish power, witnessed also the most splendid epoch of Spanish art and literature, the golden age of the Spanish stage, and a wasteful prodigality of magnificence in the Court such as, with the exception of that displayed by Philip's son-in-law, the Roi-soleil, the world has never seen equalled. The Elizabethan age in England may have approached it in literary strength, although even that cannot show such a galaxy as Lope de Vega, Calderon, Velazquez, Murillo, Tirso de Molina, Moreto, Quevedo, Guevara, Montalvan, and their host of imitators. The history of the reign has never yet been adequately or even fairly written. Isolated portions and detached incidents or personalities have been dealt with, and stray fragments now and again bring vivid pictures of the sumptuous Court before us. Spanish writers, of late years particularly, are fond of dwelling with microscopic minuteness on the incidents and adventures of the time that happened at particular spots in the capital ; but the topographical-historical style, first introduced by Mesonero Romanos, and now so popular, pleasant reading as it is, does not attempt to do more than amuse by presenting romantic and detached pictures of a bygone age, and all that can be claimed by the writers is that materials are gradually being collected and brought to light by them from contemporary sources which will be invaluable to the future serious historian of the reign.

The British Museum contains many hundreds of unpublished manuscripts bearing upon the subject—copies of official documents, letters, and "relations" from Philip's Court, petitions and statements of grievance addressed to the King, and vast collections of miscellaneous papers in Spanish, Portuguese, and French, most of which have not yet been consulted for historical purposes. Amongst a great mass of rather dry official documents of the period, most of them copies, I recently came across a small, compact group of papers, all originals, telling a curious, plaintive little story, nakedly enough, it is true, but not without a pathos of its own. There is nothing historically important in it, or in the fact that it discloses probably for the first time since it happened, but a quaint side-light is thrown by some of the documents on the way in which Court intrigue was conducted, and also, curiously enough, on the opinion of the highest authorities of those times as to the best way of bringing up a child, by which it will be seen that, allowing for difference of climate and national habits, no great change has taken place in this respect in the two centuries and a half that have passed since the papers were penned.

Philip had succeeded to the throne on the death of his father in March, 1621. He was only sixteen, and Olivares at once plunged him into such distractions as the then most dissolute capital in Europe could afford. By a strange coincidence the paper in the Museum (Egerton MSS., 329) which precedes the group of which I wish to speak is a lengthy and solemn letter, dated only a few weeks after the young King's accession, addressed to the Count-Duke by the Archbishop of Granada, remonstrating with the all-powerful favourite for taking the boy-king out in the street at night. "People," he says, "are gossiping about it all over Madrid, and things are being said which add little to the sovereign's credit or dignity." Madrid even now is fond of scandal, but in the beginning of the seventeenth century, isolated from the world as was the capital of the Spains, its one absorbing pursuit from morn till night was tittle-tattle, and the long raised walk by the side wall of the church of St. Philip, fronting the Oñate palace in the Calle Mayor, was a recognised exchange for the scandal-mongers. The Archbishop says, in his bold and outspoken letter, that not only have these people begun to whisper things that were better unsaid, but the example shown by the King and his minister in scouring the streets in search of adventure is a bad one for the people at large, and he reminds Olivares of the anxiety of the late King on this very account, and his dread that his heir was already before his death being inducted into dissipation. The answer to the bold prelate's remonstrance is just such as might be expected from the insolent favourite. He tells him in effect that he is an impertinent meddler, and ought to be ashamed, with his rank, and at his age, to trouble him with the vulgar gossip of the street. The King, he tells him, is sixteen and he (Olivares) is thirty-four, and it is not to be expected that they are to be kept in darkness as to what is done in the world. It is good that the King should see all phases of life, bad as well as good. He (Olivares) never trusts the King with any one else; and the favourite finishes his answer by a scarcely veiled threat that if the Archbishop does not mind his own business worse may befall him. No doubt the prelate took the warning, for Olivares was not scrupulous, and had a short and secret way with those who incurred his displeasure.

The small group of original papers coming after this begins with a memorandum unsigned, but evidently written by Olivares to the King some nine years subsequently, namely, early in the summer of 1630. It says that it is high time that measures should be taken at once to put a boy, whose name is not given, out of the way, as he is now four years old, and it is of great importance that he should be concealed, and all communication broken off between him and the people with whom he has been. The writer goes on to say that he has considered deeply how this is to be done, and that there are objections to be found in every solution that presents itself, but he thinks on the whole the best way will be to entrust him secretly to the care of a gentleman of his acquaintance named Don Juan Isassi Ydiaquez, who lives at Salamanca. He is a person of education, has travelled all over Europe, and could bring the lad up as his own. It will be necessary to see this gentleman first, and the writer proposes to summon him to Court without telling him the reason, so that " Your Majesty " may see him and then decide for the best. Across this document is written in Philip's uncertain, poetic hand : " It appears very necessary that something should be done in this matter and I approve of what you suggest.—P."

Presumably Ydiaquez was sent for and approved of, as the next document in the series is of a much more formal character, being a notarial deed drawn up by the Secretary of State, Geronimo de Villanueva as prothonotary of the kingdom, who was, with the exception of Olivares, the principal confidant of Philip's intrigues.[1] This deed, dated

[1] He was with difficulty rescued from the direst vengeance of the Inquisition a few years afterwards in consequence of his too ready co-operation in the King's amorous tendencies. Don Geronimo was patron of the convent of San Placido, next door to his own house in the Calle de la Madera in

June 1, 1631, recites that his Excellency Don Gaspar de Guzman, Count of Olivares, Duke of San Lucar, Grand Councillor of the Indies, Councillor of State, and Master of the Horse, delivers

Madrid, and had inflamed the King's mind with stories of a very beautiful nun who was an inmate of the convent. Philip and his favourite, the Count-Duke, insisted upon seeing this paragon of loveliness, and Don Geronimo, exerting his authority as patron, procured them entrance in disguise to the parlour, where, as was to be expected, his Catholic Majesty fell violently in love with the beautiful nun. The interviews in the parlour were constant but, with the grating between the King and his flame, unsatisfactory, and, by dint of bribes and threats, Don Geronimo managed to break a passage from the cellars of his own house into the vaults of the convent, by means of which, notwithstanding the prayers, the entreaties, and appeals of the abbess, the King was introduced into the cell of the unfortunate nun of whom he was enamoured. He found her laid out as if she were a corpse, surrounded with lighted tapers, with a great crucifix by her side, but not even this availed, and the sacrilegious amours continued so long that the news reached the ever-open ears of the Holy Office. The Grand Inquisitor, a Dominican friar called Antonio de Sotomayor, Archbishop of Damascus, privately took the King to task, and obtained a promise that the offence should cease. Don Geronimo was seized by the officers of the Inquisition (August 30, 1644), and taken to Toledo, where he was accused of sacrilege and other heinous crimes against the faith. The evidence was full and conclusive, and Don Geronimo's life was trembling in the balance, when the Count-Duke boldly went to the Grand Inquisitor one night with two signed royal decrees in his hands, one giving the Archbishop 12,000 ducats a year for life on condition of his resignation of the Grand Inquisitorship, and the other depriving him of all his temporalities, and banishing him for ever from all the dominions of his Catholic Majesty. The Grand Inquisitor naturally chose the former, and resigned next morning. Pressure was put on Pope Urban VIII. by the Spanish Ambassador, and very shortly an order arrived from Rome that the whole of the documents and evidence in the case were to be sealed up and sent in a box by a messenger of the Holy Office to his Holiness himself for decision. The messenger chosen was one of the Inquisition notaries called Alfonso Paredes. The Count-Duke, under various pretexts, delayed this man's departure for some a boy named Francisco Fernando, aged over four years to Don Juan Isassi Ydiaquez, this boy being the person referred to but not named in his Majesty's warrant, under his sign manual, addressed to Don Juan Isassi, and countersigned and delivered to him by the Secretary of State. The deed directs that Don Juan is to bring up the boy and educate him in conformity with the instructions to be given to him by the Count-Duke, by his Majesty's orders, and Don Juan himself undertakes in the deed to deliver up the person of the said Don Francisco Fernando when required, and to obey implicitly in all things the directions of the Count-Duke with regard to him. He promises to bring him up and rear him as he is ordered to do in the royal warrant. The deed is signed by the Count-Duke, weeks, and in the meanwhile had good portraits of him painted and sent by special messengers to all the ports in Italy where he was likely to land, and orders were sent to the Spanish agents to capture him at all risks. On the night of his arrival at Genoa, by the connivance of the authorities, he was seized, gagged, and carried off to Naples, where he was imprisoned for the rest of his life, condemned to perpetual silence on pain of instant death. The box of papers that he bore was sent privately to the King, who, with Olivares, burnt the contents without even opening the packet. The new Grand Inquisitor, who was a creature of the Queen, a Benedictine monk named Diego de Arce, was not to be entirely balked, and although no evidence now existed, he had the prothonotary Don Geronimo Villanueva brought from his prison in Toledo, where he had languished for two years, and placed before the tribunal of the Inquisition. He was stripped of his arms, accoutrements, insignia of rank and outer clothing, and sat upon a plain low wooden stool, and then, without any evidence being given or statement of specific offence, was condemned for irreligion, sacrilege, superstition, and other enormities, and, by the mercy of the Holy Office, was absolved from all this on condition that he fasted every Friday for a year, never again entered the convent, and gave 2,000 ducats to the poor through the monks of Atocha.

Isassi, the King's secretary Carnero, and two servants, and is attested in notarial form by Villanueva, as prothonotary of the kingdom.

Then comes the King's warrant, under Philip's own sign manual, in the fine old Spanish form:—

"The King—Don Juan Isassi Ydiaquez. The Count-Duke will deliver to you a boy in whose education and virtuous bringing up you will serve me well and with absolute secrecy, following therein all the orders given to you by the Count-Duke. I, the King."

It is clear that this Don Francisco Fernando was no ordinary babe of four to require the personal attention of all these high and mighty gentlemen in sending him to school. Philip had one child by his wife at this time, the chubby youngster Don Baltasar, who for all time will prance on his stout bay cob on the canvas of Velazquez, and only the year previous, in 1629, there had been born to the King, by the beautiful actress, Maria Calderon, the idol of the Spanish stage, a boy who in the fulness of time was to become that second great Don John of Austria, the last virile man of his race; but Don Francisco Fernando was the first-born, and apparently his mother was of far superior social rank to the jaunty "Calderona," so that he was no doubt, baby as he was, destined for great things. The instructions given by the Count-Duke to Don Juan Isassi with regard to the care of his charge are minute to the last degree, and reflect in every line the great importance that is attached to the identification of the child. The long document begins by saying that the boy delivered to Don Juan is the illegitimate son of the King by the daughter of a gentleman, and was born in the house of his grandparents, between eleven and twelve at night, on May 15, 1626. Don Francisco Eraso, Count of Humanes, took the midwife, and was present at the birth; conveying the infant as soon as it was born to the house of Don Baltasar de Alamos y Barrientos, Councillor of the Treasury, where a nurse was awaiting him, and the child had there remained until its delivery to Don Juan. After impressing upon Don Juan the need for the most exquisite care to be taken of the child's life and health, and arranging for the nurses and doctor who have had the care of him to accompany him to Salamanca for the first few months of the change, the Count-Duke instructs Don Juan to seek a good doctor to be kept at hand permanently, who is not to be told who the boy is unless his services are required, and in the meanwhile is to receive a good salary. "His Majesty," says Olivares, "has confided this care to me, and I depend upon you to carry out the task."

First of all the child was to be well taught in religion and morality; secondly, on no account was he to learn who he was, and if his attendants have already told him incautiously he is to be allowed to forget it, and "neither by word nor behaviour is he to be made to think that he is not an ordinary person;" thirdly, he is to be taught polite learning and languages, particularly Italian and French, to dance, fence, and play tennis, and, when he is a little older, to ride. He is to be treated familiarly and without ceremony, and, "in short, to be educated and brought up with the virtues and nobleness of royalty, and the study, modesty, knowledge, and temperance of a private person." Don Juan is to send a weekly report to the Count-Duke through his secretary Carreras, but to take care that this is done with the utmost secrecy, and on no account is the child to be shown to any one without a written order. As secrecy is of the first importance 500 (ducats) a month only are ordered to be paid, besides the doctor's fees, and Don Juan is to devise some means for the secret payment of this sum. A coach is to be secretly got ready to meet the Count-Duke and the child on the night and at the place which may be appointed for the delivery; and then, after another urgent injunction of secrecy and care of the child's religious instruction, and a fervent prayer that God will give to the little one "all the happiness, spiritual and temporal, which He will see is necessary and good for the realm," the proud favourite signs himself simply Gaspar de Guzman.

The hidalgo of Salamanca appears to have been quite overwhelmed at the honour done him by the charge of so important a person, and his ceremonious and verbose letter of thanks to the Count-Duke needed hardly to be prefaced by the prayer that his patron will not attribute his laconic speech to the proverbial taciturnity of his countrymen, but rather to his confusion at the greatness of the honour done him by his Majesty, for which words are inadequate to express his gratitude. His only thanks can be his faithful fulfilment of orders. He begs that the doctor who has had the care of the little one may be sent to Salamanca with him in order to consult with Don Juan's doctor, and ascertain whether he is fit to undertake so important a charge, and if not he will approach cautiously a doctor in Vitoria, named Treviño, of whom he hears good accounts. The woman who accompanies the child shall stay with him some short time, although the good hidalgo is evidently rather doubtful of this arrangement, as he adds that if she should find the horizon of their dull country life too confined for her after Madrid, or begins to kick against the discipline, other arrangements will have to be made. All care shall be taken to prevent the boy from learning who he is, and if it should get wind efforts shall be made to silence it, but the task will be a difficult one. The child shall be so reared, please God, that he shall not become abject or servile (which is most important to a royal personage), or licentious and headstrong; and the good hidalgo thereupon breaks out into a mild pedantic little joke by quoting a Latin proverb, to the effect that, to attain so great an object as this, one must be prepared to eat salt and acrid food, which, he says, will be easy for him to do, "as we all live on salt bacon and hung beef in my province." This does not sound very promising, nor does his description of the water they have to drink, which he says is bad to drink raw, particularly in the summer, and needs cinnamon or other spice to correct it. The doctor, he says, will advise whether they had better boil it with mastic or some other drug. The correspondence shall be sent weekly through "my nephew, Don Alonso Ibarra Isassi, the eldest of the lads I took to Madrid with me. He is a good, prudent, and modest lad, and a correspondence between us as uncle and nephew will arouse no suspicion." As for the 500 ducats a month payment, the good hidalgo says his cheeks burn with shame as he writes or even thinks about them; "but if your Excellency should deign to order them to be paid to me they might be sent without attracting notice through the treasury at Vitoria or Burgos."

So the little child is sent to Salamanca, and with him goes the ponderously learned Dr. Cristobal Nuñez, who wraps up the simplest facts in the most complicated and pedantic technical phraseology, and, what is far more troublesome for the present purpose, writes a shockingly bad hand. His first document is a microscopic report of the constitution and temperament of the child, and the simple history of his baby ailments. The description is most curious; and, if any doubt existed as to his paternity, every trait indicates the character and appearance of a son of the sovereign race of Austria. "He is," says the learned doctor, "of melancholic, choleric temperament, wilful and passionate, but playful when he is pleased, and respectful to those he thinks his superiors. He is of sound constitution, being the offspring of young and healthy parents; possesses superior intelligence for his age; a wonderful memory, which gives great hope if he be well trained. He is slow of speech, and expresses himself with great difficulty, stuttering and lisping; and is so backward on his feet that he has only just learnt to walk. His person is so perfect and beautiful, that the mind of a sculptor never imagined anything better; he has a lovely, fair, red and white complexion, and full grey eyes. He is grave and thoughtful—not dull or sad, but full of childish humour; quick to laugh and quick to cry. He is," says the doctor, "high of spirit, courageous, and pugnacious, impatient of contradiction; and, if his speech be not at once understood, he flies into such ungovernable rage as to make it dangerous to thwart him, and he should rather be coaxed to obedience than forced."

Like all his forbears, he is described as a great eater, and very fond of sweets; and it is not surprising to learn that he has all his short life suffered from over-eating and indigestion, and for long past has had quartan ague. The drastic remedies of the times were endured by the child, the doctor says, "without weeping, as if he knew they were for his good"; but the learned medico confesses that all his own prescriptions had done the babe less good than what he describes as an old wife's remedy of anointing the stomach and spine with ointment and saffron.

The child's usual mode of life is carefully described. Between eight and nine in the morning he had a fowl's liver and a little loaf, or else some bread or cake sopped in broth, or bread and jam and a cup of water. At twelve o'clock broth with sippets of bread or half of the breast of a fowl, or sometimes some forcemeat balls, as he likes a change, and demands it. When he gets tired of this he may have a little loin of mutton or the leg of a fowl. He is also very fond of a piece of bacon between two slices of bread, and of quince marmalade, jams, and sweets. At five o'clock he "packs his wallet," as the doctor calls it, by a meal of bread and jam, and a cup of water. He is put to bed at nine o'clock, and sleeps with his nurse. The learned Don Cristobal then enters into a most verbose disquisition as to the fitness of the locality chosen for the temperament of the child, and arrives at the conclusion that the choice has been a wise one, although the roundabout method of argument founded on wise talk about blood and humours and vapours and the like seems rather beside the mark to a modern reader. The sum of it all is, however, that Don Juan de Isassi's house stands healthily, if somewhat bleakly, on high ground about three bow-shots from the town, and joining the great convent of the Suceso, the house itself being a good one, surrounded by its own grounds.

Thus far the doctor has only spoken of the constitution and past management of his late charge; but the next document, which bears the same date as the preceding one (June 18, 1630), lays down an elaborate plan for the future rearing of the child. He recommends that he should be allowed to play after his early supper, and not be sent to sleep before nine at night, unless he feels sleepy. He is to be woke at eight, if he is not already awake, and is to be given his light breakfast of a fowl's liver and cake, a rasher of bacon and bread and broth, or a roasted egg. At eleven or twelve he is to dine on forcemeat balls, made of two parts chicken, one part mutton, and one part bacon, with a little pie or broth with sippets. Sometimes, instead of forcemeat balls, he may have the leg of a fowl, which, if he likes it, will be enough for him, with a little bread soaked in broth, or he may have a mouthful of mutton with chicken broth. It will be well, says the courtly doctor, that the gentleman himself should be consulted occasionally as to whether he preferred the fowl or the sausages, or roast or boiled food. He is to sleep about an hour and a half after dinner, and play in the afternoon; but great care must be taken to keep him out of the sun, and his early supper may be as heretofore, only somewhat later; a biscuit or two with jam, a small egg, such as the fowls of the province lay, or sippets in broth. A curious and somewhat elaborate little dish is recommended for occasional breakfast or supper. "Take," says the doctor, "a half-dozen almonds or melon seeds, and press the juice from them, which mix with a little barley-cream and some good broth. This must be boiled, and sugar and sponge-cake worked into it until it is a smooth paste, which may be served with half a beaten egg over it, and will make a nice light supper." It will be good to excite the appetite by variety, and as the child gets older he may sometimes be given coarser food, and trout or other fresh fish. He must drink fresh spring water boiled with viper-grass, or mixed with cinnamon, according to the weather. He is always to have some fruit for dessert, unless it disagrees with him; but much care must be taken to guard him from excess; and he is to be specially sparing in drinking. Full common-sense directions are given with regard to his dress, and if he needs medicine his food must be reduced by one half, and a decoction of mallow and camomile, honey and oil administered. Red Alexandria honey is also recommended, quinces, oil of wormwood, and a variety of other remedies for simple ailments.

There is yet another document from the doctor giving some further rules, apparently in answer to special questions. In it he again learnedly describes the child's constitution, his weak stomach and aptness to catch cold, inherited from his parents, his tendency to hydrocephalus, and his almost continuous series of ailments since he was born, which, says the medico, would have killed him but for his strong constitution. From seven years old he was to eat fish and other Lenten fare, and at twelve years must be taught to fast. Above all, he is not to be brought up delicately or coddled, but encouraged to run and romp. Great care must be taken that he is not exposed to the cold, but he must be well wrapped up even in summer. Drugs are to be given sparingly, if at all : mallow, camomile, sweet almonds, black sugar or honey if wanted ; but he is not to be constantly dosed with red honey and other things as children usually are, and if he is really ill he is not to be lowered or bled much ; by which it will be seen that Dr. Cristobal Nuñez, pedantic as he was, differed somewhat from the usual type of sangrados of the time. All this was between the 1st and 18th of June, 1630, and it is to be supposed that the poor babe of the house of Austria lived his little life in and around the "Casa Solariega" of the Salamancan hidalgo for the next few years, although no record remains of it here.

The next document of the series is a letter, dated nearly four years afterwards, March 17, 1634, from the Secretary of State, Geronimo Villanueva, to Don Juan Isassi Ydiaquez, saying that his Majesty had received with the deepest grief the news of the death of Don Francisco Fernando, who showed such bright promise for his tender years, and his Majesty highly appreciates all the care that has been taken of his education. The body is to be brought with the utmost secrecy in a coach to the royal monastery of

St. Lorenzo (the Escurial), where it is to be buried, and advice is to be sent by confidential special messenger to Madrid when the corpse should arrive, in order that one of the King's stewards may be there to receive it. All the other arrangements for the burial are made. The four years had apparently not been unprofitable ones to the hidalgo, as the next time his name appears he is a knight of Santiago and lord of the town of Ameyo, as well as of the castles of Isassi and Orbea. The date of the document is April 15, 1634, and again it is a notarial deed attested by the prothonotary of the kingdom, Don Geronimo Villanueva, setting forth that Don Juan Isassi Ydiaquez delivered the body of Don Francisco Fernando, son of his Catholic Majesty Philip IV., whom God had taken to himself, to the Marquis of Torres, the Bishop of Avila, and other nobles appointed by the King to receive it. The delivery was made in the porch of the cathedral, and we are told that the corpse was dressed in a red gown, bordered with gold, and lay in a coffin of black velvet. The coffin, which had been borne by Don Juan Isassi and his servant to the porch, was thence carried to the great hall of the monastery by certain of the King's gentlemen-in-waiting, and after the religious ceremonies had been performed, was taken to the vault by the monks of the Order and laid to rest. And so ended a little life which, like that of his half-brother Baltasar, if it had been spared, might have stayed the decay of the Spanish branch of the House of Austria. It is true that Don John of Austria survived, and for a short time snatched his poor brother, Charles the Bewitched, from the clutches of his foolish mother and her low-born favourite, Valenzuela, but who knows whether the strong, masterful spirit of the baby of four whom it was dangerous to thwart might not, if he had grown to manhood, have done more than his younger brother to keep the reins of power when once he grasped them. Poor trembling, white-faced Charles the Bewitched, with his leaden eyes and monstrous projecting jaw, a senile dodderer at thirty, wanted a strong, masterful spirit like this to hold him up and shield him from the vultures that fought over the carcase before the poor creature was dead.

But it was not to be, and the forgotten babe of the sovereign house was put with so many other princely corpses in that horrible "rotting place of princes," off the black marble stair of the regal pantheon of the Escurial, where, not so very many years ago, I saw a ghastly heap of princely and semi-princely skulls and leg-bones gathered up as they had fallen from the rotting coffins to the floor. There, all undistinguished from the others, probably enough rests still, his very name never published, and his short existence hardly known till now, Don Francis Ferdinand of Austria, one of the last male members of the Spanish branch of the sovereign house, which in four generations descended from the highest pinnacle of human greatness to contempt, disgrace, decrepitude and decay.

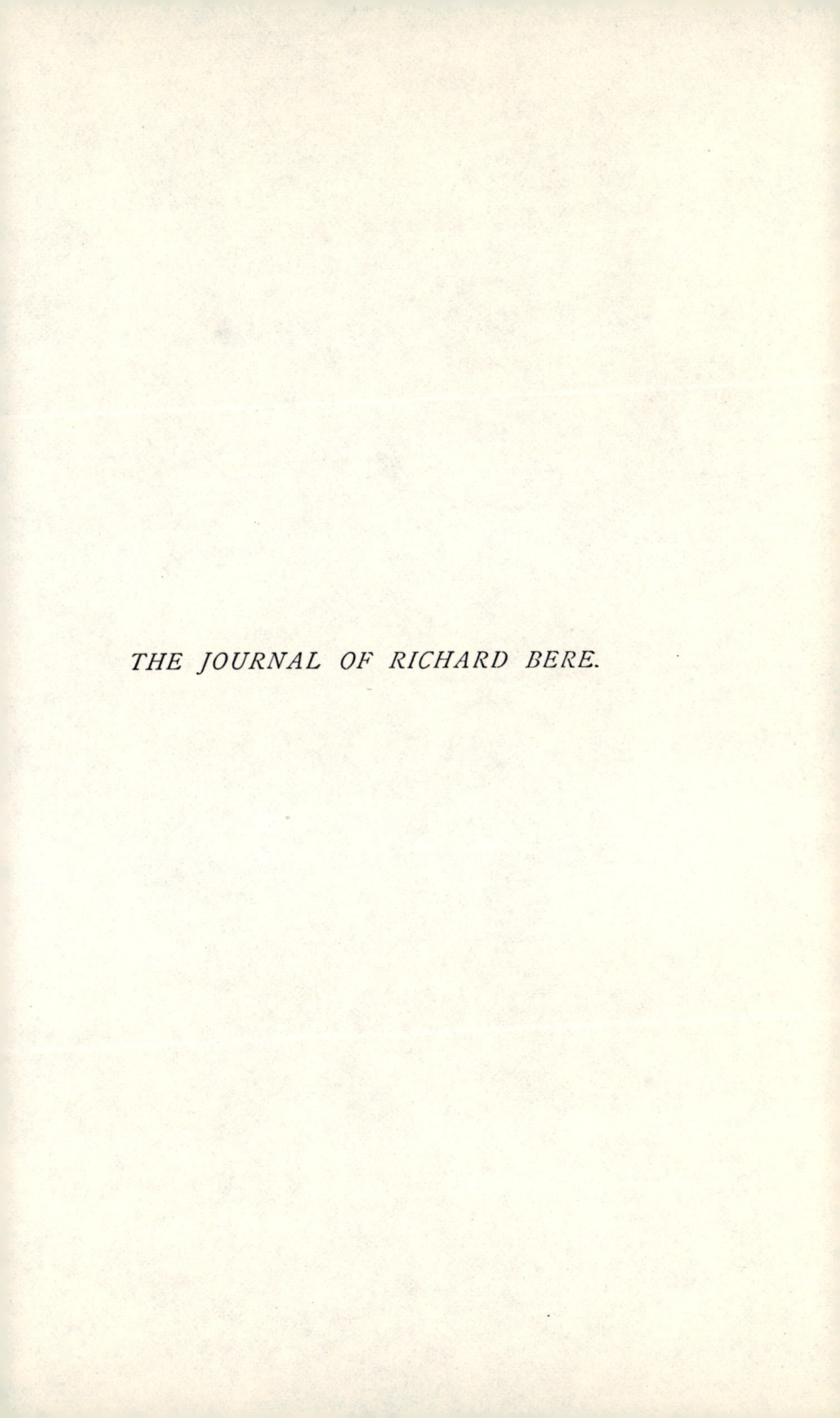

*THE JOURNAL OF RICHARD BERE.*

## THE JOURNAL OF RICHARD BERE.[1]

IN the course of a recent search amongst the Sloane MSS. at the British Museum for a document of an entirely different character I chanced upon a manuscript which, so far as I have been able to discover, has never yet been described in print or received the attention it appears to deserve. It is a long, narrow book like an account book, in the Sloane binding, containing 244 pages of cramped and crowded little writing in faded ink on rough paper, recording the daily—almost hourly—movements of a man for eleven years, from the 1st of January, 1692-3, to the middle of April, 1704. It is written in Spanish—Englishman's Spanish, full of solecisms and English idioms, but fair and fluent Castilian for all that, and the diarist, thinking no doubt his secrets were safe in a language comparatively little known at the time, has set down for his own satisfaction alone, and often in words that no amount of editing would render fit for publication, the daily life of one of the dissolute men about town, who roistered and ruffled in the coffee-houses and taverns of London at the end of the seventeenth century. Few men could hope to possess the keen

[1] *The Gentleman's Magazine*, November, 1891.

observation and diverting style of Samuel Pepys, or the sober judgment and foresight of stately John Evelyn, and this last contemporary diarist of theirs certainly cannot lay claim to any such qualities. He rarely records an impression or an opinion, and as a rule confines himself to a bald statement of his own movements and the people he meets day by day; but still, even such as it is, the diary is full of quaint and curious suggestions of the intimate life of a London widely different from ours. The familiar names of the streets, nay, the very signs of the taverns, are the same now as then, but in every line of the fading brown ink may be gathered hints of the vast chasm that separates the busy crowded life of to-day from the loitering deliberation with which these beaux in swords and high-piled periwigs sauntered through their tavern-haunting existence. It strikes the imagination, too, to think that the man who thus sets down so coarsely and frankly the acts of his life must have listened, with however little appreciation, to the luminous talk of wondrous John Dryden at Will's coffee-house, most certainly knew the rising Mr. Addison, and probably met Matthew Prior at his old home at the "Rummer" tavern, which the diarist frequented.

There is nothing in the manuscript directly to identify the writer, and probably the indirect clues furnished by references to his relatives have never before been followed up to prove exactly who the author was. The task has not been an easy one, and has started me on more than one false scent ending in a check, but at last I stumbled on evidence that not only absolutely identified the diarist, but also explained many obscure passages in the manuscript.

From the first page to the last the writer refers to Danes Court, near Deal, as the home of his brother, and he himself passes the intervals of his dissolute life in London in visits to his Kentish kinsman. Now Danes Court had been for centuries in the possession of the ancient family of Fogge, and I at once concluded that the writer of my diary was a younger member of the house. Indeed, encouraged therein by Hasted, the great authority on Kentish history, I went so far as to establish to my own entire satisfaction that the diarist was a certain Captain Christopher Fogge, R.N., who died in 1708, and was buried in Rochester Cathedral, and I was confirmed in this belief by the fact that the wind and weather of each day is carefully recorded as in a sailor's log-book. But somehow it did not fit in. Constant reference is made to a brother Francis, and no amount of patient investigation in county genealogies and baptismal certificates could unearth any one named Francis Fogge. So I had to hark back and try another clue. Brother Francis was evidently a clergyman and a graduate of King's College, Cambridge, and towards the end of the diary the author visits him at the village of Prescot, near Liverpool.

Sure enough the rich living of Prescot was in the gift of King's College, Cambridge, and further inquiry soon showed that a certain Francis Bere, M.A., was rector from 1700 until his death in 1722. This of itself was not much, but it led to further clues which proved the monumental Hasted ("History of Kent") to be hopelessly wrong about the Fogge pedigree and the ownership of Danes Court at the time, and the whole question was settled more completely than I could have hoped by the discovery, in the "Transactions of the Kent Archæological Society for 1863," of a copy of the copious memoranda in the old family Bible, written by the stout cavalier, Richard Fogge, and his son John, with the notes attached thereto by Warren, the Kentish antiquary in 1711, in which the family history is made clear. This was good as far as it went, and proved the surname and parentage of the author of the diary, but did not identify him personally. Certain references in the manuscript, however, sent me searching amongst the Treasury Papers in the Record Office, and there I found a set of papers written in the same cramped, finnicking hand as the diary, which set my mind at rest, and proved beyond doubt or question who was the methodical rake that indiscreetly confided the secret of his "goings on" to the incomplete oblivion of the Spanish tongue.

The writer of the diary was one Richard Bere, whose father was rector of Ickenham, near Uxbridge, and who was born at Cowley, near there, on the 28th of August, 1653. His sister Elizabeth had married in 1679 John Fogge, who subsequently succeeded to the Danes Court Estate, and, on the fly-leaf of the Fogge family Bible referred to, John Fogge, who was evidently proud of the connection, sets forth that his wife's grandfather had been "Receiver General of ye Low Countries; her uncles, one of them was in a noble imploy in ye C Clarke's office, ye other being one of ye clarkes of ye signet to King Charles II., a man acquainted with all Xtian languages. Ye other now alive is rector of Bendropp in Gloucestershire, who has an Estate. Her mother was one of ye family of Bland, of London, eminent merchants at Home and Abroad." Richard Bere was born only a year after his sister, so that the statement as to her relatives will hold good for him also. He had been Collector of Customs at Carlisle, but apparently had allowed his Jacobite leanings to be too evident, and had been dismissed from his office a short time before he began the diary, leaving his accounts at Carlisle still unbalanced and in arrear. How he learnt Spanish I do not know, but he had evidently been in Spain before his appointment to Carlisle, probably in the navy, or in some way connected with shipping, as, in addition to the careful noting of the wind and weather all through the diary, he shows great interest in the naval events of his time. His uncle's remarkable proficiency in "all Xtian tongues" may also perhaps partly explain his own knowledge of the Spanish language. His family in old times had been a wealthy and powerful one, seated at Gravesend, Dartford, and Greenhithe in Kent, but had lost its county importance long before the date of the diary. The widow of one of his uncles, however, still lived at Gravesend at the time he wrote, and one of his father's sisters, who had married a man named Childs, also lived in the neighbourhood, and on her husband's death went to live with her niece at Danes Court.

The diary commences on the 1st of January, 1692-3, when Bere was living at Mr. Downe's in

London, but the detailed entries begin on the 9th of the month, when he went by tilboat from Billingsgate to Gravesend. Here, after visiting his aunt Bere and his kinsman Childs at Northfleet, he slept at the inn, and started the next morning in a coach to Canterbury. The next day he continued his journey to Danes Court on a hired mare, and then after a few days rest, "without seeing anybody," begins a round of visits and carouses with the neighbouring gentry. All the squires and their families for miles round march through the pages of the diary. Mr. Paramour, of Stratenborough; Mr. Boys, of Betshanger, "my uncle Boys," who was probably Christopher Boys, of Updowne, uncle by marriage to John Fogge; "my uncle Pewry," who was rector of Knowlton, but whose relationship with the diarist is not clearly discoverable; Mr. Burville, rector of the Fogge Church of Tilmanston, and a host of other neighbours come and go, dine and drink, often staying the night, and in a day or two entertain John Fogge and his brother-in-law in return. The latter records the fact, but unfortunately does no more, and little is gathered of the manner of their lives at this period of the diary, except that they did a prodigious deal of visiting and dining at each others' houses. One of the most constant visitors to Danes Court is the aged Lady Monins, of Waldershare Park, the widow of the last baronet of the name, and Richard Bere appears to be as often her guest at Waldershare. The round of dining and visiting is broken in upon by a visit on horseback with brother John Fogge to the assizes at Maidstone, where the latter has a lawsuit which he loses, and Richard returns to

Danes Court alone, leaving his defeated brother at Canterbury. On the 12th of April the diarist records that he first saw the swallows, and on the 20th, as instancing the uneventful life in this remote part of the country, it is considered worth while to register the fact that "whilst I was digging in the garden with Carlton a man passed on horseback." A few days afterwards neighbour Carlton's daughter is married, and then "my nephew Richard was first sent to school at Sandwich, Timothy Thomas being master." Richard, the heir of Danes Court, was about twelve years old at the time, and, as we shall see later on, turned out badly and completed the ruin of the fine old family, of which he was the last male representative in the direct line. Timothy Thomas, who was a distinguished scholar and M.A. of Sidney-Sussex College, Cambridge, was headmaster of the Sandwich Free School and brother to the rector of St. Paul and St. Mary, Sandwich. He seems to have been always ready for a carouse at the hostelry of the "Three Kings" at Sandwich or elsewhere with the father or uncle of his pupil.

On the 28th of April "the fleet entered the Downs, the wind blowing a gale at the time. A ship called the *Windsor* was lost. I went to Deal to see the ships, and saw five ensigns." Small details of ablutions—rare enough they seem nowadays—bed-warming, and quaint remedies for trifling ailments sound queerly enough to us coming faintly across the gloom of two centuries, but in the midst of the chronicles of this small beer of visits paid and received, of the stomach-ache, and so on, brother John receives a writ, and we feel that we are witnesses of the process by which all this feasting and revelry is completing the ruin of the ancient family that once owned broad lands and fat manors all over Kent, which founded hospitals and colleges, and was closely allied to the regal Plantagenets, but whose possessions had even now shrunken to one poor mansion house of Danes Court and the few farms around it. John Fogge's father, Richard, whose pompous Latin epitaph is still in Tilmanston Church, written by his eldest son, Edward, and scoffed at in the family Bible by the degenerate John, had been true to the King's side during the civil war His near neighbour, Sir John Boys of Betshanger, had hunted and harried the cavalier and sacked his house after the mad Kentish rising in 1648, and had frightened his favourite child to death, and for the whole of the Commonwealth period poor Richard had been plundered and well-nigh ruined. His sons Edward and John had been captured at sea by the Dutch, and Christopher had been taken prisoner by the Turks, and all three had had to be bought off with ransom. Stout old Richard Fogge therefore had left Danes Court sadly embarrassed at his death in 1680. His eldest son, Edward, died soon after, and John Fogge, the brother-in-law of our diarist, was rapidly continuing the ruin at the date of the diary. By the 30th of May Richard Bere had had enough of Danes Court, and started to Canterbury " with my brother's horse and servant, and so to Northfleet, where I visited my kinsman Childs." He mounted his horse at five o'clock in the morning and arrived at Northfleet at five in the evening, staying on the way only a short time at Canterbury to rest and drink with friend Best, at whose house he always alights when he passes through the ancient city. The distance by road is a good fifty-five miles, so Richard no doubt thought he had earned his night's rest at Uncle Childs' before starting, as he did next day, by tilboat to London. The first thing he did when he arrived was to "drink with Higgs" and send for Benson to meet him at Phillips' mug-house. Benson appears to have been a humble friend or foster-brother, as Bere calls Benson's father "my father Benson," who went on all his errands, pawned his valuables, and faced his creditors. When Benson came they started out together and took a room, where they both slept, "at the sign of the 'Crown,' an inn in Holborne," and the record thereafter for some time consists mainly of such entries as " Dined with Sindry at the 'Crown,' and drank with him all the afternoon and evening at Phillips'. Slept at Mrs. Ward's;" "Dined with Dr. Stockton, Haddock, and Simpson at the 'Pindar of Wakefield';" "Dined at the sign of the 'Castle,' a tavern in Wood Street, with many friends from the North; drank there all the afternoon, and all night drinking with usual friends at Phillips'," only that these daily entries usually wind up with the record of a debauch which need not be described, but which Richard does not hesitate to set down in such cold blood as his orgy has left him.

He appears to have had as a friend one Westmacott, who was a prison official, and a standing amusement was apparently to go and see the prisoners, who sometimes fall foul of Westmacott and his friend and abuse them. Richard also has a quaint way of drawing a miniature gallows in the margin of his manuscript on the days that he records the execution of malefactors. On the 15th of June, for instance, after giving his usual list of friends and taverns, he writes: "Seven men hanged to-day; fine and warm. Drinking at Phillips' at night; Westmacott there again." A day or two afterwards the bailiffs walk in during his dinner at the tavern and hale his boon companion, Pearce, off to jail; but Richard thinks little of it, for he goes off to drink straightway with Colonel Legge, and then passes a merry evening with Dr. Stockton and Mr. Rolfe at the sign of the "Ship," near Charing Cross.

On the 29th of June "a new sword-belt, some woollen hose, and a rosette for my hat," were bought; and soon after he leaves his lodgings at Mrs. Ward's, and thenceforward seems to sleep in taverns or inns for some time, very often winding up the entries in the diary by confessing that he was "drunk" or "very drunk."

On the 18th of July, 1693, he visits "the house of the Princess of Denmark with Mr. Wooton," and thence goes to see a fashionable friend of his called Captain Orfeur, who had a fine house at Spring Gardens, where he meets his brother, and they all make a night of it at the "Ship." By the beginning of August it is not surprising that he is ill, and decides to visit his brother Francis in the country. On the 3rd he takes horse to Biggleswade and thence to Oundle, "where I met my brother and Mr. Rosewell" (he was a fellow of "King's," and apparently a great friend of Francis Bere's). "Dined at Caldwell's, and slept at the sign of the 'Dog.'"

He stays at the "Dog" at Oundle for some days, still ill, and visits Northampton, where he is struck with the curious church, town-hall, prison, and courts of justice, and slept at the "George." From there he rides to the "Angel" at Wellingboro', and so home to London by Dunstable, where he stays at the "Saracen's Head," Watford, Rickmansworth, and Uxbridge, where he puts up at the "Swan." Being now well again, he recommences the old round of the "Horns," the "Red Cow," the "Mermaid," the "Crown," and so on, usually winding up with a roaring carouse at Phillips', and occasionally relieved by trips to Islington-wells to walk in the fields with friend Stourton, who lives near there, and who later on becomes his inseparable companion. To illustrate the methodical character of this roistering blade, it is curious to note that, as he could not well carry his cumbrous diary with him on his journey to Oundle, he has made his daily entries on a small loose leaf and has afterwards carefully transcribed them in the book, the loose leaf, however, being also bound up with the rest. On the reverse side, in English, Richard has copied the following couplet of Lord Thomond's, which seems to have struck him:—

"Whatever Traveller doth wicked ways intend,
The Devill entertains him at his journey's end,"

and to this he adds several little remedies which some travelling companion seems to have told him on the road. He scrupulously records the fact that the day is his birthday on each succeeding 28th of August, and the occasion appears to be an excuse for a burst of deeper drinking than ever, but on this first birthday mentioned in the diary, 1693, he is evidently getting hard up. He lodges with a man named Nelson, who ceaselessly duns him for his rent, and we soon learn that the faithful Benson has pawned his two rings for eighteen shillings. On the 27th of September his friend Dr. Stockton tells him "that Mr. Addison told him that I lost my place because I was against the Government, and was foolish enough to talk about it, which," says indignant Richard, "is a lie."

It sounds curious nowadays to read that he and his friends, Westmacott and others, sometimes walk out in the fields to shoot with bows and arrows, and usually return thence to the "Hole-in-the-Wall" to pass the evening.

As a specimen of the entries at this period, I transcribe that for the 30th of September, 1693, at least so much of it as can well be published. "With Metham and Stourton to the City, and dined at the 'Ship' in Birchin Lane. Vickers there, and we went together to the Exchange and met Mr. Howard; with him to the 'Fountain,' Mr. Coxum there. At five o'clock went to Sir James Edwards', and drank there two flasks of wine. Then to the 'King's Head,' where I left them and went to Mr. Pearce's house and received ten pounds. Found Stourton very drunk. Went and paid Jackson and Squires. Slept at Pearce's—drunk myself."

With the ten pounds received from Mr. Pearce Richard seems to have set about renewing his wardrobe, and duly records the days upon which his various new garments are worn. On the 26th of October "Aspin, the tailor, brought my new white breeches in the morning, and we went out to drink at the 'Bull's Head' in Mart Lane." On the second of November he recites the names of six taverns at which he drank during the day, namely, the "Bull's Head," the "Red Cow," the "Ship," the "Horns," the "Cheshire Cheese," and the "Crown," and on the 7th of the same month a dreadful thing happens to him. The constables walk off his dulcinea, Miss Nichols, to jail, and Richard is left to seek such consolation as he can find at the "Chequers," the "Three Cranes," and the "Sugar Loaf." The next day he seeks out his friend Westmacott at the "King's Head," and is taken to the prison to see the incarcerated fair one. Whilst there he "meets the man who has done the mischief." But he winds up at the "Sugar Loaf" in Whitefriars, and Phillips' mug-house, and is carried home thence in a coach too much overcome by his grief and potations to walk. On the 14th, after several more visits to the prison, he bewails that he can do nothing for Nichols, and on visiting a Mrs. Hill, that kind matron tells him that his great friend, Dr. Stockton, had told her that "I had squandered all I had over a worthless wench, and thought now to live at the expense of my friends," but the entry, unfortunately, winds up with the words: "Borrowed two pounds of Simons on my watch."

After this Richard thinks that quiet Danes Court might suit him for a time, and starts the next day, the 15th of November, as before to Gravesend by the tilboat, and, after a duty visit to his relatives, stays two nights at the sign of the "Flushing," and dines there merrily with "a clergyman named Sell and another good fellow from the North." The same companions and others go with him in the coach to Canterbury, where he stays at the "Fleece," gets gloriously drunk, and is cheated out of half-a-crown, and lies in bed until mid-day next morning, his niece, Jane Fogge, who lived with the Bests at Canterbury, coming to visit him before he was up. In the afternoon he continues his road more soberly to Danes Court on a hired horse, and the old round of visiting and feasting begins afresh. On the first of December he meets Parson Burville, of Tilmanston, and drinks Canary wine till he is drunk. On the 12th Captain Christopher Fogge meets his brother John at a friend's house and they quarrel; Uncle Childs dies, the cat is drowned in the well, three East Indiamen captains dine at Danes Court, Ruggles' wife is confined, and the daily small events of a remote village happen and are recorded much as they might happen to-day. Uncle Boys had a kinsman, presumably a brother, Captain Boys, R.N., who was Constable of Walmer Castle, where he lived, and Richard and his friends often go there to dine and visit the ships in the Downs. On the 26th of February, 1694, they all go to dinner on board the *Cornwall*, and "they gave us a salute of seven guns." They all went back to the castle to sleep, and John Fogge made a bargain with his weak-witted younger brother William about Danes Court, presumably with regard to his reversionary interest or charge upon the property. But whatever it was it did not matter much, for William Fogge died soon after. On the 25th of March, after going to Betsanger church and to the rectory to see Thomas

Boys, "Ruggles threw a poor boy out of the cart and seriously injured him," and on the next day a curt entry says: "The poor lad died at nine o'clock this morning, and was buried in the evening," but not a word about any enquiry or the punishment of the offending Ruggles.

But after five months Richard sighs again for the taverns of Fleet Street, and on the 4th of April, 1694, returns to London by the usual road by Canterbury and Gravesend, and again haunts the taverns and night-houses of the metropolis. He tries hard to borrow money from his friends, and is evidently getting anxious about his Customs accounts left in arrear at Carlisle. He is a pretty constant visitor to Whitehall about a certain petition of his, which petition, although he often mentions it in his diary, he of course does not describe or explain in a document written for his own eye alone. I have, however, been fortunate enough to find the actual document itself in the Treasury Papers at the Record Office, with all the voluminous reports and consultations founded upon it during the seven years it lingered in the Government offices. It appears that in August, 1689, the Earl of Shrewsbury, Secretary of State, had addressed a letter (the original of which is attached to Richard Bere's petition) to the Mayor or Collector of Customs of Carlisle, directing them to provide for the maintenance of certain "papist Irish soldier prisoners" who were to be kept in the castle there. The mayor refused to find the money, and Richard Bere, as Collector of Customs, had to do so, expecting to be reimbursed out of the Secret Service Fund, as provided by the Secretary of State. The prisoners were kept at Carlisle until December, 1690, and Richard spent £74 4s. on their maintenance. He was soon after suddenly dismissed from his post, and was unable to balance his accounts for want of this money, and shortly before beginning the diary had presented his petition to the Lords of the Treasury for the reimbursement of the sum, or at least that it should be handed to the Receiver-General of Customs on his account. But whilst the petition was lying in the pigeon-holes in one office, another office was only conscious that Richard was behindhand in his accounts, and on the 11th of May, 1694, there is an entry as follows in the diary: "Alone to dine at the 'Spotted Bull.' Then to Phillips', where one Petitt told me about the tolls of Carlisle, and said that the bailiffs from Appleby had a warrant to arrest me." Richard did not wait long for the bailiffs, and in less than a week had signed and sealed a bond, apparently for borrowed money to settle his toll accounts, bought a horse and a Bible, had gone to Westminster Hall "about his brother's affairs," and started off for Carlisle. He rode through Oundle, where the Rev. Francis Bere appeared still to be living, and so by Stamford, Grantham, Newark, Doncaster, Ferrybridge, and Appleby to Carlisle. Two days before he arrived at the city some choice spirits came out to meet him, and a host of friends received him with open arms after his ten days' ride. He dines fourteen times with Dick Jackson, drinks often and deeply with the Mayor of Carlisle, collects money owing to him, buys a fine new periwig of Ned Haines, and a new sword, settles up his accounts of tolls, and begs a holiday for the schoolboys, whom he treats all round, and winds up in a burst of jubilation by receiving a present of two kegs of brandy from his friend Bell, which had not paid much to the King probably, and of which, no doubt, the late Collector and his jovial companions gave a very good account. And then, after a six weeks' stay at Carlisle, he wends his way back to London again by the same road, his horse falling lame at Stamford, and the rider having to post from Grantham to Ware, and thence to London by coach. He alights at the "Bell," in Bishopsgate Street, where Benson soon seeks him with fresh clothes and a sedan chair, and takes him to his old quarter of London again.

But poor Richard's prosperity is of short duration. The borrowed money soon comes to an end, with the able and constant assistance of a certain Catherine Wilson, who has now supplanted the vanished Nichols, and by the beginning of September, 1694, Benson is taking one article after the other to the pawnshop, and bringing back sums which Richard regards as very unsatisfactory in amount. On the 6th of that month he attends what must have been rather a curious marriage at the church of St. George's, Bloomsbury, where one of Catherine Wilson's companions, named Early, was married "to a young man named James Carlile, between nine and ten in the morning." The whole of the party adjourn to the fields, and at one o'clock return to drink at the "Feathers" in Holborn, "but the knavish constables disturbed us and we went to Whitefriars; at two I went to seek Benson, but he could only bring me 5s. on my pistols." With this sum Richard finds his way back to Whitefriars, where he remained drinking till evening with the "newly married pair, Catherine Wilson, a gentleman and his wife, and a marine." He then attends a coffee-house, and winds up with a carouse at the "Rising Sun." The unfortunate bridegroom soon disappears from the diary, but the "bride" takes part in the drinking bouts for some time to come. By the middle of October Richard has apparently come to the end of his tether, and, after borrowing a half-crown on his knives, quarrels with and separates for a time from Catherine Wilson; but brother Francis and sister Fogge are appealed to for money, and when it arrives Catherine is to the fore again. A great scheme is hatched about this time with a Captain Sales and Mr. Butler, apparently relating to the tobacco duties, and the Commissioners of Customs and other officials are being constantly petitioned and visited. Sometimes the tobacco business is considered hopeful, and sometimes the contrary, but on the 7th of January, 1695, it looks very bright when the Lords of the Treasury and the Commissioners of Customs sitting together at Whitehall receive Richard and his two friends, who lay the case before them, but "Mr. Culliford spoke against us," and nothing was decided; so the trio and others who joined them go to the "Rummer" tavern at Charing Cross, and drink confusion to Mr. Culliford. A day or two days after this "a knave came to betray me to the bailiffs," and poor Richard and his friend Sales seek the shady retreat of a tavern in Fulwood's Rents. For the next few days he dodges the bailiffs from tavern to tavern, and sleeps at Bell Court, Whitefriars, and elsewhere. The "knavish bailiffs even follow friend

Sales in the hope of tracking Richard. On the 14th of January the faithful Benson brings his clothes to the new lodging in Whitefriars, and Richard ventures out " to the ' Anchor ' in Coleman Street, about the business of Andrew Lloyd and the widow. Then the 'St. John the Baptist's Head' in Milk Street, where I found Butler meeting the citizens about the tobacco business." A few days after, the business of " Andrew Lloyd and the widow" is settled somehow at the " Mermaid " in Ram Alley, and on the 26th Benson pawns all Richard's silver for £5 7s., and Richard slips out of Whitefriars at night, sleeps at the " Star," and escapes to the quiet of Danes Court, where the bailiffs cease from troubling and the spendthrift is at rest.

On the 2nd of February, 1695, scapegrace little nephew Dick Fogge comes home with a story that the small-pox had appeared at the school at Sandwich, " but it is all a lie," and the youngster is led back ignominiously the next day by his father and Tim Thomas the schoolmaster, and when John Fogge returns to Danes Court he brings news that the French are capturing English boats in the Channel. Richard is still uneasy in his mind, for on the 15th of February he dreams that the bailiffs have caught him at last, and soon afterwards begins seriously to put his Customs accounts in order. Then early in April he starts for London again, but as soon as he was on board the tilboat at Gravesend he caught sight of a bailiff ashore seeking him. It takes four hours to reach London, and the city is in a turmoil, for during the night " the mob knocked down a house in Holborn." He takes a room at

the "Green Dragon" for a day or two, and the
next night the mob burn down two houses in the
Coal Yard, Drury Lane. A false friend named
Fowler accompanies him in his search for lodgings,
which he eventually takes at the house of a cheese-
monger named Tilley in Fetter Lane, and also
goes with him to the Custom House "about my
accounts," and then on the 13th of April, after
carousing with him half the day, " the hound
betrayed me to the bailiffs," and poor Richard is
caught at last. He is at once haled off to a spunging-house, called the "King's Head," in Wood
Street, and the first thing the prisoner does is, of
course, to send for Benson, who comes with Sales
and other friends, and they have a jovial dinner of
veal with the keeper. The next day Benson brings
some money, and Richard holds a perfect levee of
friends. Some of them go off to soften the creditors,
in which they fail, and other to apply for a writ of
*habeas corpus*. A good deal of dining goes on at
the spunging-house, but on the 16th the carouse is
cut short by the removal of Richard to the Fleet.
He has a good deal of liberty, however, for he still
occasionally haunts the taverns in Fleet Street,
probably within the "rules" of the prison or under
the ward of a keeper. Brother Francis is appealed to
daily by letter, and pending his reply all the old boon
companions come in and out of the prison, dine there,
drink there, and get drunk in the vaults, Benson and
Catherine Wilson coming every day with clothes,
books, and comfort. At the end of the month of
May the parson brother, Francis, arrives, and after
a month of negotiation at the Custom House and
the law courts, and much drinking and dining as

usual, a bond is signed and sealed at the "Three Tuns" tavern, "Sales standing my friend," and Richard Bere is free again.

But imprudent Richard, after a sharp fit of the gout, soon falls into his old habits again, and on the 6th of September confesses that he got into a row at the "Dog" Tavern in Drury Lane "about drinking the Prince of Wales' health," an indiscreet thing enough considering that his Custom House accounts were still unsettled, and his own petition to the Treasury unanswered. On the 1st of July, whilst he and his friend Sales are dining at the "Crown," the constables walk Sales off to prison, "and then go to the 'Globe' Tavern and arrest his landlady, and Andrew Lloyd the author." And so the diary goes on; his accounts still unpaid, but Richard full of the tobacco business, with petitions to the King and interviews with Treasury officials. Then there is some great Irish wool scheme, which necessitates much dancing attendance on the Duke of Ormond, but does not seem to result in much. His boon companions evidently do not think much of his chance of recovering anything from the Treasury, for "they made me promise B. Skynner a new wig if ever I received my £74 4s. on the King's order."

However much Richard may drink, he is frugal enough in his eating, for from this period to the end of the diary he constantly records that for days together he has eaten nothing but a little bread and cheese, and the "one poor halfpennyworth of bread to all this intolerable amount of sack" is as applicable to Richard Bere as it was to the fat knight. And he needs to be sparing in his expenditure, for he is poor enough just now, notwithstanding his drinkings with the Duke of Richmond's steward, with Stourton at the "Rose" in Pall Mall, and his visits to Lord James Howard in Oxenden Street, for he is reduced to pawning his new lace ruffles for six shillings, and Benson could borrow nothing on his new wig, for which he had just paid (or not paid) thirty-five shillings to Rolfe, the barber. But Benson pawns his linen for ten shillings and brother Francis sends funds, so after borrowing nine shillings and sixpence on "my Bezoar stone," and going to the Temple to receive "my pension" Richard starts on the 1st of September, 1696, by hoy for Sandwich. The voyage is long and tedious, the weather being bad, but after a day and a night at sea they drop anchor, and Richard solaces himself with punch and good fellowship at the "Three Kings" at Sandwich.

On his arrival at Danes Court "John gives me a bad account of my nephew Richard, who went back to school to-day." But John certainly does not set his son a good example, for he soon breaks out himself, and on the 21st of October, "after dining with my aunt," threatens to cut his wife's throat. For months after this the diary constantly records that "John came home raving drunk"; "John from Sandwich to-day, very violent"; "John mad drunk all day"; "to Tilmaston Church twice, John there raving drunk," and so on. On Christmas Day, 1696, Richard, who as befits a parson's son, is all through an indefatigable church-goer, takes the Sacrament at Tilmanston Church, as he generally does on special days, John through all the Christmastide remaining drunk as usual. On the 18th of January, 1697, he gives his wife a black eye, and the next day it is Richard's turn, and he goes on a great drinking bout with Captain Whiston, and "got drunk and lost my white mare," whereupon the immaculate "John is very angry with me." On the 10th of February nephew Richard runs away from school again, and gets soundly whipped by his father, who remains drunk all the month. On the 15th of March tidings comes to Danes Court that the master has been lodged in Dover jail, and his wife and her brother start off next morning to find him. He has escaped somehow, and gets back to Danes Court mad drunk just as his household are returning from afternoon service at Tilmanston Church. This goes on all March, and on the 26th John borrows money from an attorney named Lynch, and seals a bond at Danes Court conveying all his goods to the lender as security, "being rabid drunk at the time." A few days afterwards "the bailiffs nearly took John, but he escaped by the quickness of his mare." Echoes of more important events occasionally reach Danes Court. On the 6th of April, 1697, news comes that the French have taken Jamaica, and that they have captured a merchant fleet and convoys off Bilbao. Soon after we hear of "French pirates infesting the Downs, and they had taken two of our ships," but the domestic troubles of the old Kentish manor house occupy most of the diary at this period; incorrigible young Richard runs away from school again and cannot be found for days; with some difficulty drunken John's accounts with Hill and Dilnot, of Sandwich, are arranged, but on the 24th of April he is lodged in jail at Canterbury on another suit, and is only released by more borrowing from Lynch, and at once goes back to his drunken career again. An entry on the 29th of April, 1697, gives another inkling of Richard's Jacobite leanings. "Walking to Eythorne I met Petitt the parson and Captain March. We drank together and went to Walker's, where a Mr. Kelly defended the bad opinion that it was lawful for people to rise against the King if he violated his coronation oath."

All through May John Fogge continued drunk, and one day falling foul of his brother-in-law, calls him a scurvy knave, and threatens to kick him out of his house. So Richard, having worn out his welcome at Danes Court, starts for town again, taking with him nephew Dick, who has just run away from school once more for the last time.

He lodges henceforward at Stokes' in Short's Gardens, and pays ten shillings a month for his room. Every morning two or three taverns are visited with Stourton, Churchill, and others, where unfortunately they are sometimes imprudent enough to drink deep to the health of King James. Metheglin and mum are occasional drinks, but brandy the most usual, and black puddings seem a favourite dish for dinner. On the 19th of October, 1697, peace is proclaimed with France, and on the 16th of the following month the King enters the City in state, and on the 2nd of December the peace rejoicings were crowned by a great display of fireworks, and a banquet given by the Earl of Romney to the King. Richard's petition after five years' waiting is favourably reported upon by the Commissioners of Customs, and during all the winter he haunts Whitehall and the ante-room of Lord Coningsby to get the recommendation carried out by the Treasury. But one obstacle after the other is raised, the papers are sent backwards and forwards, and it is fully two years longer before Richard at last receives his money. On the 2nd of December, 1697, he records the consecration of St. Paul's, and on the 15th of February, 1698, he attends his first service in the Cathedral, "from thence to the Temple Church, and so to the 'Trumpet,' where I supped on black puddings and cheese. Home at eight, when my landlady besought me to pay the rent." On the 18th of April he sees Prince George, and on the 16th of May visits the ship *Providence* from New England, and thence to the "Dolphin" tavern until three in the morning. On the 9th of June, apparently fired by the example of some of the wits he meets in the coffee-houses of Covent Garden, or in his favourite promenade at Gray's Inn Gardens, he records the fact that he wrote some satirical verses. The next day a fine new suit of clothes comes home, and he dons them with great pride. But alas! a sad thing happens. Drinking at the "Sun" with his friends, some of the latter "threw some beer over my fine garments," much to Richard's disgust. The quaint little gallowses on the margin are pretty frequent now, and the names of the wretches who are hanged are often given. On the 29th of June, 1698, Richard visits the Duke of Norfolk at St. James's House with his friends Stourton and Orfeur. "Thence to St. James's Park, to see a race between youths, where I met Churchill."

Richard becomes certainly more respectable as he gets older, and beyond a slight flirtation with his landlady, Mrs. Stokes, of Short's Gardens, we hear little of his gallantries henceforward. He is certainly more prosperous, too, in some mysterious way, owing to a voyage he makes, apparently in an official capacity, from Gosport to Flanders, for which a sum of ninety-five guineas is handed to him. He says nothing of his adventures in Flanders, where, however, he only lands at Ostend for a few days from his ship the *Good Hope*. The voyage, however, is evidently an important one for him, as he has spoken of it on and off for many months, and takes a special journey to Cambridge to see brother Francis before setting out. On the 19th of October, 1698, he anchors in Dover Roads on his return, and goes thence to Danes Court, where he stays over Christmas, and returns to London in January, 1699. His friend Churchill has now taken the Treasury matter in hand, and after many months of hope deferred Richard Bere gets his £74 4s. at last in October. But Churchill wanted paying, and on the morrow of the payment "Churchill came to me drunk, and quarrelled with me because I would not give him the money he wanted." I suspect the money was all spent long ago, for Richard has often enough gone into the City to borrow five or ten pounds "on the King's order." He is very methodical about money matters, too, for all his apparent improvidence. He has a boon companion named Henry Johnson, who during the autumn and winter of 1699 drank mainly at his expense. Every penny thus spent is noted against the date in the diary, and a neat account of the whole, headed "Expenditure on account of Henry Johnson," is bound up with the diary. From this it appears that Johnson consumed over seven pounds' worth of brandy at various taverns with Richard in about five months. On the 27th of January, 1700, Richard again visits the Duke of Norfolk; but it is rather a falling off to be told that he goes straight from the Duke's to eat black puddings at Smith's. In July of the same year he goes to see a witch called Anna Wilkes, a prisoner in the Marshalsea, and the same day he learns in the Tilt Yard that his boon companion Stourton is made Deputy-Governor of Windsor. On the 30th of July the young Duke of Gloucester dies, and one day next week Richard, after drinking punch with Mr. Van Dyk, tries to see the body of the young prince at the lying-in-state, but fails. His brother Francis is in town about the firstfruits and fees of his new fat living of Prescot, and Richard is his surety for £48 1s. 8d. to the King, and when Francis has got comfortably settled in his new rectory in July, 1701, Richard takes the ship *Providence* for Liverpool to visit him. They take a fortnight to get there; and when he arrives a gentleman comes on board and announces that brother Francis has married his (the gentleman's) sister, whereupon Richard is much surprised, and promptly borrows some money from his new connection. There are high jinks at Prescot, and Richard is in his element. He dines and carouses with everybody, from his brother's glebe-tenants to the Earl of Derby at Knowsley, gets drunk constantly, breaks his nose, loses his horse and money, quarrels in his cups with a good many of his friends, toasts King James III., and enjoys himself greatly. It is to be noted that his brother's curate generally shaved him during his stay. On the 13th of June 1702, King William's death is recorded, and soon after the diarist returns to London by road, taking up his quarters at Stokes', Short's Gardens, again. In the autumn he goes to Danes Court, where John Fogge is still usually drunk; and in October of that year a most important thing happens to Richard Bere. On the 23rd of that month he visits the aged Lady Monins at Waldershare, the next mansion to Danes Court. His sister, Mrs. Fogge, is with him; and staying with Lady Monins is a certain Lucy Boys, presumably a daughter of Captain Boys, the Constable of Walmer Castle. After dinner Richard, who was then forty-nine years of age, whispered soft words of love to this young lady, and the next day he records the fact that he sent her a tender love letter. The maiden, nothing loath, sends him an answer next day, and a few days afterwards comes herself to visit Mrs. Fogge at Danes Court. Of course Richard improves the occasion, and, as he says, "makes love again. For the next week a lively interchange of notes takes place between Danes Court and Waldershare; and on the 8th of November Lucy Boys thinks it time to go home to Walmer Castle. It is not quite in the direct road, but she called to say good-bye to Mrs. Fogge at Danes Court, and, of course, Mr. Richard Bere thought well to go in the coach with her to Walmer. "We pledged," he says, " to marry each other, and solemnly promised to marry no one else." On the 16th of December he again goes to Waldershare, and they again renew their pledge, and Lady Monins promised all her influence with her grandson-in-law, the great Earl Poulet, to forward Richard's fortunes. Early in January, 1703, Richard speeds to London with a letter from Lucy Boys to Lord Poulet in his pocket. The peer welcomes him warmly, promises him great things at the Treasury and elsewhere, and loving letters still speed backward and forward between London and Walmer. Richard is constant at Lord Poulet's levees, and at last, on the 25th of March, 1703, Richard is introduced to the all-powerful Lord Godolphin, who promises him a good office, upon strength of which he "borrows another £5 of Gawler."

But Richard complains of lameness on the very day that he saw Godolphin, and the next entry in the diary is carefully traced with a trembling hand at the bottom of the page nearly three months afterwards. Richard had fallen ill of gout, fever, and rheumatism, and had not left the room for ten weeks, "attended by Mr. Sheppery of Drury Lane, my surgeon Mr. Williams, and my housekeeper Mrs. Cockman." In July he was well enough to go to Danes Court, and on the 11th of August visited Waldershare with his sister. There, walking in the grotto, he again pledged his troth to Lucy Boys. On the 2nd of September Lucy Boys came to dine at Danes Court, and the vows were repeated. On this occasion Miss Boys showed her sincerity by handing to Richard "95 guineas, one pistole, and six shillings in silver," presumably for investment or expenditure on fitting up a home. Soon afterwards Lord Poulet came and took his wife's grandmother away on a visit to Hinton, where she died in six weeks. Richard

Bere returns to London a happy man, but in a few weeks his lady love herself comes on a visit to Lord Poulet, and then, on the 20th of November, a great change comes over the tone of the entries. "The strumpet Boys came to London. I saw her at Lord Poulet's and gave her five guineas, besides five guineas I gave her on the 26th to go to the Exchange, five guineas more I paid on her account at Mr. Stow's, and another ten pounds on account of the slut." Another entry on the 30th is still more disheartening. "I went to see the slut Boys at Lord Poulet's, and the baggage denied ever having promised to marry me at all, and now she has gone and married a stuttering parson called Woodward." Then Lord Poulet said he had never promised to do anything for him, and "treated me vilely," and the whole romance was ended.

At this time there are two entries in English as follows: "November 27, 1703. From 12 o'clock in ye morning till 7 was ye most violent storm of wind y$^t$ ever was known in England, and ye damage done at land and sea not to be estimated."

"On ye 15th, 16th, and 17th of January, 1703-4, was a very violent storm, which forced back ye fleet bound to Lisbon w$^{th}$ ye Archduke Charles, under Rooke, separating them, and did a great deale of damage."

In March, 1704, Richard is evidently making great preparations for another sea voyage. He often visits Bear Quay, and is much in the City. Trunks and new clothes seem to be brought now without much difficulty, and Benson's services are not apparently so needful for raising the wind. Richard's friend, old Mrs. Feltham, who keeps a shop in the Exchange, invites him to come and see her and drink mum, in order to ask him about making her son purser. Richard seems also to have quite a friendly correspondence with the "stuttering parson Woodward," and one is tempted to believe that Lord Poulet may after all have done something for the jilted lover. Richard's circumstances must be a good deal changed, for he can afford to leave twenty guineas with T. Bell to keep for him when he departs for Danes Court, after a merry dinner at the "Blue Posts" in the Haymarket (which he quaintly translates as "los Postes ceruleos en la Feria de feno) with Churchill and others. On the 23rd of March, 1704, he starts for Danes Court, and there the usual life of visiting and feasting is recommenced. On the 11th of April, 1704, there is an entry to the effect that he went to visit Lady Barret, and wrote to Mr. Woodward, and then the curtain drops and all is darkness, which swallows up Richard Bere and all his friends for ever. Where he went and what became of him I have been unable to discover, and the transient gleam thrown across his trivial history by his own folly, in writing down his most secret actions in a language known to many, will in all probability be the only light ever thrown upon his life. John Fogge died soon after, but his widow, Richard Bere's sister, lived at Danes Court in straitened circumstances for many years after. Warren, the antiquary, writing in 1711 (Fausett MS. Kent Archæological Society), deplores that the once fine estate was reduced even then to about fifty pounds a year only, and says that it was uncertain whether any male heir was living—thus soon had scapegrace nephew Dick drifted away from his friends. Warren says that he had been last heard of at Lisbon some years before, but on his mother's death he turned up a common sailor, sold Danes Court to the Harveys in 1724, married a certain Elizabeth Rickasie, a sister of St. Bartholomew's Hospital at Sandwich, and died on board the fleet at Gibraltar in 1740, leaving, says Hasted, an only daughter, married to a poor shepherd named Cock, and living in a lowly hovel near the manor house of which her ancestors had for centuries been masters.

# INDEX.

## A.

Acevedo, Diego de, 149, 155.
Adanero, Count de, 295.
Addison, Mr., 346, 356.
Adelphi, the, 264, 288.
Aguilar, Marquis de, 140, 155.
Alarcon, Captain, 46, 55, 59.
Alba, Duchess of, her reception by Queen Mary, 163-4, 167, 170.
Alba, Duke of, in Portugal, 13.
Alba, Duke of, 76; sent to crush the Netherlands, 93; his seizure of Egmont, 94; his failure, 98; renewed severity, 99-104; his praise of Romero, 106; retires from the Netherlands, 106-7.
Alba, Duke of, 140, 149, 153, 155.
Alba, Duke of, urges Philip II. to action against England, 183.
Alberoni, Cardinal, 255.
Albert, Archduke, in command at Lisbon, 42, 48, 50-1, 53, 56, 63, 67.
Alburquerque, 3rd Duke of, with Henry VIII. before Boulogne, 80.
Alburquerque, 4th Duke of, 93.
Alburquerque, Matias de, commands the galleys in the Tagus, 50.
Alencastro, Luis, Don, Grand Master of the Order of Christ, 46.
Aljubarrota, Portuguese victory over Castile, 218.
Allen, Father, 191, 193, 197, 198, 201.
Alonso the Wise of Castile, his decree against extravagance in attire and food, 212-13.
Alonso XI. of Castile, decrees against extravagance, 213.
Altamira, Count de, raises an army to relieve Corunna, 38.
Alvaro, Souza, Portuguese captain, 65-6.
Alvelade, near Lisbon, 56-7.
Andrada, Count de, attempts to relieve Corunna, 37, 39.
Antonio, Dom, the Portuguese Pretender, 13; flies to England, 14; his treatment by Elizabeth, 14; flies to France, 15-16; attacks the Azores, 16; again appeals to Elizabeth, 17; his concessions to Elizabeth, 18-23; accompanies the expedition, 29; lands at Peniche, 43-5; arrives at Torres Vedras, 55; at the gates of Lisbon, 56-9, 64, 67; leaves with the English, 64, 68; returns to England, 71-2.
Antwerp, sack of, in the Spanish Fury, 117-20.
Araujo, Captain, surrenders Peniche, 42.
Argüelles, Father, an exorciser, 303; his communications with the devil, 304, passim.
Armada, defeat of, 3-5; cause of its defeat, 3-4; the disaster to foretold by Mendoza, 200.
Arundel, Earl of, 149, 153, 154, 155, 162.
Arundel, Earl of, at Durham Place, 269.

## INDEX.

Arundell's rising suppressed by the aid of Spanish mercenaries, 77.
Astorga, Philip II. at, 142.
Austria, decline of the house of, in Spain, 340-1.
Authorities with regard to the wedding of Philip and Mary, 125-7, 131-6.
Azores, attacks upon, in the interest of Dom Antonio, 14-16; to be attacked by the English expedition, 22, 71; plan abandoned, 71, 72.

### B.

Bacon, Lady, 284.
Baden, Margrave of, imprisoned for debt at Rochester, 284.
Baoardo, the Venetian, his account of the marriage of Philip and Mary, 126-7.
Barlemont, Count, to betray Brussels, 115.
Basing House, Philip and Mary at, 166.
Bazan, Alvaro de, 66.
Beaton, Archbishop of Glasgow, his plans against Elizabeth, 184 *passim*.
Beauvoir, de, 108.
Bedford's, Earl of, visit to Spain to ratify the marriage contract, 128. 137, 142-3; Philip's gift to, 143-4; chooses the ship to carry Philip to England, 145; in England, 153.
Bedford, Earl of, his house in the Strand, 264.
Benavente, Philip II. at, 141-2.
Benavente, Count de, entertains Philip II., 141.
Benavente, Count de, Chamberlain to Charles II., 297, 300.
Bere, Francis, Rev., rector of Prescot, 347, 360, 371.
Bere, Richard, his parentage, 348; his adventures, 348 *passim*.
Bergues, Marquis of, 149.
Berlips, Madame, 295.
Bertondona, Martin de, Spanish naval commander, 145.
Bossu, Count, 102, 105.
Boulogne besieged by the English, 79-81.

Boys, Captain, R.N., Constable of Walmer Castle, 358.
Boys, Christopher, of Updowne, 350.
Boys, Mr., of Betshanger, 350.
Boys, Lucy, her love passages with Richard Bere, 372-5.
Boys, Sir John, of Betshanger, 352.
Braganza, Duke of, 68.
Brazil, offered to Catharine de Medici in return for aid to Dom Antonio, 18.
Brett, Colonel, at Corunna, 33; killed at Lisbon, 60.
Britain's Burse, Strand, 287.
Browne, Sir Anthony, master of the horse to King Philip, 151.
Bruce, Robert, envoy of the Scottish Catholics to Philip II., 199-202.
Butler, Sir Philip, a friend of Essex, 41.
Burleigh, Lord, his house in the Strand, 264.
Burville, Mr., rector of Tilmanston, 350, 358.

### C.

Cadiz, Drake's attack upon, 8.
Calais, the Armada in, 3.
Calderon, 253.
Caraffa, Cardinal, 197.
Cardenas, surrenders Cascaes to Drake, 62; beheaded by the Spaniards, 63.
Carew, at Durham Place, 265.
Carillo, 155.
Carlisle House, Strand, 264, 286.
Carlos, Don (son of Philip II.), 137, 141.
Carr, Captain, killed at Lisbon, 60.
Carsey, Captain, killed at Lisbon, 60.
Cary, Robert, sent by Elizabeth to warn James of the Catholic plot, 202.
Cascaes at the mouth of the Tagus, Drake at, 62-3, 64, 66, 68.
Castile, Admiral of, Prime Minister of Spain, 295-8.
Castro, Fernando de, 56.
Catharine de Medici, aids Dom Antonio, 16, 18.

# INDEX.

Catharine of Lancaster, bride of the Prince of Castile, 218.
Cave, Sir Ambrose, gives a wedding feast at Durham Place, 282–3.
Cecil, Robert, first Earl of Salisbury, his house in the Strand, 264; obtains Strand frontage of Durham Place, 267, 286–7.
Cecilia of Sweden, Margravine of Baden, at Durham Place, 283–4.
Cerralba, Marquis of, defends Corunna, 31.
Cervantes' burial-place, 75–6.
Challoner, Sir Thomas, English ambassador in Spain, 274.
Chambergo hat, 254.
Chapin-Vitelli, at Mons, 99.
Charles V., Emperor, his decrees against extravagance in dress, 223–4.
Charles II. of Spain (the Bewitched), his appearance, 291, 296; his distress, 297; the exorcism, 303 *passim*; death, 319.
Charles II. of Spain, his sumptuary decrees, 255.
Charles III. of Spain, his sumptuary decrees, 257–9.
Charles IV. of Spain, his sumptuary decrees, 259–60.
Charles Stuart's visit to Madrid, 249–50.
Chartres, Vidame de, 276.
Chatillon, French ambassador, at Durham Place, 268.
Chinchon, Count de, 155.
Churchill (1697), 368–9, 370.
Coaches, abuse in the use of, 231–2, 242–3, 244, 256.
Cobham, Lord, 153, 284.
Cobham, Lady, 284–5.
Como, Cardinal, 197.
Copetes (topknots), decree against, 253.
Cordoba, Don Antonio de, mobbed in London, 170.
Cordoba, Cardinal, Inquisitor-General (Charles II.), 316; poisoned, 316.
Cordoba, Pedro de, Chamberlain of Philip II., 149; mobbed in London, 170.

Corunna, English attack upon, 31–40, 45.
Corunna, Philip II. at, 144; the Spanish fleet at, 145–6; Philip II., departure from, to marry Mary, 147.
Cotes, Sebastian de, a conspirator against the Queen Marie Anne of Neuberg, 298.
Coventry, Lord Keeper, at Durham Place, 287.
Clanking farthingales, 251, 252.
Clarencis, Mistress Susan, 273.
Clinton, Lord, 153.
Cloth manufactory in Spain, 218, 224, 227.
Creighton the Jesuit, his action in the plot against England, 188, 189, 201.
Crisp, Provost-Marshal, 51.
Cromwell, Richard, at Durham Place, 265.

D.

Danes Court, Tilmanston, Kent, 347 *passim*.
Darcy, Lord, 153.
D'Aubigny, Duke of Lennox, joins in the plot against England, 185, 188, 190.
Derby, Earl of, 149, 153, 160, 164.
Derby, Earl of (1700), 371.
D'Este, Cardinal, 197.
Devereux, Walter (Essex's brother), 41.
Diaz, Cristobal, a Spanish captain in the English service, 85, 90.
Diaz, Froilan, the new confessor of Charles II., 299; his participation in the exorcism, 303 *passim*; confesses, 316; arrested and escapes, 317; re-captured and imprisoned by the Inquisitor-General, 318–19; released and made Bishop of Avila, 320.
Diaz de Lobo, Ruy, beheaded in Lisbon, 57.
Dormer, Jane, Countess of Feria, 158; at Durham Place 268, 273.
Drake, Sir Francis, commands the expedition against Portugal, 9,

23, 25, 26, 28, 29, 30, 31, 35, 39–43, 45–6, 62–3, 64, 66, 69, 71.
Dryden, John, 346.
Dudley, Earl of Warwick and Duke of Northumberland, 82, 91, 265–6.
Dudley, Robert, Earl of Leicester, at Durham Place, 269.
Dumblain, Bishop of, 201.
Durham Place, description of, in Tudor times, 270–2.

### E.

Ecclesiastical palaces in the Strand, 264.
Egmont's visit to Madrid, 93; his arrest and execution, 94–5.
Egmont, Count, at Durham Place, 268.
Egmont's visit to London to ratify Philip and Mary's marriage contract, 137, 139; with Philip, 140, 149, 155.
Elder, John, his account of Philip and Mary's entrance into London, 125.
Elizabeth's attitude towards Spain, 179–80.
Elizabeth of Valois, Queen of Spain, 228, 231.
Englefield, Sir Francis, English adviser of Philip II., 190.
English Catholic feeling against the Scots, 190–1, 195–6, 198.
English Catholics favour a purely Spanish attack on England, 192, 193.
English aggression against Spain, 8, 182–3.
English fashions, Spanish opinion of, 157–8, 165–7, 171.
English feeling after the Armada, 7–8.
English feeling against Philip's marriage with Mary, 137, 169–74.
English food, abundance of, 167.
English ladies, Spanish opinion of, 157–8, 166.
Enriquez, Pedro, his account of the marriage of Philip and Mary, 134–5 *passim*.

Essex, Earl of (Walter Devereux), at Durham Place, 286.
Essex, Robert, Earl of, flight from Court to join the Portuguese expedition, 27; embarks on the *Swiftsure* and escapes, 28–9; the Queen's rage thereat, 28, 35; joins the expedition at sea, 41; lands at Peniche, 43; leads the vanguard, 51–2; at Lisbon, 56, 60, 64; his humanity, 66; sends a challenge to the Spaniards, 67–8.
Ethrington, Captain, at Puente de Burgos, 38.
Expedition against Portugal: authorities hitherto known respecting it, 10; new authorities now quoted, 10, 11, 12; its constitution as a joint-stock enterprise, 9, 18, 22–8; its strength, 24–6; difficulties, 24–8; finally sails, 29; attacks Corunna, 31–40; alarm in Spain, 30–3, 39–40; the sacking of Corunna, 33–5; arrival at Peniche, 43–7, 51; attack on Lisbon, 60–6; withdrawal, 63–8; sails from Cascaes, 70; return to England, 71; reasons for its failure, 72.

### F.

Fadrique de Toledo, 98, 100, 101, 103–4.
Fashion in hair-dressing, 250, 253–4.
Fashion of dress in Spain in time of Philip II., 230–4; in the time of Philip III., 238–9; in the time of Philip IV., 247–54.
Female extravagance in dress, Philip IV.'s fulmination against, 251–3.
Fenner, Captain, with the English at Corunna, 32.
Ferdinand and Isabel, their decrees against gold and silver tissues, 220; limiting the use of silk, 221.
Fernando de Toledo, prior, commands the Spanish army to relieve Lisbon, 30, 39, 61.
Fernihurst (Gray, Laird of), 185.

# INDEX.

Feria, Count de, 140, 149, 155; marries Jane Dormer, 158; urges Philip to attack England, 180; at Durham Place, 267-8, 269, 272, 273.
Feria, Countess de. *See* Dormer.
Figueroa, Spanish special envoy, 149.
Finch, Lord Keeper, at Durham Place, 287.
Fitzwalter, Lord, accompanies Bedford to Spain, 137, 142, 143; in England, 153.
Fogge family of Danes Court, 347 *passim*.
Fogge, Captain Christopher, 347.
Fogge, Edward, 352.
Fogge, John, of Danes Court, 348, 352, 366-7, 368, 372, 375.
Fogge, Richard, Cavalier, 348, 352.
Fogge, Richard, heir of Danes Court, 351, 363, 366, 367, 375-6.
Folch de Cardona, Antonio, a member of the Queen's party, 301, 313, 316, 318.
Folch de Cardona, Lorenzo, Member of the Council of the Inquisition, 301, 313, 318-19.
Fouldrey, Dalton-in-Furness, proposed place of landing for the Spanish invasion, 192.
Francisco Fernando, the illegitimate son of Philip IV., 328-41.
French ambassador de Foix at Durham Place, 282.
French fashions, revolt against, in Spain, 255.
Froude's account of the marriage of Philip and Mary, 126, 130, 131 *passim*.
Fuentes, Count de, commands the Spaniards in Lisbon, 55-6, 65, 67, 72.
Fulford, Captain, at Puente de Burgos, 38.

## G.

Gafas (horn spectacles), 254.
Gage, Sir John, 154.
Gamboa, Sir Peter, a Spanish captain, murdered in London, 77; enters the English service, 82-3; pensioned by Henry VIII., 86; his treachery to Romero, 88-9; his brilliant charge at Pinkie, 90.
Gardiner, Bishop of Winchester, 155, 161, 174.
Garter, the investure of Philip with, 149, 150.
Genlis' troops massacred at Mons, 99.
Germaine de Foix, Queen of Aragon, 221.
Gilimonas, the, leaders of the ladies' revolt against the sumptuary decrees, 252-3.
Glimes, de, Flemish captain in the Spanish service, killed, 109.
Godolphin, Lord, 373.
Golilla, invention of the, 248, 249, 255, 260.
Gomez, Ruy, Philip II.'s favourite, 146, 149.
Gonsalves de Ateide, commands the Spaniards at Peniche, 42-3.
Gonzaga, Cardinal, 197.
Goodwin, Captain, wounded at Corunna, 35.
Granada, Archbishop of, protests against Olivares leading Philip IV. into dissipation, 326-7.
Granvelle, Cardinal de, his attitude towards the plot against England, 187, 189.
Grey, Lady Jane, married at Durham Place, 265.
Grey, Lord, in command at Boulogne, 81.
Guaras, Antonio de, 77, 88.
Guarda-Infante (flattened farthingales), decrees against, 251-3.
Guedejas (side locks), 250; decrees against, 253-4.
Guevara, Captain, hanged for murder at Smithfield, 77.
Guise, Duke of, his plans against England, 184 *passim*.
Gutierre, Lope de Padilla, sent to receive the English envoys, 139, 149.
Guzman, Captain, at Torres Vedras, 47, 51, 55, 70.
Guzman, Diego de, Spanish ambassador in England, 182; at Durham House, 282, 285.

## H.

Haarlem, siege of, 102-4.
Haddington, siege of, 90.
Hamilton, Lord Claude, appeals to Philip II., 199.
Haro, Juan de, a Spanish captain in the English service, 78, 82.
Hawkins, John, at Durham Place, 269.
Heneage, Sir Thomas, 285.
Henry, King-Cardinal of Portugal, 12, 13.
Henry IV. of Castile, 219.
Henry VIII. attacks Boulogne, 79-81 ; his death, 90.
Hinder, Captain, at Puente de Burgos, 38.
Holt, Father, the Jesuit, his action in the plot against England, 186.
Horn, Count, with Philip II. in England, 149, 155 ; his arrest and execution, 94-5.
Hostages, French, in England, 276.
Household of an ambassador at Durham Place, 274.
Howard, Lord Admiral, with Philip and Mary, 155 ; proposes an expedition to Portugal, 9.
Howard, Lord James (1696), 366.
Hugo's, Victor, distortion of history, 294.
Huntingdon, Earl of, sent by the Queen to seek Essex, 28.
Huntly, Colonel, at Corunna, 33-4.
Huntly, Earl of, appeals to Philip II., 199.
Hunsdon, Lord, 284.

## I.

Infantado, Duke of, 249.
Ireland, the Armada on the coast of, 5.
Isassi Ydiaquez, Juan de, takes charge of the child of Philip IV. (Francisco Fernando), 328 *passim*.
Ivy Lane, Strand, 263, 286.

## J.

Jaime I. of Aragon, his enactment against extravagance, 211.
James VI. of Scotland, plan to carry him to Spain, 185 ; his duplicity, 186 ; his religion, 186, 192, 193-5, 197, 201.
Jara, near Lisbon, 55.
Jewels brought to England by Dom Antonio, 14-17.
John I. of Castile, his sumptuary decrees, 218.
John II. of Castile, 219.
Juana la Loca, Queen, 141 ; her sumptuary decree, 222.
Juan, Don, of Austria, 114, 120 ; seizes Namur, 120.
Juan José, Don, of Austria, 254, 292, 307, 340.
Juan of Portugal, Philip's brother-in-law, death of, 138.
Julian, Captain. *See* Romero.

## K.

Katharine of Aragon at Durham Place, 266.
Kett's rising, suppressed by the aid of Spanish mercenaries, 77.
Kildare, Earl of, 164.
Kingston, at Durham Place, 265.
Knollys, Francis, sent by the Queen to seek for Essex, 27.

## L.

Lane, Colonel, at Lisbon, 60.
Leganes, Marquis de, a conspirator against the Queen Marie Anne of Neuberg, 298.
Leicester, Earl of, and Dom Antonio's jewels, 14. *See also* Dudley, Robert.
Lethington (William Maitland, Laird of), at Durham Place, 269.
Linen, manufacture of, in Spain, 227.
Lisbon, English attack on, 45-6 ; Spanish force fall back, 47 ; terror in the city, 47-50, 54-5 ; attempts to betray the city, 57-8 ; night attack on the English, 60-61 ; withdrawal of the English, 63-66 ; distrust of the Spaniards, 65.
Lloyd, Andrew, "the author," 363, 365.
Lope de Vega, 253.

# INDEX. 383

Lopez, Dr. Ruy, 15, 17.
Louvres, near Lisbon, 55.
Lumay, Count de la Mark, 103.
Lumley, Lord, at Durham Place, 269.

## M.

Madrid in the sixteenth and seventeenth centuries, 231-44, 242-3, 251-5.
Maineville, de, sent by Guise to Scotland, 190-1.
Margaret of Parma, 93.
Mariana, Queen Regent of Spain, 254, 292, 307.
Marie Anne of Neuberg, Queen of Spain, 292, 295, 300, 301; discovers the exorcism, 313-16.
Marie Louise of Orleans, Queen of Spain, 292.
Marriage of Philip and Mary, feeling against it in England, 137, 167-74; hard conditions imposed by the English, 138; great preparations in Spain, 140-1; voyage of Philip, 147-53; his first interview with Mary, 154-7; the ceremony at Winchester, 160; the banquet, 161-3; after the marriage, 164-74.
Mary, Queen, her first present to Philip, 139; at Winchester, 152; her presents to Philip, 152-3; her first interview with Philip, 154-7; her appearance, 156-7; her splendour at the marriage ceremony, 160; at the banquet, 161-3; her reception of the Duchess of Alba, 164.
Mary Stuart, proposal to marry her to Don Carlos, 181; her adhesion to Spain, 184-5, 188-9, 196, 198.
Mason, Sir John, 91.
Massino, Captain, attempt to murder him in the Strand, 276, 277.
Master of Santiago, Regent of Castile, his denunciation of extravagance in attire, 220.
Matilla, confessor to Charles II. of Spain, 295; his fall and death, 300-1.

Matthew, Toby, Bishop of Durham, at Durham Place, 267.
Medici, Cardinal de, 197.
Medici, Pietro de, ordered to raise mercenaries for the Spanish service, 39.
Medina Celi, Duke of, 140, 155; sent to replace Alba in the Netherlands, 98.
Medina Sidonia, Duke of, his return to Spain from the Armada, 5.
Medkirk, Colonel, at Lisbon, 60.
Melino, Guise's envoy to the Pope, 192, 196.
Mendovi, Cardinal, 201.
Mendoza, Bishop of Segovia, Inquisitor-General (Charles II.), 317; contest with the Inquisition, 318-19; dismissed, 319.
Mendoza, Bernardino de, Spanish ambassador in England and France, 14, 105, 186-9, 198-99, 200.
Mendoza, Iñigo de, 155, 162.
Merino sheep introduced into Spain by Catharine of Lancaster, 218.
Middleburg besieged by the Gueux, 107; Romero's attempt to relieve, 107-10.
Middleton, Captain, at Puente de Burgos, 38.
Milford Lane, Strand, 263.
Mondragon, Spanish commander in Middleburg, 107-8, 119.
Monins, Lady, of Waldeshare, 350, 372-3.
Montague, Viscount (Browne), at Durham Place, 269.
Monterey, Count, conspirator against the Queen Marie Anne of Neuberg, 298.
Montigny, at Madrid, 94.
Montreuil, besieged by the English, 79, 80, 81; Romero's duel at, 83-6.
Mora, Cristobal, deserts from the English service, 82; challenges Gamboa, 83; his duel with Romero, 83-6.
Moors, sumptuary rules for, 213.
Morton, Earl of, 185.
Morton, Earl of (the younger), appeals to Philip II., 199.

# INDEX.

Murder attempted from Durham Place, 276–7; escape of the criminal by the water-gate, 278.

## N.

Naarden, the massacre at, 100–1.
Nantouillet, Provost of Paris, a hostage in England, 276, 278.
Navas, Marquis de, sent to England with Philip's first present to Mary, 139, 146, 148, 164.
Negro, Sir Pero, a Spanish captain in England, 78, 90.
Noailles, de, French ambassador, his account of the marriage of Philip and Mary, 128–31; his efforts against the match, 130, 137.
Norfolk, Duke of, besieges Montreuil, (1544) 79–80.
Norfolk, Duke of (1698), 369, 371.
Norris, Sir Edward, at Corunna, 34; wounded, 38.
Norris, Sir John, commands the land forces of the expedition against Portugal, 9, 23, 25, 26, 35–6, 41–3, 45–6, 51, 55, 58, 62; withdrawn from Lisbon, 64–6; arrival at Cascaes, 66.
North, Lord, 153.
Northumberland, Duke of, makes use of the Spaniards to overawe Somerset, 91; dismisses them, 91. *See also* Dudley.
Nuñez, Cristobal, Dr., his orders for the rearing of a child (Francisco Fernando), 335–9.

## O.

Odonte, Francisco de, letter from Lisbon, 58–9.
Olivares, Chamberlain of Philip II., 149.
Olivares (the Count-Duke), Minister of Philip IV., 247, 249, 326–7; his orders for the rearing of Philip's child, 330–3.
Olivares, Count de, Spanish ambassador in Rome, 197.
O'Neil, Shan, at Durham Place, 269, 276, 281.
Orange, Prince of, 98, 105, 114.
Orfeur, Captain (1698), 354, 369.

Oropesa, Count de, Spanish Minister, 295.
Osorio, Captain, 109.
Oviedo, Bishop of, refuses to participate in the exorcism, 303.

## P.

Pacheco, Don Juan, 165.
Paget, Charles, Guise's envoy to England, 192.
Paramour, Mr., of Stratenborough, 350.
Parma, Duke of, his share in the defeat of the Armada, 5; his negotiation with the Scotch Catholics, 200.
Pembroke, Earl of, 152–3, 161, 164; buys Durham Place (1640), 287.
Penalties for infraction of the sumptuary laws, 214, 216–17, 218, 241, 247, 256.
Peniche, the English at, 43–7, 51.
Perez, Ensign, deserts to the Scots, 90.
Persons, Father Robert, the Jesuit, his action in the plot against England, 186, 198, 201.
Pescara, Marquis de, 140, 149, 155.
Peter the Cruel of Castile, his sumptuary decrees, 217–18.
Pewry, rector of Knowlton, 350.
Philip II. accepts the match with Mary at his father's bidding, 138–9; his journey to Valladolid, 138; splendour of his outfit, 140; his reception of the English envoys, 142–3; splendid departure from Corunna, 144–7; voyage and arrival in England, 147–9; his gracious manner, 148; at Southampton, 149–52; journey and arrival at Winchester, 152–4; his first interview with the Queen, 154–7; his splendour at the wedding, 160; at the marriage banquet, 161–3; his attention to Mary, 166; his departure from England, 174.
Philip II., his reception of the news of the disaster of the Armada, 6; his action on the

# INDEX. 385

news of the English expedition, 30, 44.
Philip II. and the Flemish nobles, 93-4.
Philip II. and the Portuguese succession, 13.
Philip II., his character, 177.
Philip II., his attitude towards England, 8-9, 178-83, 184, 188, 190-5, 197-8, 202.
Philip II., his splendour in apparel, 225-6; his sumptuary decrees, 228, 229, 230, 234-5.
Philip III., his sumptuary decrees, 238-44.
Philip IV., his appearance and character, 323; Spain under his rule, 234-5; his youthful dissipation, 326-7; adventure in the convent of San Placido, 328.
Philip IV., decrees against extravagances in apparel, 247-54.
Philip V. of Spain, his sumptuary decrees, 255-6.
Pole, Arthur, at Durham Place, 269, 281.
Pole, Cardinal, 267.
Portocarrero, Cardinal, forwards the intrigue against the Queen Marie Anne of Neuberg, 297 *passim*.
Portuguese succession, claimants to, 12, 13, 14.
Portuguese feeling towards the English expedition, 43, 47-50, 53-5.
Poulet, Earl (1700), 373-5.
Poynings, at Durham Place, 265.
Prior, Matthew, 346.
Puente de Burgos, fight at, 38.

## Q.

Quadra, Bishop, urges Philip to make war on England, 180.
Quadra (Bishop of Aquila, Spanish ambassador) at Durham Place, 273; complaints of his conduct, 275; facilitates the escape of a criminal, 277-8; Cecil's attempt to dislodge him, 278-9; his defence of his conduct, 280-1; expelled from Durham Place, 281.
Quevedo, 253.

## R.

Raleigh, Sir Walter, 28, 35; at Durham Place, 266, 267, 271, 286.
Ravenstein, Austrian envoy, at Durham Place, 273.
Redondo, Count de, beheaded in Lisbon, 67.
Relations between England and Spain. *See* Spain.
Renard and the marriage of Philip and Mary, 137, 148; his plan to marry Elizabeth to the Duke of Savoy, 178.
Requesens, Grand Commander, Alba's successor in the Netherlands, 107-10, 111, 114.
Richmond, Philip and Mary at, 166.
Riots in Madrid against the sumptuary decrees, 237, 252, 257-9.
Rivalry between Spanish and French ambassadors, 282-3.
Robles, Gaspar de, his account of the siege of Haarlem, 104.
Rocaberti, Inquisitor-General (Charles II.), 302; his share in the exorcism, 303 *passim*; death, 313.
Rodas, Jerome, Spanish member of the Flemish Council, 115, 119; his head demanded by the Flemings, 120.
Rome, intrigues in, respecting the invasion of England, 197-201.
Romero, Julian, his origin, 78-9; enters the English service, 82; sent to Scotland, 82; at Calais, 83; accepts Mora's challenge to Gamboa, 83; the duel, 83-6; rewarded by the kings of France and England, 86; in London, 87; arrested for debt, 87-8; accused of treason, 88-9; at Pinkie and Leith, 90; dismissed the English service, 91; surrenders Dinant to the French, 92; bravery at St. Quintin, 92; in Italy, 93; sent to Flanders, 93; aids in the arrest of Egmont, 94-5; his severity, 95-6; returns to Spain, 95-6; rumoured intention of attacking

## INDEX.

England, 97; again sent to Flanders, 98; at Mons, 98-9; his account of affairs in the Netherlands, 99; his cruelty at Naarden, 100-1; his behaviour at Haarlem, 102-4; his march of vengeance through Holland, 105; begs for leave to return home, 106, 111; his unsuccessful attempt to 'relieve Middleburg, 107-10; his letter to Requesens, 112-13; again in the Netherlands, 114; sent by the Flemish Council to pacify the mutinous Spaniards, 115; his share in the "Spanish Fury," 116-20; his head demanded by the Flemings, 120; marches out of Flanders, 120; to return from Italy in command, 120; dies on the way, 120.

Romney, Earl of (1697), 368.

Ronquillo, Francisco, a conspirator against the Queen Marie Anne of Neuberg, 298, 302.

Ruffs, decrees against, 243-5.

Rusticucci, Cardinal, 197.

Ruthven, Raid of, 190.

Rutland, Earl of, 153.

### S.

Saint Ferdinand, King, in Seville, 212.

Salablanca, a Spanish captain at Boulogne, 81.

Sampson, Captain, at Corunna, 33.

San Anton, gate of, Lisbon, 60.

Sancho de Avila, Spanish commander in Flanders, 76; at Egmont's arrest, 94; in the Spanish fury, 116-20; his head demanded by the Flemings, 120.

Sancho Bravo, Spanish officer in Lisbon, 59-60, 65.

*San Felipe*, galleon captured by Drake, 8-9.

San Roque, monastery, Lisbon, 60.

Santa Cruz defeats Strozzi at the Azores, 16, 18; offers to invade England, 194, 200, 202.

Santa Catalina, gate of, Lisbon, 60.

Santander, arrival of the Armada in, 5.

Santiago, Philip's reception at, 142-3.

Santorio, Cardinal, 197.

Sanzio, Cardinal, 197, 201.

Savoy, the, Strand, 264.

Scottish Catholics appeal to Philip, 186-9, 199; proposal to invade England in the interest of Spain, 199-200.

Sebastian, King of Portugal, 12.

Seymour, at Durham Place, 265; grants Durham Place to Elizabeth, 265. *See* also Somerset.

Shrewsbury, Earl of (1689), 359.

Sidney, Colonel, at Puente de Burgos, 38.

Sidney, Lady, at Durham Place, 269.

Silk manufactory in Spain, 220-1, 224, 227.

Sirleto, Cardinal, 197.

Sixtus V., Pope, subsidises the Armada, 5; joins in the plot against England, 196-203.

Somerset, Protector, 90-1.

Sotomayor, Inquisitor-General, rebukes Philip IV. for his sacreligious amour, 329.

Southampton, the landing of Philip II. at, 149.

Spain, relations with England, 177 *passim*.

Spaniards, their discontent at their position in England with Philip II., 153, 161, 164-7, 168, 169, 170, 171-4.

Spanish accounts of the coming of Philip to England, 132-7.

Spanish extravagance in dress, 223-4, 229, 245, 249.

Spanish Fury, the, 115-20.

Spanish mercenaries in the English service, 77-8; at Boulogne, 80-4; fresh bodies recruited, 82; sent to Scotland, 82-3; at Boulogne and Calais, 83-4; sent to Scotland, 89-90.

Spanish nation clamours for revenge for the defeat of the Armada, 6-7.

Spanish troops in Flanders mutiny

## INDEX.

for pay, 114-15; plot to seize Brussels, 115; massacres at Alost, &c., 115-16; the Spanish Fury, 117-20; marched out of Flanders, 120.
Spanish succession, intrigues respecting, 292-4.
Spencer, Master of the Ordnance at Corunna, 34.
Spes, Guerau de, Spanish ambassador, 182.
Squillaci, Marquis de (Esquilache), his attempt to suppress the Chambergo and cloak, 257-9.
Stanhope, his letters from Spain about Charles the Bewitched, 291, 296, 304.
Stourton, Deputy - Governor of Windsor (1700), 368-9, 371.
Strand, the, in Tudor times, 264, 270-1.
Strand Lane, 263.
Strange, Lord, 153, 161.
Stukeley, Thomas, his proposed invasion of Ireland, 96-7; at Durham Place, 269.
Suffolk, Duke of (Brandon), 80.
Sumptuary enactments in England, 208.
Sumptuary enactments in Spain, 208 *passim.*
Surrey, Earl of, 153.
Sussex, Countess of, 284.
*Swiftsure,* the, sails surreptitiously with Essex on board, 28, 35, 41.
Sydenham, Captain, sad death of, at Corunna, 37.

### T.

Talbot, Lord, 153.
Tassis, J. B., Spanish ambassador in France, 185, 188, 194-5.
Taverns in London (1693), 353-5, 356-7, 360.
Thomas, Timothy, M.A., headmaster of Sandwich School, 351.
Throgmorton's plot, discovery of, 195.
Titles, decree of Philip II. against, 236-7, 242.
Torres Vedras, on the road to Lisbon, 51-2.
Trains, decree against, 216.

Treason against Elizabeth at Durham Place, 269, 273.
Tunstal, Bishop of Durham, at Durham Place, 266-7.

### U.

Umpton, Colonel, at Corunna, 33.
Underhyll, Edward, the hot-gospeller, at Queen Mary's wedding, 126, 161-2.
Urraca, Juan Antonio, a conspirator against the Queen Marie Anne of Neuberg, 298.

### V.

Valenzuela, favourite of Mariana, Queen Regent of Spain, 309.
Valladolid, rejoicing and mourning at, 138; Philip's departure from, 141.
Van Dyk, Mr. (1700), 371.
Vargas, Alonso de, Spanish commander in Flanders, 115-16, 117.
Vigo burnt by the English, 70.
Villa Dorta, Count de, pursues the English, 65-6.
Villanueva Geronimo, Minister of Philip IV., 328; punished by the Inquisition for sacrilege, 329, 339.
Villa Sirga, Sir Alonso, a Spanish captain murdered in London, 77, 90.

### W.

Waldershare Park, 350, 372-3.
Walloon collars, 247-8.
Walsingham, Secretary, 9, 15, 35, 97.
Wedding feasts, decrees against extravagance at, 213, 216.
William III., death of, 372.
Williams, Sir Roger, aids Essex to escape, 28, 35, 41; takes part in the attack on Lisbon, 42, 51-2, 56-8, 64, 68.
Williams of Thame, Sir John, 149.
Willoughby, Lord, 153.
Winchester, Marquis of, 153, 162; at Durham Place, 269.
Windebank, Captain, 107.
Wingfield's account of the Portuguese expedition, 10 *passim.*

Wingfield, Anthony, at Puente de Burgos, 38.
Wingfield, Sir Edward, 41.
Wingfield, Captain Richard, 33.
Woodward, Parson (1700), 375.
Worcester, Earl of, 153.
Wotton, Dr., 92.
Wyatt's rebellion, 128, 137.

Y.

Yorke, Colonel, at Corunna, 37; at Lisbon, 55, 60.

Z.

Zeeland lost to Spain, 110.